The B

Channel Islands

Peter & Fionnuala McGregor Eadie

A&C Black • London
WW Norton • New York

BLUE GUIDE

Third edition, July 1998.
Reprinted February 2000.

Published by A & C Black (Publishers) Limited
35 Bedford Row, London WC1R 4JH

Maps and plans drawn by John Flower and Map Creation Ltd
Illustrations © Peter McClure

ISBN 0-7136-3852-4

Published in the United States of America by
WW Norton and Company Inc.
500 Fifth Avenue, New York, NY 10110

Published simultaneously in Canada by
Penguin Books Canada Limited
10 Alcorn Avenue, Toronto
Ontario M4V 3BE

ISBN 0-393-31797-X USA

Cover photograph of the Seigneurie, Sark by Paul Mellor. **Title page drawing** shows a statue-menhir, La Gran'mère de Chimquière, St. Martin's churchyard, Guernsey.

Peter McGregor Eadie has written many guide books and has contributed to numerous newspapers and periodicals. He is a former Chairman of the British Guild of Travel Writers. He wrote the *Blue Guide Malta and Gozo*. **Fionnuala McGregor Eadie** is an intrepid traveller, like her husband, and has assisted him in the research for many books. They live in Caversham, near Reading.

Printed and bound in Great Britain by Butler and Tanner, Frome and London.

Contents

Bailiwick of Guernsey 97

Sark 138

Herm and Jethou 147

Alderney 150

Index 158

Maps and plans

Introduction

The Channel Islands are steeped in a history which is closely linked to that of England and France through centuries of turbulence. With the fall of France in 1940 the islands were occupied by Germany for five years until the end of the war. That was over 50 years ago and several new statues and museums have marked the celebration of the 50th anniversary which has taken place since the publication of the last edition.

By and large the Channel Islands are a holiday venue for the whole family, with long sandy beaches, rocky coves, country walks and megalithic and medieval ruins. They attract nearly two million visitors annually.

Nestled up to the coast of France, these islands enjoy long continental summers and mild winters. This Blue Guide provides a detailed account of the various attractions available to readers and takes them back in history some 70,000 years to the Stone Age and then forward to the present day. It tells about the artists, writers, soldiers, sailors and statesmen who have made these beautiful islands famous.

We are grateful to Dr I.A. Kinnes of the British Museum and to Mr Robert Burns, until recently Assistant Curator of the Guernsey Museum for their account of the archaeological and early history of the islands. Thanks go also to Heather Sebire, the Archaeology Officer of the Guernsey Museums and Galleries for additional comments and information.

Invaluable advice and assistance have been given cheerfully by the staff of the Jersey Museum, by the staff at La Hougue Bie in Jersey and by Peter Sarl, Director of Museums, Guernsey. The editors are most grateful.

No guide of this sort can be written without the assistance of colleagues within the tourist industry. We would therefore like to thank the Jersey Tourist Board team in London led by Diane Needham, as well as Michael Tait in Jersey. In Guernsey we would like to thank Evan Ozanne and Tony Carey. In Sark we would like to thank Colin and Sheila Guille. In Alderney thanks go to David Jenkins and Simon Le Lièvre.

Finally, our appreciation goes to Nicholas Dobbs of Condor Ferries for his help with surface facilities and information on ferry services and package holidays to the Channel Islands. Similar thanks go to British Midland Airways and Aurigny Services for their assistance and information on the air transport side.

It is, above all, the welcoming, friendly and helpful people of Jersey, Guernsey, Alderney, Sark and Herm, with their pride in their island heritage and their infectious enthusiasm for all the visitor can enjoy, that calls us, and so many others, back again and again.

While striving always for accuracy, we are well aware of the difficulty of avoiding errors and any suggestions for correction and improvements will be welcomed.

Many changes have been incorporated into this latest edition of *Blue Guide The Channel Islands*. These are aimed at giving information in a more readily accessible form and to extending commentary in a way which we hope will provide both an interesting read and will serve to enhance the visitor's stay in these enchanted isles.

Practical information

Geography, language and climate

The Channel Islands, called by the French 'Les Iles Anglo Normandes', are made up of the bailiwicks of Jersey and Guernsey. The Bailiwick of Jersey includes Jersey and two groups of rocky islets, the Ecréhous and the Minquiers, sovereignty over which was granted in 1953 by judgement of the International Court of Justice in the Hague. The Bailiwick of Guernsey includes the islands of Guernsey, Alderney, Sark, Herm and Jethou.

Once part of the Duchy of Normandy, the Channel Islands lie far closer to France than to England, nestled up against the Cherbourg Peninsula, in the Gulf of St. Malo. The inhabitants, by and large, are derived from Norman stock and the spoken tongue used to be a Norman-French patois. It may still be heard in Sark and some country parishes. Today the first language is English and everyone speaks it, but the memory of earlier origins is still retained in the islander's toast to 'The Queen, our Duke'.

Description of each of the islands is provided at the beginning of the appropriate section. For a comparison of size of each island the acreage and populations are: **Jersey**, 28,717 acres and 85,150 inhabitants; **Guernsey**, 16,062 acres and 58,681 inhabitants; **Alderney**, 1962 acres and 2297 inhabitants; **Sark**, 1274 acres and 550 inhabitants. **Herm** covers 450 acres and supports a family community. **Jethou** is only 4.4 acres, is privately owned and not open to the public.

Climate

A weather chart for Jersey is set out below, based on averages over a 30-year period (degrees Celsius).

	Highest maximum temperature	Mean maximum temperature	Average sunshine hours
January	14.4°C	7.9°C	67.4
February	16.7°C	8.1°C	89.4
March	21.1°C	10.6°C	150.1
April	26.1°C	13.1°C	198.5
May	28.9°C	16.2°C	245.5
June	31.1°C	18.9°C	255.2
July	35.0°C	20.7°C	248.4
August	35.6°C	20.6°C	231.9
September	33.3°C	19.0°C	169.9
October	25.0°C	15.8°C	127.5
November	18.3°C	11.7°C	73.5
December	16.1°C	9.3°C	57.3

Jersey is the most southerly, sunniest and warmest of the Channel Islands. It has the best sunshine record in the British Isles, with an average of eight hours a day in summer. The average yearly sunshine is 1915 hours. The average summer sea temperature is 17.1°C (62.8°F) recorded in deep water. The yearly average rainfall is 84.8cm. Temperatures experienced in the various islands differ only by one or two degrees. Comparative figures with those above show that the mean maximum temperature for Guernsey in June is 17.1°C with 18.9°C in July, 18.7°C compared with 20.7°C and in August 19.0°C compared with 20.6°C. The advantage here is due mainly to the fact that Jersey slopes down from north to south and in Guernsey it is the other way. The bailiwicks of Jersey and Guernsey are unquestionably the sunniest spots in the British Isles.

Getting there
Listed below are direct scheduled flights from the UK and Ireland. At the time of going to press many of these flights operate throughout the year.

To Jersey by air

Airport	Operator	Reservations
Alderney	Aurigny	01481 822886
Belfast	British Midland	0345 554554
Birmingham	British Midland	0345 554554
	Jersey European	0990 676676
Blackpool	British Airways Express	0345 222111
Bristol	British Airways	0345 222111
Cardiff	Manx Airlines	0345 256256
Derry City	Jersey European	0990 676676
East Midlands	British Midland	0345 554554
Edinburgh	British Midland	0345 554554
	British Airways Express	0345 222111
Exeter	Jersey European	0990 676676
Glasgow	British Midland	0345 554554
Humberside	Air UK	0345 666777
Leeds/Bradford	British Midland	0345 554554
Liverpool	British Midland	0345 554554
London, Gatwick	British Airways	0345 222111
Gatwick	British Airways Express	0345 222111
Gatwick	Jersey European	0990 676676
Heathrow	British Airways	0345 222111
Stansted	Air UK	0345 666777
Luton	British Midland	0345 554554
Manchester	British Airways Express	0345 222111
Newcastle	British Airways Express	0345 222111
Newquay	British Airways Express	0345 222111
Norwich	Air UK	0345 666777
Plymouth	British Airways	0345 222111
Southampton	Air UK	0345 666777
Teesside	British Midland	0345 554554
Cork	Manx Airlines	(01) 260 1588
Dublin	Manx Airlines	(01) 260 1588
	Jersey European	0990 676676

To Guernsey by air

There are flights to Guernsey from many UK airports. At the time of going to press many of these flights operate throughout the year.

Alderney	Aurigny	01481 822886
Birmingham	Jersey European	0990 676676
Bournemouth	Islanders	01202 481081
Bristol	British Airways Express	0345 222111
Cardiff	British Airways Express	0345 222111
Dublin (via Jersey)	Delta Travel	00 3531 874 7711
Dublin (via Jersey)	J Barter Travel	00 352 2181 1855
East Midlands	British Midland	01332 810741
Edinburgh	British Airways Express	0345 222111
Exeter	Jersey European	0990 676676
Glasgow	British Airways Express	0345 222111
Jersey	Aurigny	01481 822886
Leeds/Bradford	Air UK	0345 666777
London, Gatwick	Jersey European	0990 676676
Gatwick	British Airways Express	0345 222111
Heathrow	Air UK	0345 666777
Manchester	British Airways Express	0345 222111
Newquay	British Airways Express	0345 222111
Norwich	Air UK	0345 666777
Plymouth	British Airways Express	0345 222111
Southampton	Air UK	0345 666777
Southampton	British Airways Express	0345 222111
Stansted	Air UK	0345 666777

To the Channel Islands by sea

The Condor Express Ferries operate between Poole and Guernsey and on to Jersey twice daily throughout the high season, and five days a week throughout the rest of the year. The new generation of wave-piercing catamarans has given a new dimension to car ferry travel. Whereas the conventional service used to take around 9 hours to travel to Guernsey and 11 hours to Jersey, the Condor Express takes 2 hours 30 minutes to Guernsey and 3hours 45 minutes to Jersey. The catamaran carries 774 people and 185 cars at 41 knots. There is an open deck above and comfortable seats with tables below deck and a duty-free shop. Self service food and drink is also available. Latest information on fares can be obtained from central reservations ☎ 01305 761551. The company also produces a brochure available from your local travel agent. There is an Apex fare (limited number available) for those who book 30 days prior to departure, which offers a 10% reduction on the standard fare. There is also a range of special day trips and tours on offer throughout certain periods of the year which are worth enquiring about. Finally a brochure called Condor Holidays to Jersey and Guernsey provides a wide range of inexpensive packages. For more information ☎ 01223 516789. If you are staying mainly at either Jersey or Guernsey you can book to take your car over for the day or longer to the other island, or go as a foot passenger.

People who travel regularly to the Channel Islands can make a 20% saving by becoming members of Condor's 'Islander Club'. Membership at the time of going to press is £50 for a full 12 months for a car and passenger discount.

There are also three services a week by Condor from Jersey to Sark return which takes three quarters of an hour. This service runs from early April to late October. The **Isle of Sark Shipping Company** in St. Peter Port Guernsey provides a 45-minute service between Guernsey and Sark on many days of the week from the end of March to the end of October. As dates of sailing vary ☎ 01481 724059 for precise information to match your requirements. Many day excursions are available.

Subject to weather conditions there are three daily services throughout the season from Guernsey to Herm by **Herm Seaways** and **Herm Express**. Bookings for these sailings can be made at the kiosk on the Albert Pier in St. Peter Port. Several other air and surface carriers link the Channel Islands with the Continent.

National Express provide combined coach/sea fares to the Channel Islands between 1 April and 31 October, from four different zones: (a) Hamshire, (b) London and Sussex, (c) Midlands, Cambs., Beds., Notts., Herts., (d) S. Yorks., Norfolk. For more information ☎ 0990 808080. Money saving rail/sea tickets are available from all parts of the UK and can be booked at your local station.

Getting around

By car

Visitors are advised to bring with them the same documents they should have easily available in the UK, ie driving licence, vehicle registration, certificate of insurance, road fund licence and MOT. A nationality plate must be displayed. On Guernsey no vehicle may exceed 35mph during the off peak season and 25 mph during the high season. On Jersey the speed limit is 40mph except on certain roads which have lower speed limits marked. Motorcyclists and their passengers must wear helmets.

The AA and the RAC have offices in both Jersey and Guernsey. Parking regulations in Jersey demand that you purchase scratch cards and put them in your window. These can be obtained from many places and are easily available at your hotel desk where staff will explain how you use them. At the time of going to press each scratch card costs 20p, and usually, but not invariably, this provides you with one hour's parking.

Parking regulations in Guernsey public car parks and side streets usually have the time limit marked up for which you are allowed to stay in any particular space, and it is necessary to purchase (65p) a parking display card, available from the police or from petrol stations, which you put in your front window marking the time of arrival.

Note that certain **box junctions** in the Channel Islands, usually denoted by cross-hatched yellow marking, have a sign instructing visitors to filter in turn. This clever idea keeps traffic flowing faster in busy congestion areas and is rigidly adhered to. Regulations regarding driving are similar to those existing on the mainland.

Petrol is about one third cheaper than on the mainland, so if you travel with your own car, take advantage of the saving by filling up over there. No cars are allowed on Sark, but watch out for the tractors, they can travel quite fast.

Hire cars, motorcycles and bicycles. Lists of vehicle hirers are available from the relevant tourist information offices. Generally, drivers must be over 20 and under 70 years old to drive in the Channel Islands. The 70-year rule is not enforced with most car-hire companies. Where it is, separate cover can be arranged enabling drivers over this age to hire a car. Hirers must produce a current driving licence. In Jersey there are 34 car-hire companies, six scooter- and moped-hire companies and nine bicycle-hire companies. In Guernsey and Alderney there are approximately 25 car-hire companies altogether, three scooter- and moped-hire companies and ten bicycle-hire companies. On Alderney there are also (golf) buggies for hire that can be used for travel on the roads. Caravans are not permitted on the island, also there are no car ferry services to Alderney.

In Sark, only **bicycles** can be hired and as many visitors arrive by boat each day, there can be a big demand. **Avenue Cycle Hire** stock some 500 bikes of all kinds and sizes. You can book in advance on ☎ (01481) 832102. The other popular mode of transport is by **horse and carriage**. These are lined up for hire at the top of Maseline Hill above the port. It is a steep walk up the hill and a tractor with carriages like those at a childrens' fair (fondly referred to as the 'toast rack') will run the visitors to the top of the hill. It is inexpensive and frankly quite worth taking.

Taxis

Taxis, compared to the UK, are comparatively inexpensive. In Jersey the first 236 metres is charged at £1.40 for up to four people. Each additional 368 metres is 20p extra. There is a baggage charge of 10p per bag if carried else-where than in the passenger compartment.

For night calls there are two further tariffs, one for between 23.00–02.00 and another between 02.00–07.00. They are fairly minimal increases. Where the vehicle is hired for a journey from any seaport in Jersey or from the airport there is an extra charge of 20p and for each person carried in excess of one carried an extra charge of 10p. At the time of going to press expect to pay approximately £6 from the airport to the centre of St. Helier.

The taxi fare from Guernsey Airport into St. Peter Port is approximately £5. There are taxi ranks at the airport, harbour, shopping area (Town Hall) and the Weighbridge.

On Alderney the return fare for one person from airport to hotel is approximately £4.

Tour operators

There is a very substantial number of tour operators who package holidays to the Channel Islands and many of them can be found by visiting your local travel agent. Full lists are available from both the Jersey and Guernsey Tourist Boards.

Among the leaders are Premier Holidays, Preston Holidays, Saga Holidays, Travelsmith, and Delta Travel (Ireland).

Saga, whose holidays are for anyone over 50, is well represented in Jersey and Guernsey, and have flexible travel arrangements. Single bookings carry no extra charges. They also offer special rate return travel with National Express from some 1200 departure points throughout the UK. In Jersey, Saga offer their special packaged holiday from late April to mid-July, and from the end of August until late September. Their holidays include a guided coach tour of the island, and optional excursions to Herm, Sark, and France. The leading hotel on this tour is the **Grouville Bay**, which has beautiful views over the Royal Jersey Golf Club, and is close by the harbour town of Gorey, with many attractive restaurants, and conveniently placed for visiting the imposing Mont Orgueil Castle. A courtesy bus operates into St. Helier three times a week, and there are big savings to be had for those wishing to extend their stay.

In Guernsey there are three hotels to choose from, including the popular **St. Margaret's Lodge**, convenient to St. Peter Port and the airport. The food, the wine and the service are excellent. Again a coach tour of the island is included and there are several optional excursions. Saga's Channel Island packages begin in early April and run to mid-July and begin again at the end of August and run to the end of October. Great savings can be had for extended holidays. For more information and bookings freephone 0800 300500.

Visitors wishing for an all-inclusive short break in Alderney should take a look at the 'Aurigny Alderney Breaks from Southampton' brochure, listing some seven properties. (Central Reservations ☎ 01481 822886.)

Hotels

The Channel Islands have accommodation to suit a wide range of budgets. For the Bailiwick of Jersey contact the States of Jersey Tourism, Liberation Square, St. Helier, Jersey JE1 1BB ☎ (01534) 500777, or the Jersey Tourism and Information Office, 38 Dover Street, London W1X 3RB, ☎ (0171) 493 5278.

Official lists are obtainable for the Bailiwick of Guernsey from the Guernsey Tourist Board, PO Box 23, Guernsey, ☎ (01481) 726611.

Bailiwick of Jersey

Tourism is Jersey's main industry. The island authorities work to ensure that all registered establishments maintain high standards. The States of Jersey Tourism Committee is responsible for the annual inspection and grading of all registered premises.

There is a Hotel Register and a Listed Register of guesthouses and farms. Hotel Register establishments are graded between one to five suns. A one sun hotel provides simple accommodation with limited facilities and services. The standard of facilities and services can be assessed by the number of suns, so that four and five sun hotels provide all the services of top class hotels. Bedrooms are well appointed and restaurants offer varied menus and a comprehensive wine list.

Listed Register provides a range of standards of comfort and service shown by the one to three diamond symbols. They are usually small premises from 4 to 24 bedrooms and in the main are managed by the resident proprietor. The emphasis here is on friendly service in a homely atmosphere.

Booking your holiday. The *Where to Stay* booklet is the official directory of the Jersey Hotel and Guest House Association and is available from the States of Jersey Tourism Offices in London or St. Helier (see above for details). This publication makes it very easy for the visitor to book directly by telephone, fax or letter with any of the properties listed. This booklet also carries information on holiday villages, self-catering establishments and campsites. It provides information on hotels and guesthouses suitable for the disabled.

Many hotels feature a travel inclusive price panel. This unique service offered directly by those establishments provides an advantageously priced method of travelling to the island either by air or by sea. It is a worry free method of booking your holiday requirement whilst benefiting from a high level of personal service.

Another way of booking is through Jersey Tourism's own central reservation system Jersey Link (☎ 01534 500888). This service is particularly useful if you are making last minute arrangements. It is totally free of charge with reservation staff supplying details of properties, their location, facilities and prices. Once your final decision has been made, there is an option which allows you time to make the travel arrangements. To complete this booking you have to pay a non-refundable deposit equivalent to the price of the first night's stay.

Additionally there are many specialist tour operators that offer holidays to Jersey, details of which can be obtained from your local travel agent.

Bailiwick of Guernsey

All establishments offering holiday accommodation in the Bailiwick, including Alderney Sark and Herm, are graded in the *Where to Stay* booklet available from the Guernsey Tourist Board. Hotel grades are indicated by crowns ranging from five down to one. Guesthouse and self-catering accommodation are graded A, B, C, with A representing the highest grade. **Campsites** with addresses are also listed.

Booking your holiday

The *Where to Stay* booklet makes it simple for you to book direct with the properties listed. Many of them will make transport arrangements by air or surface at reasonable prices if requested. Tour operators also package holidays at advantageous prices and for this service see your local travel agent. For late bookers, Alderney has an accommodation hot-line to advise which of their establishments have vacant rooms (☎ 01481 824242). Guernsey also has an accommodation service informing what establishments have vacancies (☎ 01481 723555). They can make firm bookings on your behalf if you make the booking in the Tourist Information Centre.

Eating out

Jersey names nearly 100 restaurants in her official literature, and the Tourism Committee holds an annual Good Food Festival Award, the results of which are made available to enquirers at the Tourist Board in Liberation Square.

Longueville Manor, a 5-sun hotel and a founder member of the Relais et Chateaux organisation, whose head chef Andrew Baird formerly worked at the Ritz in London, offers an excellent menu. The à la carte fare changes according to the seasons, and the four course set menu changes every day to make the most of the fresh produce available in the market. The main oak panelled dining room displays an array of trophies awarded for the establishment's cuisine. These include the Jersey Gold Merit Award for exceptional standards in food service and accommodation within their grade.

An 'in place' in St. Brelade is the **Sea Crest Hotel and Restaurant**. Owners Julian and Martha Bernstein, have a natural touch which makes it one of the best sea food restaurants on the island. It is advisable to book in advance. This is another Gold Merit Award establishment.

The Atlantic, the Channel Island's sole member of the *Small Luxury Hotels of the World* has undergone a major refurbishment and the large west facing windows in the restaurant offer fabulous and romantic views of St. Ouen's Bay through landscaped gardens. Excellent lunch and dinner menus attract visitors and residents alike. Particularly recommended are the medallions of monkfish and lobster glazed with tarragon hollandaise and lobster sauce.

Another corner of the island where you can eat exceptionally well is the **Village Bistro** in Gorey Village. It is run by the owners, chef David Cameron and his wife, and is filled with locals every night, so you must book to be sure of a place. AA and Michelin recommended, the menu is extensive and all dishes are cooked to order. Prices are moderate.

There is an official *Eating Out* guide to Guernsey, Alderney, Sark and Herm, available from the various tourist information centres, which lists a full range of restaurants in the Bailiwick, and also keys them according to price. The range of restaurants in Guernsey is substantial, and you could eat out in a different venue every night for a month. The majority of eating out places in Guernsey are found around St. Peter Port but wherever you are on the island, there will be a good restaurant nearby. The local fish is excellent, usually freshly caught each day. The cost of wine should be less than in the UK because the proprietor does not have to pay VAT. Having said that, comparatively the prices are not that much cheaper than on the mainland because the development of offshore finance has led to prosperity and a high standard of cuisine demanded by executives who are involved in this business. If you have to eat out on a budget, there are many good bar restaurants, serving proper meals, which are very popular, and on weekends and holidays they can become very busy indeed. It is therefore advisable to get there early to find a comfortable seat.

The hotel restaurant in **St. Margaret's Lodge Hotel**, that lies between the airport and St. Peter Port on the main Forest Road has a good table d'hôte menu, with a fine selection of starters, main courses and desserts. There is also an à la carte menu with many specialities prepared by the chef, using locally caught fish, and locally grown vegetables. The restaurant has won many awards and recommendations. Here value for money and gourmet food combine to give a good evening out. Prices for the table d'hôte menu with coffee is around £16 per head. Last orders are taken at 21.30, and there is a comprehensive and reasonably priced wine list.

At the **Idle Rocks Hotel**, Jerbourg Point, the bar restaurant has one of the best sea views in Europe. It serves excellent fish and chips and most of the main dishes cost around £5. There is also, for only £2, a children's selection.

The **Waterfront Restaurant**, right by the Guernsey Tourist Board Information Office in St. Peter Port, has a selection of shell fish dishes and among the specialities are two choice starters, crab bisque laced with brandy, and grilled garlic oysters. Another good option is the chargrilled steak and salad. Prices are moderate, with main dishes averaging around £10–£12 at dinner time.

The **Steak and Stilton Restaurant** is also on the waterfront, close to Marks and Spencer. As the name suggests, it has a variety of steak cuts, from around £8–£10. It also has an equally good selection of fish dishes in much the same price category, as well as less expensive pastas, all served with a salad.

On **Alderney** good food is to be found in many of its restaurants. **The**

Moorings is a popular venue with the locals and has an open terrace overlooking Braye Bay, and for light meals, is very reasonably priced. It also has an indoor restaurant.

The hotel **Chez Andre** in St. Anne, besides being a very comfortable AA 3-star hotel has an excellent table d'hôte dinner menu and wine list. The author started with a freshly caught small lobster Thermidor and for the main course chose a large plaice with chips and vegetables. There was a good selection of desserts to choose from and coffee and peppermints. The bill for food was £14.95, quite a bargain. Recommendations include Egon Ronay, Logis of Great Britain, Johansens, and Ashley Courtenay.

Just a few yards down the same road, the Georgian House offers a Grand Plateau Fruits de Mer. It includes a whole crab (approx 4lbs), whole lobster (approx 1.5lbs), half a dozen Herm Island oysters, king prawns and other shell fish in season with salad and new potatoes. The table groans under the weight and the bill per person is £27.50 and the chilled Muscadet sur lie is £11.50 per bottle.

Sark caters very much for those who like to get away from it all and eat freshly caught seafood, and hence most of the hotels provide a very good and varied menu. Day visitors often choose to eat in the sunny secluded gardens of the 400 year old farmhouse which has been converted most attractively into **La Sablonnerie Hotel** on Little Sark. Much of the produce comes directly from the farm itself and is tastefully prepared, and as one would expect, freshly caught fish and Sark lobster are both popular. A complete list of places to eat is available from the Tourist Information Officer in Sark.

Herm Island has the excellent **Ship Restaurant** at the White House Hotel.

General information

Shopping and customs
The Channel Islands have much to offer shoppers. There are lower rates of duty on drinks, cigarettes and perfume, making them far cheaper than on the mainland. There is also no VAT, making a 17½ per cent reduction on most other articles. The shops are crammed with a wide choice of goods, particularly jewellery, clothes, leather, wines, spirits, photographic, radio, TV and general electrical equipment. Local products of interest are Guernsey and Jersey knitwear, pottery and woodcraft. Many will also wish to take home a carton or two of Jersey or Guernsey cream. Early closing day in Jersey and Guernsey is Thursday.

The Customs and Excise Department allow the following amounts of duty-free goods upon return to the mainland. Tobacco goods: 200 cigarettes or 100 cigarillos or 50 cigars or 250 grammes of tobacco; alcoholic drinks: 1 litre of spirit or liquer or 2 litres of fortified or sparkling wine plus 2 litres of still table wine; perfume: 50 grammes (60cc or 2 fl. oz); toilet water: 250cc (9 fl. oz). By far the lowest duty reduced prices for spirits are to be found in Alderney, where Old Chelsea Gin is £5.60; Tsarvich Vodka £5.50; Bardinet Napoleon £6.00; Claymore Scotch Whisky £5.95 and Pimms No1 £7.50. All are one litre bottles.

Battle of Flowers festival
Jersey and Guernsey are famous for their Battle of Flowers. In Jersey this annual carnival is held on the second Thursday in August. The word 'Battle' is now a

misnomer because the crowds are so large that competitors no longer pull the floats to pieces and pelt one another with blossoms after the parade. The parade in St. Helier has dozens of floats decorated with flowers, a beauty queen, bands with drum majorettes and a full collection of carnival figures. In Guernsey the Battle of Flowers is usually held on the third Thursday in August at Saumarez Park. These festivals are magnificent occasions. The flowers have to be picked and arranged for the floats in just 24 hours if they are to look fresh. Flower arrangers work round the clock and both events are well worth attending. Full details are announced in the local press.

Bank Holidays
Bank Holidays are the same as in England with the inclusion of an extra day, Liberation Day on 9 May.

Banks and currency
The hours of business for the banks in Jersey and Guernsey are from 09.30–15.30 Monday to Friday. Listed below are the main groups.

Jersey: **Barclays**, Library Place; Lloyds, 9 Broad St; **Midland**, Library Place, National Westminster, Library Place; **Royal Bank of Scotland**, Eagle House, Colomberie—all in St. Helier.

Guernsey: **Barclays**, 6/8 High St; **Midland**, 13 High St; **National Westminster**, 35 High St; **Royal Bank of Scotland**, High St; **Lloyds**, Smith St —all in St. Peter Port (09.30–15.30 weekdays). Alderney: **Lloyd's**, Victoria St; **Midland**, Victoria St; **National Westminster**, Victoria St—all in St. Anne (10.00–13.00 and 14.30–15.30). There are no cash dispensers on Alderney.

Sark: **Midland** and **National Westminster** (10.00–12.00 and 14.00–15.00 Mon–Fri).

Currency is the same as on the UK mainland although the Bailiwicks of Jersey and Guernsey mint their own coins and print their own notes. Coins are 1p, 2p, 5p, 10p, 20p, 50p, £1 and £2. Notes are £1, £5, £10, £20 and £50. Alderney has a range of coins it has produced for special events mainly the size of the old Crown or 5 shilling piece.

English money is acceptable in both Bailiwicks. Both Bailiwicks accept each other's notes and coinage but these are not accepted in shops on the UK mainland.

Post office
The Channel Islands' telephone and postal services are similar to those on the mainland. Local telephone books will provide the numbers required for local services. The main **Jersey post office** is on Broad St in St. Helier. The main **Guernsey post office** is on Smith St in St. Peter Port. Both Jersey, Guernsey and Alderney produce regular and interesting issues of stamps. Those wishing to purchase should visit the Sales and Service counter in the post office in Jersey, the Philatelic Bureau by the main post office in Guernsey, and the main post office in Victoria St, St. Anne in Alderney.

Medical attention
Bailiwick of Jersey. UK National Health Insurance does not apply in Jersey. Visitors from the UK may consult a doctor, free of charge at the Morning Medical Clinic at the General Hospital, Gloucester St, St. Helier, between 09.00 and

12.00 Monday to Friday from May to September and on Saturday from 10.00 until 11.30. From October until April (inclusive) the clinic operates on Monday, Wednesday and Friday from 09.00 to 11.00. There is no service on Bank Holidays.

Visitors who are prescribed medicines will be required to pay a nominal price for each item, and must bear the cost of consultation with a doctor in general practice. Further information is obtainable from The Controller, Social Security Department in St. Helier.

Bailiwick of Guernsey. There is no National Health Service in the Bailiwick but visitors from Britain are covered under a reciprocal arrangement with the United Kingdom and can receive free medical treatment if staying less than three months. The same applies to **Alderney**.

Electricity
240 volts a.c. and sockets fit standard equipment used in the UK.

Television and radio
Services are the same as those available on the mainland of the UK. Continental programmes are picked up on radio channels and with special aerials French TV broadcasts from Caen are easily received and in some cases programmes from further afield. There are also BBC Radio Jersey, BBC Radio Guernsey, Island FM, and Channel TV.

Newspapers
Weather permitting, UK newspapers are available on day of printing. Local papers include: *Alderney Journal* (fortnightly); *Guernsey Evening Press* (daily); *Guernsey Globe*; *Guernsey Weekly Press*; *Weekender*; *Evening Post* (Jersey, daily); *Weekly Post* (Jersey).

Useful telephone numbers
States of Jersey Tourism, St Helier ☎ 500700, London ☎ (0171) 493 5278. **States of Guernsey Department of Tourism and Recreation** ☎ 723552 (general enquiries) ☎ 723555 (accommodation).
Sark Tourism Officer ☎ 832345.
Alderney Tourism Office ☎ 822994.
Police: Jersey ☎ 999; Guernsey ☎ 725111; Alderney ☎ 822731; ☎ Sark 999.
Fire Brigade Jersey ☎ 999; Guernsey ☎ 724491; Alderney ☎ 882672; Sark ☎ 999.

History

Archaeology and early history

The Channel Islands are, and were, a microcosm of European culture; close enough to France to be in the mainstream yet separate and distinctive. The visitor will find much of archaeological interest, some of it of a kind to be seen nowhere else.

For much of the period covered here, until the coming of the Normans, there are no written records and when they do occur, in the last few centuries, they are few and unhelpful. From the first hunters, foraging northwards to the glacial fringes, to the beginnings of civilisation, the material remains of man's activities are all that survive to tell the story. With each successive generation this record has become progressively fragmentary and defaced. From the pieces that survive we have attempted to reconstruct the past. The pieces are there and accessible in the Channel Islands: in the countryside, in the museums and archives. This is our own interpretation: it does not preclude yours.

Palaeolithic man

The earliest evidence for man's presence in the Channel Islands comes from the site of La Cotte de St. Brelade, a cave on the south-west coast of Jersey. Excavations since 1910, and particularly a recent series by the late Professor McBurney, have revealed a series of superimposed layers of occupation debris covering some 70,000 years of the Palaeolithic or Old Stone Age period. From preliminary results it is possible to say that Jersey, still connected to the French mainland at this time, was part of the territory of hunting-groups living off the great herds of mammoth and woolly rhinoceros.

La Cotte de St. Brelade is the richest Palaeolithic site in the British Isles and one of the most important in Europe. Over 140,000 stone artefacts have been recovered as well as extraordinary quantities of mammoth and rhinoceros bones left as midden deposits. The stone industries, of Mousterian and earlier type, provide evidence for the range of hunting and gathering activities, and most importantly for the extent of movement by these groups in pursuit of big game. Raw materials from as far afield as Belgium have already been identified. Actual human remains, of Neanderthal type, were also recovered in the earlier work. The cave therefore provides unique testimony for a little-known period, but after the end of its occupation, perhaps around 50,000 BC, only a few scattered finds of stone tools indicate the continuing presence of man in Jersey.

As the Ice Age glaciers retreated the face of Europe changed. In the new dense forests man exploited large resources of game supplemented along coasts and rivers by rich harvests of fish and shellfish. This, the Mesolithic or Middle Stone Age, seems to be a blank period for the Channel Islands, as much of the land used for their camps is now eroded or submerged, although some flintwork might be of this date.

The first farmers

In about 5000 BC radical changes overtook this placid hunting existence when, in the Neolithic or New Stone Age, the first farmers moved into Western Europe. A stable supply of food from cultivated crops and domestic animals brought great changes. For the first time permanent village settlement was possible, and given this permanence, it was now possible to plan for the future. Forests were cleared for plough and pasture and there is little doubt that within 1000 years the landscape had been transformed to a state familiar to, but unconsidered by, the present day: patchworks of fields, an occasional block of woodland, scattered villages and farms. Although their presence can be inferred, settlements of the period are notoriously difficult to locate since the wooden buildings have long since decayed, leaving no trace above ground. Jersey, however, has evidence for the first farmers at two sites, both producing rich inventories of pottery and flint tools closely comparable to those of northern France. Beneath the Gallo-Roman shrine and early Bronze Age walls at the Pinnacle were a series of large hearths but no trace of buildings: perhaps, then, a place of communal ritual at the foot of the great rock spire recognised in the place-name. On the other side of the island the disturbed traces of another site lie beneath the castle of Mont Orgueil.

The rising sea-levels after the Ice Age have drowned much of the evidence but at low tides on some parts of the coasts submerged forests can be seen and Neolithic artefacts have been found.

More recently the picture of early settlement has been transformed by excavations at Les Fouaillages on Guernsey. Here, a small and insignificant mound has yielded evidence of an unmatched sequence of complex activity surrounding rites of the dead (see below).

These first farmers came to Jersey on foot from Normandy across a low marshy land bridge. Within the last 4000–5000 years the sea-level has risen by as much as 10m so that the Jersey peninsula has become an island. The other islands have been detached for much longer, although Guernsey and Herm were one during this period. Thus, while the first farmers simply walked to Jersey in search of land, the other islands could be reached only by boat, a hazardous undertaking for families with their domestic animals and seed corn, but enforced, perhaps, by land hunger. Much fine agricultural land, more extensive than the combined areas of the present islands, now lies beneath the Atlantic.

One aspect of these settlers does survive in spectacular form. Neolithic farmers along the Atlantic coasts constructed great stone monuments, megalithic tombs, for their dead. These usually consisted of a slab-built chamber covered by an impressive mound of earth or stones (fig. 1), itself often of elaborate construction. These were both tomb and temple: family vaults used for as much as 1500 years and a focus for rituals of life and death, central places and declarations of ancestral and territorial rights for the peasant communities that laboured to erect these great monuments.

Their prominence in the landscape, when more recent generations had forgotten their original purpose, has made them highly vulnerable parts of our prehistoric heritage; obvious stone quarries and impediments to the passage of the plough. Many have been destroyed: on Guernsey, for example, place-name evidence suggests the former existence of over 40 chambers of which no trace now remains. With the growth of antiquarian interest over the past 200 years

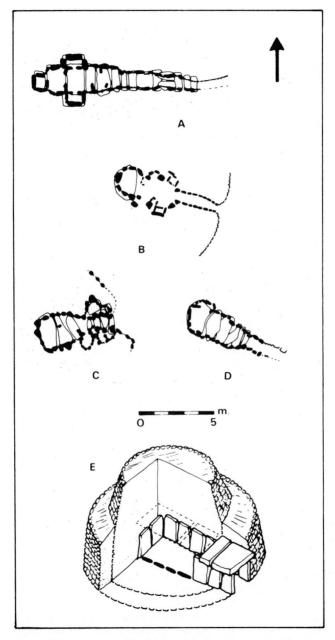

Figure 1: *Passage graves.* A. *La Hougue Bie*; B. *La Pouquelaye de Faldouet*;
C. *Le Déhus*; D. *La Varde*; E. *idealised reconstruction.*

the chambers became a prime source of skulls and artefacts for the collector's cabinet and many were pillaged. Even the tomb itself could become a portable curio: in 1788 the extraordinary Mont de la Ville structure which stood near Fort Regent in St. Helier was presented to a retiring governor of Jersey and is now to be seen in Berkshire parkland near Henley.

Much vital evidence was thus destroyed, but improvement came with the activities of the remarkable Lukis family of Guernsey in the Victorian era. Although far short of modern standards, excavations in the tombs were controlled and recorded with some care, and the results still form the basis of our knowledge of the period.

Many of the tombs are now ruined and it can be difficult to visualise them in their original state. The most distinctive form is that known as the Passage Grave, an architectural style derived closely from north-west France. In this the chamber expands from a narrow entrance to a broad inner end, where most of the burial deposits were made, and the whole is covered by a large circular mound. Although normally walled and roofed by granite slabs, other techniques are known. La Sergenté, on the west coast of Jersey, is dry-stone built, the walls originally rising to a beehive-like dome. Elsewhere on Jersey sites such as Mont Ubé and Les Monts Grantez are good examples of the normal style. Recent excavations of the mound around the chamber entrance suggest that complex construction was involved, the rituals involving extensions and platforms.

Undoubtedly the most spectacular of Jersey sites is La Hougue Bie. The mound is formidable, 54m in diameter and still 12m high: an astonishing tribute to the industry and skill of its builders 5000 years ago. It covers a massive chamber, 20m long, which is approached by a splayed entrance denoting a forecourt where rituals associated with the dead are likely to have taken place. The walls are carefully built of granite uprights supplemented by dry-stone walling, and support huge slab roofing. The chamber expands at the inner end and has three side-cells in cruciform plan, most probably reserved for particular families within the community. The stones were collected from several different sources, not necessarily those most convenient to the site, and involving transport over-land by man-hauled sledge or rollers for as much as 6km.

A recent series of excavations in the early 1990s included investigative work on the mound itself which was found to consist of a rubble deposit. There were no further chambers discovered but several phases of entrance were revealed and the impressive stone façade has been left exposed after the removal of the concrete tunnel that had been built in the 1920s.

On Guernsey there are no sites as impressive, but the passage graves at La Varde, Le Trépied and Le Creux ès Faies are well worth a visit. The finest example is Le Déhus where a circular mound, with traces of its original surround of upright stones, covers a fine chamber 10m long. Two side-cells lie at each side of the access passage and in the inner chamber is the rare feature of a central supporting pillar. The most remarkable feature is an extraordinary carving on the underside of the second capstone from the rear. Although difficult to discern, experiments with torchlight at the right angle should make the outlines clear. The representation, unique in ancient Europe, is of a human figure with face and arms, wearing a belt or girdle and holding a bow and, perhaps, arrows (fig. 3C).

Another magnificent example of Neolithic human representation, this time

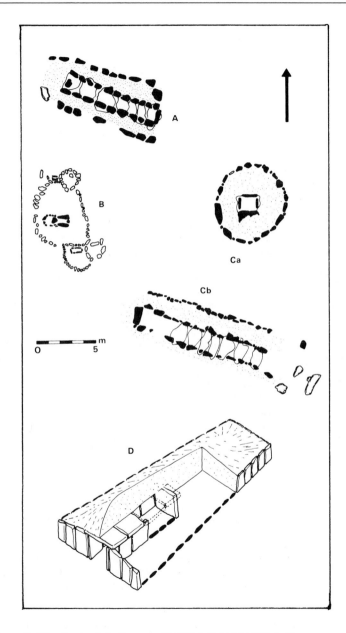

Figure 2: *Other tombs.* A. *Le Couperon*; B. *L'Islet*; C. (a & b) *Ville ès Nouaux*; D. *idealised reconstruction of a gallery grave.*

with analogies in southern Brittany, stands in Castel churchyard (fig. 3A). It is a granite pillar, carved in relief and unmistakably female with a pair of breasts, a necklace and girdle and some form of crown or headdress. The type is known as a statue-menhir, and was presumably an idol or goddess figure. One such in Brittany was associated with a Neolithic burial mound but the original context of that at Castel is unknown. It was found in 1878 beneath the chancel floor in the church and may well have been placed there to nullify or Christianise its pagan imagery.

Another figure stands at the gate of St. Martin's churchyard (fig. 3B). It is similar to that at Castel in size and outline and also has a pair of breasts in high relief. The original carving has, however, been modified in style suggesting Celtic or Roman workmanship. Facial features were added with a frame of ringlets beneath some sort of elaborate buttoned cape. It once stood within the churchyard, not necessarily in its original position, but in the 19C it was broken in two by an evangelistic churchwarden. After protests by the parishioners, whose reverence for 'La Gran'mère' was still marked by May Day offerings of flowers and wine, it was repaired and re-erected, albeit outside consecrated ground.

There are other tomb types. On Jersey, at Villes-ès-Nouaux and Le Couperon, there are long rectangular chambers originally set beneath wedge-shaped mounds with stone kerbs (fig. 2). These are again closely matched in northern France. Elsewhere there are purely local forms, already proclaiming the individuality which still characterises the islands. Notable among these is the complex arrangement of stone rings and small chambers of cists seen at L'Islet on Guernsey (fig. 2). This combination of received styles and local adaptation and invention can be seen also in the pottery, tools, and ornaments of the period.

The smaller islands are less rewarding for the amateur of prehistory. At least a dozen chambers survive on Herm, notably in the area of Le Grand and Le Petit Monceau, but are mostly ruined and overgrown. The depredations of Victorian military engineers on Alderney have left little to be seen although the tomb at Tourgis is worth a visit.

There remains one class of visible antiquity which seems to be of Neolithic date. These are standing-stones, or menhirs, which occur singly or in small groups. They range in height from about 1m to 3.5m, the tallest being La Longue Roque in western Guernsey. The group of three on the Quennevais in western Jersey are among the more interesting of the class. Their function is unknown but suggestions have included territorial markers, signposts and grave memorials. Many have certainly been carted away for building-stone.

The remaining impression, then, of the first farmers in the Channel Islands is of small, prosperous communities, very much in control of their environment. They had the surplus resources and religious compulsion to commemorate their dead and themselves in great monuments which remain impressive across five millennia. When one considers that the 62 sq km of Guernsey still exhibit ten tombs in reasonable condition and that at least another 50 are known to have existed, the achievement becomes even more astonishing.

Les Fouaillages

The mound at Les Fouaillages (see p.20) was expected to cover a simple but, it was hoped, intact megalithic chamber. Detailed and complete excavation yielded a very different story and work continues on unravelling its complexities.

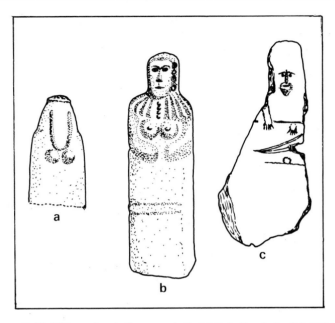

Figure 3: *Neolithic carvings in Guernsey. A. Castel; B. La Gran'mère; C Le Déhus.*

On a low plateau, then with a fertile soil cover, the first farmers chose a location for the rituals and commemoration of their dead. Their village, as yet undiscovered, must lie nearby under the modern dunes. The first structures were not spectacular: a pair of small cairns covering miniature vaulted cists, hitherto known only in Brittany. In and around these lay shattered decorated pots like those at the Pinnacle. Immediately, 1000 years was added to the agricultural history of Guernsey. For the first time, too, stone-built monuments could be attributed to this stage, precursors of the megalithic tomb tradition.

Within a short time came a major remodelling. The western cairn was levelled, and it and its partner were covered by a wedge-shaped mound of cut turfs with a monumental slab façade and boulder walls along each side. Throughout the mound, dumps of fine pottery and flintwork were carefully placed and around the western end deliberately broken schist bracelet fragments were set at regular intervals. The centre of the façade gave access to a rectangular turf-walled chamber, perhaps originally with a wooden roof. Sadly, acid soils have prevented the survival of bone, so the specific nature of the deposition of the dead remains unknown. This format of long mound and 'organic' chamber can be matched rarely elsewhere, but nowhere as early as this, so that we weave yet another thread in the complex web of monumental tomb development.

Again there were structural changes. Two massive marker slabs were slid into the end of the turf chamber and formed the rear of a cist of low slabs. At its front two wooden posts were set, marking an entrance and perhaps with the rear slabs supporting a flat roof. A complete decorated pot was placed within, presumably to accompany the dead. Another stone structure, slab-built and roofed, and about the size of a dog kennel, was inserted at the outer end behind the façade and the rest of the turf chamber was filled with dark earth containing much pottery and flintwork.

Finally, and still at a time before any other monument had been built in the islands, both chambers were carefully in-filled and the entrance gap in the façade was closed by a large slab.

For 1500 years attention switched elsewhere as the great stone tombs were built and used. Then, at the end of the Neolithic period, the users of a new style of pottery, the Beakers, known widely throughout Western Europe, established a settlement with small wooden houses alongside the already-ancient mound. On its crest they built a new and extraordinary structure. A massive semi-circular emplacement of earth and boulders was set against the existing façade and on this and the eastern end of the mound were placed two concentric boulder rings. Within them was a small stone and wooden rectangular enclosure and here again it seems that bodies had been placed, accompanied by a spectacular set of eight barbed and tanged arrowheads. Their workmanship is exceptional, and they had been made as four pairs, two of flint from the chalk of Normandy, two of the fine honey-coloured flint from Grand Pressigny, 300km away in central France.

At the end of use, the area was in-filled and this and the eastern end of the old mound were covered by a round mound of turf, again rich in finds. From about 2000 BC no activity can be shown, although the abandoned settlement had come under the plough. During the Iron Age the mound assumed a new function, as the corner marker for a laid-out system of fields defined by ditches and stone-faced banks, indicative of a new approach to land ownership. This system seems to have continued in use until a massive sand-blow in early medieval times brought abandonment and created the dunescape familiar today. The dunes protected the site from the depredations of agriculture and ensured its survival; and this is presumably true of many others on L'Ancresse Common. During the German occupation extensive sand quarrying, which would have brought destruction, fell short of the mound by a mere half metre.

The spectacular and important results of this excavation are a tribute to the interest and dedication of the States and people of Guernsey. The monument has been preserved in its third structural stage as a permanent demonstration of a remarkable achievement.

The Bronze Age

Little is known of the Bronze Age in this area. Evidence from elsewhere suggests that agricultural prosperity continued and that trade in the essential copper and tin became widespread. Part of the early settlement at Les Fouaillages has been investigated and comparable material has been recovered at other sites, especially beneath the dunes at Les Blanches Banques, Jersey. The stone ramparts at the Pinnacle are of this period; they seem to enclose some form of votive shrine at the foot of the rock. A small farmstead of later date has been excavated at La Moye, Jersey, with one or more stone-walled round houses. Little, however, is known of the conditions of daily life.

Bronze Age earthworks were excavated at Jerbourg (see below) and some coastal sites yielded pottery which indicates settlement, but these sites have yet to be excavated.

Some burials continued to be made in the tombs of their Neolithic ancestors, but new structures are rare. In the earlier part a few stone-lined graves or cists are known, some beneath small earthen mounds. Later, small cemeteries of cremations in simple urns occur, as at La Hougue Mauger on Jersey.

A few bronze implements have been found casually but a better indication of trade links along the Atlantic coast comes from two massive hoards of bronzes from Jersey and Alderney (Blanches Pierres and Longy Common). These large deposits of broken tools, and weapons as scrap-metal most probably represent the accumulated wealth of a community, stored as the village treasury in a pit or large pot.

The most splendid single object is a massive gold neck-ring or torc found in digging house foundations in Lewis Street, St. Helier and to be seen in the Jersey Museum. It is a solid gold bar, twisted into spiral curves, with a length of 140cm and weighing three-quarters of a kilogram. Almost certainly of Irish manufacture and dating to around 1000 BC, it is a remarkable witness to long distance trade contacts and the wealth and finery of a largely silent age.

The Early Iron Age

Tangible evidence for the earlier phases of the Iron Age in the Channel Islands is sparse. The lasting influences of the Bronze Age in neighbouring Brittany were perhaps reflected here also and the delayed nature of any observable change could well demonstrate the 'backwater' situation of this part of Europe. The first artefacts that may be said to come under an Iron Age heading were found in deposits made in the upper blown sand horizon of the megalithic site at Ville-ès-Nouaux, St. Helier. Here a small urnfield was discovered, which contained, among other tall-shouldered pots, a situlate jar with finger impressed decoration around its shoulder. This typical Hallstatt vessel is almost certainly the first real indication that we are entering a new phase. During recent excavations at the Ile Agois off Jersey, a similar jar was discovered in the make-up of a hut bank which the excavators consider dates to the 6C BC. A more substantial site from this early period was discovered in 1968 at Les Hougettes in Alderney where local archaeologists found a pottery manufacturing complex, which, by Channel Islands' standards, was of large proportions. Working platforms surrounded by a wall were situated among traces of other huts. Large quantities of coarse pottery were found, including many vessels similar to the Hallstatt types; among them were some with finger applied decoration on the shoulders. Bronze Age tweezers and razors were also discovered, illustrating the tenacity of earlier traditions at the site, which radio-carbon dating places c 490 BC. This Alderney site is at present unusual among Early Iron Age sites in the islands, in that it shows signs of permanence. More typical, perhaps, is the habitation site recently discovered in the centre of St. Helier where a small rescue excavation revealed a building of roughly oblong shape. In this building were a series of hearths each sealed by a layer of sand indicating sporadic, perhaps seasonal, occupation. The pottery was fine quality, well fired and burnished and bearing, in some cases, decoration in curvilinear style of La Tène type. Radio-carbon samples give a date of c 350 BC for this site.

The fortified sites built on the coasts of the larger islands produce the first visible remains of the period and both Jersey and Guernsey have their share of defensive earthworks. In Jersey, Le Catel de Rozel is the most noticeable. The site today consists of a single bank, some 6m in height, cutting off the tactically important strong-point between Rozel and Bouley Bay. Cliffs on the north western and eastern sides and a steep valley on the south, guard this important earthwork. Excavations at Catel de Rozel in the late 1980s found the earliest occupation to belong to the Neolithic-Early Bronze Age. However, the construction of the main rampart took place in the Middle Iron Age (c 400–100 BC). The dating evidence from the pottery and other finds was slight. Evidence that the earthworks were eroding was confirmed.

A smaller earthwork may be seen at Frémont Point, where a single bank with an outer ditch and counterscarp bank, has a causewayed entrance. A short excavation here in 1963 confirmed the existence of these features but the finds made were not suitable for dating purposes. At the castle site of Mont Orgueil large-scale excavations in recent years have shown the existence of Iron Age defensive work. However, the extensive medieval and post-medieval fortifications make interpretation of these earlier features difficult.

In Guernsey, excavations at Vale Castle provided an unexpected bonus with the discovery of a double-banked hillfort dating to 600–500 BC lying beneath the late medieval defensive structures.

The largest of the Guernsey earthworks is at Jerbourg, but recent excavations have demonstrated that Iron Age usage of this earthwork was negligible. The complex series of defensive banks built here was commenced in the late neolithic period, and were added to during the Bronze Age; more modern additions were made during the 14C as a result of the wars with France. In World War II the German forces created a battery and bunker system over the peninsula. There is a smaller double-banked earthwork at Jerbourg Point, not yet tested by excavation.

Further earthworks have recently been discovered at La Moye, at Corbière, where a single bank with double ditch cuts off the tiny promontory from the mainland. This site has not yet been excavated and it is possible that any early deposits will have been destroyed by the mass of German concrete which sits squarely upon it. Recent years have also seen the discovery of two earthworks in Sark: one is at the northern end of the island close to Les Boutiques, and a much smaller earthwork exists close to Port Gorey in the south of Little Sark.

The La Tène and Gallo-Roman periods

The wholesale granite quarrying activities carried out in Guernsey throughout the last century revealed the remarkable and well-known series of Late La Tène warrior burials. Small stone-lined cists, each some two metres by half a metre and buried about a metre deep, were found on high sloping ground in the west of the island at Le Catioroc, Les Issues, Richmond and La Hougue-au-Compte. Fortunately most of the material recovered has been preserved and can be seen at the Guernsey Museum and Art Gallery. The range of luxury goods discovered includes swords and scabbards, shield fittings, spears, knives, glass, amber, jet and bronze rings together with a range of pottery comprising cordoned urns and graphite decorated vessels of Hengistbury B type. The presence of these grave goods is the first indication of the existence of a wealthy and powerful minority among the local inhabitants. Recent years have seen a vast increase in our knowledge of this period in Guernsey. A settlement site of the Late La Tène period was discovered and excavated at King's Road, St. Peter Port. A circular defensive ditch enclosed a site with round post-built houses and a wide range of pottery, including cordoned and graphite-coated varieties, was discovered. A short distance from the site a graveyard of the same period was also discovered. The acidic soil had destroyed most of the organic evidence from most of the graves, but one grave made up for any disappointment. This contained a warrior burial, including a sword, shield, spear, knife, and a pair of scissors and razor in a textile bag. This material, which has been conserved in laboratories at Oxford University, will throw much new and important light on Late Iron Age burial practices. It is also on display at Candie Museum.

By contrast, evidence for this period in Jersey is slight. Some sherds of graphite decorated ware were found at the Ile Agois and pottery of La Tène type was found on Maîtresse Ile, one of the group of small islets lying some 12km south of Jersey. Two glass beads of La Tène type, both chance finds from St. Aubin, can be seen at the Jersey Museum.

In Guernsey, the cordoned vessels found in the warrior burials have some affinities with pottery found in 1976 at the Tranquesous, St. Saviour's. This important site, the largest inhabited area so far known in the Channel Islands, was discovered from cropmarks revealed during the dry summer of that year. Covering several hectares, the settlement consists of a minimum of 15 circular huts, each surrounded by a penannular ditch. A series of ditched enclosures, designed possibly for livestock marshalling and a double-ditched trackway bordering the site to the east, complete the settlement pattern. An occupation ranging from around 50 BC until AD 75 is indicated by the pottery and other finds. Metalworking, both iron and non-ferrous, was carried on and traces of salt distillation were also found; these industries indicating a permanent, ordered and relatively comfortable existence. Excavations in Brittany at Alet (modern St. Malo), have provided the strongest parallels for the pottery found at the Tranquesous and it would seem that its inhabitants, if not actually members of the Coriosolite tribe, which occupied that part of Gaul, were at least closely allied to them. Imported pottery at the Tranquesous includes Samian, Terra Nigra and amphorae from Northern Italy and from Spain. The strong influence of the Coriosolites over the Channel Islands at this time is reinforced by the coin evidence from the islands. Le Câtel earthwork in Jersey has been the scene of a series of discoveries of several major coin hoards, mostly comprising Coriosolite staters. The largest, some 12,000 strong, has been interpreted as being the mint of a large community possibly moving ahead of the Roman military activity across the water. Similarly, a major hoard found at La Marquanderie in St. Brelade is composed mainly of coins of the Coriosolites with a sprinkling of other Gaulish tribal coins including those of the Redones, Aulerci Cenomaci, Osismi, Baiocassi and Abrincantui—all near neighbours. This last hoard, and one discovered in 1957 at Le Catillon, Grouville, contained among the Gaulish issues British coins of the Durotriges. This connection, coupled with the many finds of Coriosolite coins and pottery in the catchment area of Hengistbury Head, would indicate that it was this tribe, rather than the Veneti from west Brittany, which controlled the trade between north-west Gaul, the Channel Islands and southern Britain.

The salt-working or briquetage sites, which probably belong to this period, do however present something of a dating problem. Sites have been found in Guernsey and in Herm, the best surviving examples being at Fort Grey and at Le Crocq Point, both on Guernsey's western coast. Finds consist of the coarse distillation vessels and of the hand bricks and other props used in the extraction process. The Guernsey Museum and Art Gallery possesses a small blue glass bead found at Le Crocq in 1912 and a recent trial excavation here revealed, besides the usual material, a hearth complete with the remains of two domestic cooking pots of non-diagnostic type. All that may be safely inferred is that these sites were probably in use during the period 150 BC to AD 150.

An intriguing find belonging to this period, now sadly lost, is the hoard containing Scythian phalerae or horse ornaments, found in Sark in 1718. The finds, now known only from contemporary illustrations, are considered to have been deposited around 40 BC.

The Roman period

The recent discoveries of the Roman waterfront site at La Plaiderie and of a Roman shipwreck in St. Peter Port harbour have completely transformed our knowledge of this period. The site at La Plaiderie comprised two stone warehouses with tiled roofs, and yards and drainage gullies associated with this small warehouse entrepôt. Coins, glass and other items indicate a life for the site from c AD 150 until c 400. The wealth of material recovered will take several years to research.

Recent observations as the town market is re-developed have produced large quantities of Roman material. These two fortuitous discoveries suggest that Roman St. Peter Port, hardly known 20 years ago, may have been a naval base policing the busy shipping lanes; piracy, after all, has long been a feature of these seaways.

The shipwreck recently raised by Dr Margaret Rule dates to the late 3C AD. It was a large vessel built with oak timbers which had burnt and sank just off the present harbour mouth of St. Peter Port. Originally it would have measured some 23m in length, with a width of 5.5m. The boat was flat bottomed and at its rear was a small cabin with a tiled roof. Conservation of this crucially important wreck is at present in progress. The story of the Plaiderie site and the Gallo-Roman wreck are told in the Maritime Museum at Castle Cornet.

Recent excavations under the market in St. Peter Port, in what was the Bonded Stores, has revealed further evidence of the Roman occupation of Guernsey. Extensive Roman finds have been located in the areas that survive under the massive Victorian footings. Pottery, both fine and coarse wares, glass and tile have been recovered in abundance mainly dating from the middle of the 1C AD. An earlier phase of the site has also been excavated, producing a brooch of 'Langton Down' type from AD 100.

The main contenders for inclusion as actual Roman sites are the small fort known as the Nunnery, in Alderney, and the square building, identified variously as a watch-house or Gallo-Roman shrine, at the Pinnacle in Jersey. The Nunnery, a small square fortification with corner bastions, contains Roman brickwork in herring-bone style and is certainly situated in an area which has produced substantial amounts of Roman artefacts. In 1889 Baron von Hugel unearthed a large quantity of pottery, ornament and other artefacts in association with a coin of Commodus (AD 180–191) but unfortunately much of this material is now lost. It is possible that the Nunnery is an outlier in the line of Roman Gaulish shore forts erected during the late 3C AD to combat the growing Saxon menace. The Pinnacle site in Jersey revealed a ring-neck flagon together with a coin of Commodus. Recent work on the material from the original excavation has brought to light sherds of two black-burnished bowls of Dorset manufacture, produced between AD 250 and 400.

Roman coin hoards are scarce and known only from the two larger islands. In Jersey 18 antoniniani dating from 253 to 268 were found at the Ile Agois and another hoard found in 1848 at the Quennevais consisted of approximately 400 folles dating from 290 to 354. The only hoard from Guernsey was found at Jerbourg and consisted of 16 coins dating from 290 to 354. Chance finds of single coins are known from most of the islands and it is noticeable that these are usually of the 3C–4C and often from Alexandrian mints.

A Roman Doric pillar in granite, with an inscription added in the 6C or 7C and subsequently carved with a strapwork design in the early medieval period, may be seen in the church of St. Lawrence in Jersey. Whether this originally stood in a Jersey Roman building can only be a matter for conjecture. Samian pottery has been discovered at various places in the islands, usually under circumstances unsatisfactory for accurate dating. A lion's head mortarium of the 2C was found recently at Grandes Rocques, Guernsey, in redeposited soil; Samian is known from the upper levels of some megalithic tombs excavated during the last century.

The Dark Ages

In common with many other areas of the Armorican Peninsula and the south west, information with regard to the so-called Dark Ages is sparse. Fact and legend intermingle to leave the picture both cloudy and fragmented and archaeology has done little, so far, to throw more light upon it.

The vacuum left at the end of Roman rule was almost certainly filled by Breton overlordship. However, the conditions noted by Professor P.R. Giot as existing in Armorica almost certainly existed in the islands also and the poverty of the indigenous population, coupled with the local tradition of re-using the granite from which habitations were made, has left little for the archaeologist to discover. Recent excavations at the Ile Agois have investigated the huts interpreted as belonging to a small eremitic community, perhaps of the 7C or 8C AD. A small hoard of coins struck by Charles the Bald of France between 864 and 877 was found in the 1920s somewhere on the site. Pottery from this little-known period is extremely scarce and is represented by one sherd of found in Alderney and ascribed to the 6C or 7C.

The comings and goings of the various saints associated with the islands are well documented, although firm evidence to back up the legends is lacking. Little or no archaeological investigation has been carried out on the island churches, although recent work has been carried out on the Ecréhous, off Jersey, and Lihou Priory, off Guernsey. The recurring stories of the translation of holy relics from the islands to places of safety in Brittany during this period indicate the turbulent and unsettled nature of the times. Inscribed stones from the Dark Age period do exist and form the best evidence to be seen today. A re-used 8C Celtic cross was discovered in 1976 built into the wall of a farmhouse at Les Messuriers, St. Peter's in Guernsey and a stone bearing an inscription of the period may be seen at the Vale Church, also in Guernsey.

The Viking raids and the pre-Norman period

Increasing activity by Viking bands in the area of the Channel Islands would obviously have some effect upon the islands. It has been suggested that the promontory fort at Jerbourg contains components dating from this period, in a similar fashion to the earthwork at La Hague Dyke on the Cherbourg peninsula, but recent excavations have not borne out this contention. Two main bands of Viking raiders vied for supremacy in the area: those based upon the estuary of the Seine and another powerful group based upon the Loire. Raiding started around 814 to 820 and carried on sporadically, until in 911 Rollo, chief of the Seine band, was ceded the future Duchy of Normandy by Charles the Simple of France. The Treaty of St. Clair-sur-Epte, however, did not include the Channel Islands and it was not until 933 that Rollo's son, William Longsword, gained the victory against the Breton lords which forced Raoul, King of France, to cede to him the Contentin and Avranchin. Although not specifically mentioned, the Channel Islands must surely have been ceded to William at this time.

What effect did this tumultuous and violent episode have upon the islands? The wealth of the area, such as it was, was not quickly renewable and their attraction as the targets for repeated raids would have been limited. We can assume that here, as in other parts of Britain and Ireland, small parties would have settled and lived alongside the local Breton population. The sprinkling of place-names of Scandinavian origin in the islands might lend weight to this theory. Farming was probably carried out from widely separated long-houses and, although no building directly attributable to the period has yet been discovered, three later examples will serve as models. At Old Street, in St. Helier, a long-house dating from the 12C or 13C has been thoroughly excavated. Here, as in Brittany and Wales, stone or rubble walls supported a clay and thatch roof under which both people and their livestock lived, separated merely by a flimsy partition. A similar building was discovered at Cobo in Guernsey and these simple buildings with their central hearths can have changed but little from those of earlier date. An interesting find from the Cobo house, dated by its pottery to the 12C or 13C, was a bone gaming piece finely carved with a sleeping dragon or serpent. This piece almost certainly belongs to an earlier, Carolingian period and was perhaps a chance find made by an inhabitant of the later building.

Excavation in 1986 of a small group of oval buildings at Grandes Rocques has shown direct and striking parallels with early 12C settlements in Brittany. The huts were approximately 5m long by 3m wide, with a single door and a central hearth. Much pottery has been discovered on the site, the first of this type on the Channel Islands.

With this incorporation of the islands into the Norman sphere we come to a period of slow growth and relative unimportance. The towns, as we know them, probably started their growth at this time. Rescue excavations in St. Helier denote a concentration of occupation there during this period. This type of rescue has been carried out in St. Peter Port more recently, where, thankfully, development has left much of the delightful town unscathed, but several recent large developments have revealed further evidence of the medieval town. However, further knowledge of this early medieval phase must await future discoveries and excavations.

Ian Kinnes, MA, PhD, FSA of the British Museum. R.B. Burns, former Assistant Curator, Guernsey Museum, with additional material by Dorothy Sebire, Archaeology Officer, Guernsey Museums and Galleries.

History from Norman times

In 933 Duke William I, nicknamed 'Longsword', added the Channel Islands to the Dukedom of Normandy. One hundred and thirty-three years later Duke William II, the 'Conqueror', defeated King Harold at the Battle of Hastings and pronounced himself King William I of England. Ever since then, except for a few short breaks, the Channel Islands have been associated with the Crown of England, or, as an islander will tell you, from a chronological standpoint, England has been associated with the Channel Islands.

The Normans brought with them a code of laws, called *Le Grand Coutumier*, which were excellent for the defence of human rights and which remain the basis of the Common Law of the Channel Islands. The most unusual of the Norman legal survivals is the '*Clameur de Haro*' based upon calling for justice in the name of Rollo, 'Ha-Ro', the revered father of Duke William 'Longsword'. Any citizen feeling himself wronged by some action has only to go down on his knees and cry before the appelant and two witnesses '*Haro! Haro! Haro! A l'aide, mon Prince! On me fait tort*' [Help! my prince, they are wronging me], and then repeat the Lord's Prayer in French. Instantly, whoever is committing the alleged wrong must desist until the case is tried before a court.

Clameur de Haro

The power of this law is best exemplified in ancient chronicles when the cry was raised against the dead body of William the Conqueror. The story behind the event is that William, when erecting the Abbey of St. Stephen at Caen, which he intended for his own sepulchre, failed to pay one man for his house site which had been requisitioned during the development. Later, when the body of William was brought to its resting-place, the grave was in that part of the grounds where the house had stood. During the funeral rites the house owner raised the Haro for justice and it was only when the King of England paid compensation that the body could be laid to rest.

The Dukes of Normandy owned considerable estates in the Channel Islands and there were a few royal fiefs. Most of these were small and the seigneurs were required only to pay tax, but some of the larger ones were expected to render Knight service in time of war. Certain seigneurs were also burdened with fascinating obligations. For instance, the Seigneur of Rozel was expected when the Duke paid a visit to the island to ride into the sea up to his horse's girth to welcome him. Duties paid to seigneurs of fiefs were usually levied in the form of livestock, such as geese and chickens, and produce such as eggs, vegetables and corn. Tenants were expected to fulfill certain duties on the seigneur's land in return for which they were allowed to use the seigneural mill for grinding their corn. Other large landowners included a number of religious houses in Normandy.

Although the loss of the Duchy by King John in 1204 to King Philip of France 'plucked a valuable feather from the wing of English power', it did in the long run consolidate the insular power which remained. Most of the inhabitants of the Channel Islands were probably unaffected by the period of upheaval and had little hostility towards the English realm. On the other hand they may well have feared the French as the enemy at the door of the Dukedom. Several important families who owned land in the Channel Islands and in Normandy no doubt had problems with their allegiance and had to make decisions regarding their future homes, based on financial expediency.

King John soon realised the importance of not alienating the inhabitants because of the proximity of France and he is believed to have actually visited Jersey to grant special concessions. He wisely left Norman Law practically unaltered and the ecclesiastical scene undisturbed by allowing the islanders to remain under the ruling diocese of Coutances and restoring the rights and possessions of Norman abbeys. King Henry III, when he succeeded to the throne, confirmed the decision of his father and it is recorded that in 1230 he visited Jersey.

The Customs and Privileges of the Islands were again confirmed by Charter by Edward III and they have been re-affirmed by every English sovereign since.

In 1338 the French laid siege to the Channel Islands, captured Castle Cornet and conquered Guernsey, Sark and Alderney. Seven years later the English recaptured Castle Cornet and Guernsey was liberated. In 1356 it was again taken by the French but the victory of the English at the Battle of Poitiers led to the Treaty of Calais, in which the French abandoned all claim to the Channel Islands.

Bertrand du Gueslin, one of France's great soldiers, attacked Gorey Castle with 2000 gendarmes and 600 bowmen in 1373 but failed to penetrate beyond the outer wards. In 1461 this practically impregnable fortress did fall to the French through the connivance of Queen Margaret herself, a French princess and Lancastrian 'Red Rose'. The castle surrendered to Carbonnel, the representative of her cousin, Pierre de Brézé. The latter was appointed by Louis XI, Lord of the Islands. In ordinances of this period, we find references to Gorey Castle as Mont Orgueil (Mount Pride), so great was the impression given by this fortress. This apt name has remained to the present day. King Edward IV, a Yorkist 'White Rose', recaptured Jersey in 1468 through the exploits of Vice-Admiral Sir Richard Harliston.

Towards the end of the 15C a period of neutrality arose between the monarchs of England and France. In 1483 a Papal Bull was issued and posted on the cathedrals of Canterbury, London, Salisbury, Nantes, St. Pol de Léon, Treguier and the church of St. Peter Port. This declared that the Channel Islands, their harbours and surrounding waters 'as far as the sight of man goes, or the eye of man reaches', were to be treated as neutral in times of war and that enemy ships should remain immune from attack within these perimeters. Disobedience of this command would lead to excommunication. The Bull prevented foreign powers from attacking the islands and the English from using them as a military base and although neutrality was occasionally breached, the islands were able to live on the margin of international conflicts until the Bull was abolished in 1689 by an Order in Council.

From early Norman times the Channel Islands pertained to the Diocese of Coutances, although several unsuccesful efforts were made to transfer authority. In 1499 Pope Alexander VI cancelled his last transfer from the Diocese of Coutances to that of Salisbury and issued a further Bull transferring the islands to the Diocese of Winchester. Even so in 1500 Richard Le Haguais made sure that he was appointed to the Rectory of St. Brelade not only by the Bishop of Winchester but also by the Bishop of Coutances. The transfer can only really be said to have taken place when an Order in Council in 1569 confirmed a previous letter of Queen Elizabeth I on this matter. With the accession of Elizabeth to the throne the islands became firmly Protestant. Calvin himself succeeded in appointing two of his pupils as Rectors of the Town Churches of Jersey and Guernsey.

Sark, which was at the mercy of the French and pirates for three centuries, was colonised during the reign of Elizabeth I by Helier de Carteret, Seigneur of St. Ouen. He was granted all rights and privileges for a twentieth part of a Knight's fee, on two conditions—that within two years Sark should be occupied by at least 40 men, and that the land should remain in Carteret's family unless the Crown granted otherwise. It was on the basis of 40 tenancies that life on Sark was henceforth fixed, and the 16C feudalism of Sark has survived with limited modification to the present day. The colonists transformed the island into a prosperous community and Helier was able to report that Sark defences were now secure. The Queen showed her pleasure by making Sark a Fief Haubert, which meant that the Seigneur owed homage only to the sovereign and had to supply, if called for, a horseman with a coat of mail or 'haubert'. Certain customs still persist, such as the right of the seigneurs to own the only pigeons and the only bitch on the island.

To this period belongs the re-entry of Alderney to the full community of islands. In 1559 it was granted to George Chamberlain, son of the Governor of Guernsey, the English having abandoned its fortification just a few years earlier, on the grounds that it would be of 'no annoyance at all to the enemy, nor any benefyte or proffite to the realme but a mere gulfe of charges to no purpose'.

The Chamberlain family retained governship (except for a short period when rights were sold to the Earl of Essex) until 1643, just after the start of the Civil War.

During the English Civil War Guernsey supported the Parliamentarians and Jersey, mainly because of de Carteret, the Royalists. The friendly rivalry which exists between the two islands even today probably arose from this polarisation of loyalties. Jersey twice gave refuge to the Prince of Wales (later to become Charles II), and when his father Charles I was executed by Cromwell, Charles II was proclaimed the new king in the Market Place (now the Royal Square) in St. Helier. When the Parliamentarian forces arrived in 1651 to take over Jersey, Sir George Carteret withdrew to defend Elizabeth Castle. The invaders first captured St. Aubin's Fort and then Mont Orgueil which was not constructed to withstand cannon fire. The Royalists held out for 50 days at Elizabeth Castle until a mortar exploded the arsenal. Castle Cornet in Guernsey was also held by the Royalist Lieutenant-Governor, Sir Peter Osborne, who withstood almost nine years of siege. Continuous bombardment from the castle forced the Court, which was no longer Royal, to move its venue to Elizabeth College. In the end this last Royalist garrison marched out with the full honour of war in December 1651.

King Charles II was restored to the throne in 1660 and was for the second time proclaimed King in the Market Square of Jersey. During his reign, partly due to the influence of Sir George Carteret, five scholarships became reserved for Channel Islanders at Pembroke College, Oxford.

In 1781 the French made their final bid to capture Jersey when Baron de Rullecourt landed by night at La Rocque. The Lieutenant-Governor, surprised in his bed, surrendered but not so the 24-year-old Major Peirson, who ignored orders and attacked the French in the Market Place. Strong in personal courage and tactical skill he defeated the enemy and died in action. His body lies buried in the Parish Church of St. Helier. Baron de Rullecourt was also killed and was buried in the churchyard.

The defeat of Napoleon at Trafalgar in 1805 and at Waterloo in 1815 ended the threat of further French invasion and many ex-naval and army personnel now settled in the Channel Islands. The 18C boom in privateering stimulated the growth of the ship-building industry in the islands but this was phased out with the advent of steamships. Even so, Victoria's reign heralded great development in the Channel Islands despite several bank failures. It was an age of prosperity for the islanders; quarrying stone and oyster farming flourished. During this period the cider-making industry continued to thrive and by 1832 over half a million gallons were exported annually from Jersey alone.

Royal visits continued through to the 20C with George V and Queen Mary visiting Jersey and Guernsey in 1921 and the Prince of Wales (later Edward VIII) arriving in 1935.

In the summer of 1940 the Germans occupied the Channel Islands and stayed until May 1945, when they were forced to surrender to the Allies. During this period the island became part of Hitler's notorious Atlantic Wall.

German Occupation

The 'Atlantic Wall' was Hitler's title for a line of fortifications which covered the coastal stretch from Normandy to the Spanish border. This wall was the defensive rampart which the Germans built between 1940 and 1944 to protect their western front. The enormous project required the movement of 28 million cubic metres of earth and consumed 11 million cubic metres of concrete. In the Channel Islands alone 613,000 cubic metres of reinforced concrete were poured into what became one of the most comprehensive defence layouts ever devised; each cubic metre took an average of 70 man hours. Most of these defences have survived intact as the islands were by-passed in the Allied invasion of June 1944.

In October 1941 Hitler issued a directive for the consolidation of the Channel Island defences and Organisation Todt became responsible for the construction work. Fritz Todt paid a visit and supervised the setting up of OT commands in Alderney, Guernsey and Jersey. Each island was treated as a separate defence sector with its own Fortress Commander. Guernsey had 11 strongpoints and 53 defence nests, each code-named, around its perimeter. There were 15 coastal batteries, the largest with four mounted 30.5cm naval turreted guns with a range of 32km at Le Frie Baton on high ground in the west. The core of the artillery defence was 36 10.5cm guns grouped in batteries and placed between strongpoints. Aerial protection was provided by 31 batteries of anti-aircraft weaponry. Along the cliff line of the south coast were a line of observation posts flanked on the west by four 22cm guns at Pleinmount and on the east by four 22cm guns at Jerbourg. Famous sites were re-fortified to modern standards of warfare at Castle Cornet, Vale Castle, Fort George and Fort Hommet. With remarkable camouflage and ingenuity, observation platforms were added to Vale Mill tower and Fort Saumarez. In addition to permanent defences, extensive field works were employed which included anti-landing obstacles on the beaches, barbed wire, mine fields, flame throwers and trench systems. Extensive rock tunnelling was carried out in both Guernsey and Jersey to provide underground hospitals and ammunition dumps.

Jersey was also ringed with 13 strongpoints and 52 resistance nests with batteries of guns ranging from 8 to 22cm. A particular problem was the protection of the large beaches at St. Ouen and St. Aubin's. The concrete anti-tank wall with a concave profile presented to the beach which would turn an invading tank on its back was one essential form of defence. St. Ouen's, with its 6km beach, was flanked by a 15cm battery in the north at Etaqueret and by a 22cm battery at La Moye in the south. St. Helier was protected by 15cm guns on an unusual elevated emplacement with a ramp for bringing up ammunition at Noirmont. Open emplacements covered other approaches. Elizabeth Castle by the harbour entrance had several anti-aircraft emplacements, two casemates for 10.5cm guns, an observation post, searchlight installations and bunkers. Mont Orgueil, Fort Henry, St. Aubin's and many existing Martello towers were also fortified.

Alderney seems to have received the greatest attention because of its small size. It has 13 strongpoints and 12 resistance nests. Eleven of the 13 19C forts which overlook the north and east coast were fortified. Besides five major coastal batteries, there were 21 anti-aircraft batteries. In addition, there were extensive fieldworks and anti-tank walls.

Finally, in case of attack from the mainland one 8.8cm battery was installed on Sark. Despite all these ant-like preparations, very few sections of the 2865km Atlantic Wall were ever tested in battle.

The Channel Islands today

Since World War II tourism has grown to be a major industry and the forward thinking of the Channel Islanders has resulted in value for money for visitors. Purchases are free of 15 per cent VAT and liquor, wine and cigarettes are cheap. Summers are long in this most southern section of the British Isles. The winters are mild and in spring the flowers are an attraction in themselves. In summer the visitor can choose to make individual arrangements or select a package holiday; in the winter and early spring, winter week and weekend breaks are growing in popularity. Jersey is also one of the key conference venues of Europe.

Government

The Channel Islands, along with the Isle of Man, have a unique relationship with the United Kingdom. Although they are not part of the UK, the British Nationality Act of 1948 declares that 'a citizen of the United Kingdom and colonies may, if on the grounds of his connection with the Channel Islands or the Isle of Man he so desires, be known as a citizen of the United Kingdom, Islands and Colonies'.

Between 1204 and 1415 the Islands were governed by the King of England in Council through a Warden. However, after the loss of Normandy the islanders were allowed to continue to adhere to Norman customs and laws. From 1415 to 1470 the Crown was represented by a Lord of the Isles. After this date separate Governors were appointed for each Bailiwick and this continued to the mid 18C, when the duties came be to carried out by Lieutenant-Governors. Lieutenant-Governors, the personal representatives of the Queen, act in person for the Sovereign on most official occasions and are in command of military matters. Each is entitled to sit and speak but not to vote in the Assembly of the States.

Other Crown appointments in Jersey include Bailiff, Deputy Bailiff, Dean, Attorney General, Solicitor General, Vicomte and Receiver of Her Majesty's Revenues. In Guernsey they include Bailiff, Lieutenant Bailiff, Dean, Her

Majesty's Procureur and Her Majesty's Comptroller. The last two posts fulfil the duties of Attorney and Solicitor General respectively. The States of Deliberation also has a Bailiff who is a High Court Judge and ex officio President (Speaker) of the States of Deliberations. Twelve Conseillers are chosen by universal suffrage from both the electorate of Guernsey and Alderney. Thirty-three Deputies and two representatives from Alderney also sit in the States of Deliberations. Ten Douzaine representatives are elected anually by each Parish Council.

The States of Election in Guernsey (the electoral college) elects the twelve Jurats of the Royal Court. In the States of Election the Bailiff presides and the college comprises Jurats of the Royal Court—12 Conseillers, 10 Rectors, 24 Douzaine representatives, HM Procurer, HM Comptroller, 33 Deputies and 10 Douzaine representatives who have seats in the States.

In Alderney the Chairman of the Court and the six Jurats are appointed by the Secretary of State for Home Affairs. The States have a President elected at a separate presidential election, who holds office for four years. The elections are staggered so that six members are elected every two years. The senior civil servants, the Clerk of the States and the States Treasurer are appointed to their office with the approval of the Secretary of State for Home Affairs. The Clerk of the Court is also appointed under the same arrangement.

In Sark, the Seigneur appoints three officers (subject to the approval of the Crown through the Lieutenant-Governor of Guernsey) of the Seigneural Court. They are the Senéchal, who is the Magistrate, President of the Chief Pleas and Chief Administrator with authority over the Seigneur himself in civil cases; the Prévôt, who acts as Sheriff, Sergeant of the Court and gaoler; and the Greffier—Registrar and Clerk to the Court and to the Chief Pleas. The Chief Pleas is a tiny legislature which meets three times a year. It is composed of the Seigneur, Prévôt, Greffier, Tenants and Deputies of the People.

Bailiwick of Jersey

Jersey is the largest of the Channel Islands and covers 115sq km. With two groups of islets, the Ecréhous and the Minquers, it comprises the Bailiwick of Jersey. The main island slopes towards the south, has a verdant centre and possesses over 32km of the finest sandy beaches in Europe. It is approximately rectangular in shape with an average length of 15km and average width of 8km. The south coast stretches from **Corbière Point** to **La Rocque Point** and has two bites out of it, a small one on the west side creating **St. Brelade's Bay** and a larger one in the centre creating **St. Aubin's Bay**. On the east side of St. Aubin's Bay is the capital port of **St. Helier**. The west coast runs north from Corbiére Point and incorporates the enormously long sandy beach of **St. Ouen's Bay**. The north coast has a rugged coastline descending to several bays and stretching from **Grosnez Point** to **La Coupe Point**. The east coast descends from La Coupe Point, past the famous castle of **Mont Orgueil** and the attractive little port of Gorey to **La Rocque Point**.

Just over 160km from the south coast of England and only 24km from France, which is clearly visible from the east coast, Jersey is the sunniest spot in Britain. The Gulf Stream flows in its direction and the prevailing wind is south-west so that spring comes early and autumn lingers.

The following **bus routes** take the visitor to different beaches and points of interest on the island from the main bus centre at Weighbridge in St. Helier:

Rte 1:	Gorey Pier via East Coast Road
Rte 1A:	Gorey Pier via St. Clement's Inner Road*
Rte 1B:	Gorey Pier via Georgetown, Grouville Arsenal and Church
Rte 2C:	Circular Route: St. Helier to St. Helier via Longueville, Grouville Church, Grouville Station (Golflinks), Fauvic Crossroads, St. Clement's Church, Samarès Manor, Jersey Recreation Ground
Rte 3:	Rozel Bay via Five Oaks and St. Martin
Rte 3A:	The Zoo via Faldouet and St. Martin's Church
Rte 3B:	The Zoo via St. Saviour's Church and Five Oaks
Rte 4:	Les Platons via Trinity Church and Bonne Nuit Bay*
Rte 5:	St.Mary's Church via St. John's Church and Jersey Pearl*
Rte 6:	First Tower and Pomme D'Or Farm via St. Saviour's Road and Rouge Bouillon
Rte 7:	Devil's Hole via St. Lawrence's and St. Mary's Churches
Rte 7B:	Plémont via St. Lawrence's Church, Hamptonne Farm, Jersey Flower Centre, and St. Mary's Church
Rte 8:	Plémont via Millbrook (Glass Church), Tesson Chapel (for German Hospital), St. Ouen's Parish Hall (Shire Horse Farm and Grosnez)
Rte 8A:	Greenhill via Millbrook (Glass Church), German Underground Hospital and Living Legend*
Rte 8B:	Links Living Legend, Jersey Pearl, Zoo and Gorey*

Rte 9:	Grève de Lecq via Millbrook (Glass Church), Bel Royal, Beaumont, St. Peter's Village (Motor Museum)
Rte 12:	St. Brelade's Bay and Corbière via St. Aubin and Red Houses*
Rte 12A:	St. Ouen's Bay/L'Etacq via St. Aubin
Rte 14:	St. Brelade's Bay via St. Aubin*
Rte 15:	Jersey Airport via St. Aubin
Rte 18:	Le Marais Estate via Havre Des Pas
Rte 19:	La Pouquelaye and Chestnut Lea
Rte 20:	Five Oaks, La Hougue Bie and St. Catherine
Rte 21:	Victoria Village via Nicholson Park
Rte 22:	Rue des Près and Plat Douet Road
Rte 23:	Zoo via Five Oaks*
*Rte 4	Includes Bouley Bay*
*Rte 5	Includes St. Mary's Church*
*Rte 12-	Includes Portelet*
(*summer only)	

Bus number to a selection of destinations:

Airport	Rte 15
Battle of Flowers Museum	Rte 9A & 12A
Bonne Nuit Bay	Rte 4
Butterfly Farm	Rte 7
Bouley Bay	Rte 4 (summer only)
Corbière Lighthouse	Rte 12
Devil's Hole	Rte 7
General Hospital	Rte 5, 19
German Underground Hospital	Rte 8,8A
Glass Church	Rte 8, 8A, 9, 12, 12A, 15
Golf (La Moye)	Rte 12, 12A
(St. Clement)	Rte 1, 2C
(Grouville)	Rte 1, 2C
Grève de Lecq	Rte 9
Gorey Castle	Rte 1, 1B
Hamptonne Farm	Rte 7, 7B
Jersey Flower Centre	Rte 7, 7B
Jersey Pearl	Rte 5
La Hougue Bie	Rte 3A, 20
L'Etacq	Rte 12A
Lavender Farm	Rte 12, 12A, 15
Living Legend	Rte 8A
Potteries (Gorey)	Rte 1, 1B
Quennevais	Rte 15
Race Course	Rte 8
Rozel Bay	Rte 3
St. Aubin	Rte 12, 12A, 15
St. Brelades Bay	Rte 12
St. Ouen's Bay	Rte 12A
St. Peter's Motor Museum	Rte 9
Zoo	Rte 3A, 3B, 23

All buses are non smoking by law and are one-man operated. Passengers are requested to have the correct fare when booking. Special five-day and six-day commuter fares are available as well as Explorer tickets for seven consecutive days, three consecutive days, and one day. The **Central Bus Station** is at Weighbridge in St. Helier ☎ 21201.

   Tantivy Coach at 10 The Parade and Blue Coach Tours at 70–72 Colomberie, St. Helier run morning, afternoon, evening and full day tours to a variety of destinations. For more information ☎ 38877 and 22584.

Highlights

St. Helier
Jersey Museum and Barreau-Le Maistre Art Gallery devoted to the study and preservation of Jersey's history, antiquities and natural history. The gallery collection includes works connected with the island by subject or the artist's birth.

Elizabeth Castle. The site of this fortified castle began life as the retreat of St. Helier, son of a Belgian noble who arrived here in the 6C, and played an important role in the history of the island.

Royal Square. The original market place of the town until 1803. An attractive square with plenty of benches shaded by horse-chestnut trees.

St. Helier's Parish Church. The reddish granite Town Church is the burial place of Major Peirson who died saving Jersey from the French in 1781.

Fort Regent. Overlooking the town and harbour from the east and built during the Napoleonic scare but now in leisure mode it houses a comprehensive sports, entertainment and leisure complex.

Open air market. Held every Saturday in Hope Street.

Occupation Tapestry Gallery. Houses tapestries of the German Occupation, stitched by members of the island's 12 parishes to mark the 50th anniversary of the island's liberation in 1945.

Maritime Museum. Newly opened and devoted to Jersey's great maritime achievements.

Highlights in the Parishes
St. Brelade's Parish Church. With an idyllic position overlooking the bay, the exquisite little church of St. Brelade and the Fisherman's Chapel beside it are two of the most interesting churches, architecturally and historically, in Jersey. Bus Rte 12.

Corbière Lighthouse, St. Brelade. The lighthouse, built in 1874 is 500m offshore and can be reached by the causeway between half-ebb and half-flood tides. Bus Rte 12.

La Hougue Bie, Grouville. One of the finest passage graves in Europe, dating from 3500BC. There is an impressive mound some 13m high crowned with two medieval chapels. Bus Rte 3A, 20.

Eric Young Orchid Foundation, Trinity. Landscaped gardens with 28,000sq ft of glasshouse with magnificent displays of award winning cultivated orchids. Bus Rte 21.

Jersey Zoo and Wildlife Preservation Trust. Not just another zoo according to its inspired founder Gerald Durrell. It is a sanctuary for many threatened species in the world today and has as its appropriate mascot the dodo, hunted to extinction by man. Bus Rte 3A, 3B, 23.

Hamptonne Country Life Museum, St. Lawrence. A wonderful evocation of times past takes place in this restored manor and farm. The staff dress in traditional clothes and talk of their life on the farm at all levels of the social scale. Great fun. Bus Rte 7, 7B.

German Military Underground Hospital, St. Peter. It took nearly three years of slave labour by wartime prisoners to build this hospital which was never used for its purpose, but many of the prisoners died of exhaustion and malnutrition, or in the frequent rockfalls which occured in hewing this grim memorial out of the solid rockface. Rte 8A.

Jersey Flower Centre, St. Lawrence. Acres of flowers and plants. Flowers can be packed and sent on for the customer. Jersey carnations are sent all over the world and cuttings can also be bought. Rte 7,7B.

The Glass Church, Millbrook. St. Matthew's Glass Church is uniquely decorated with Lalique glass. Rte 8, 8A, 9, 12, 12A, 15.

Gorey Castle, St. Martin. Dubbed 'Mont Orgueil' by the Duke of Clarence, brother of Henry V, because of its proud position, the castle was built by the English as a stronghold beginning in the 12th century. Rte 1, 1A, 1B.

Kempt Tower, St. Ouen. This martello tower now houses the island's centre of information about Jersey's flora and fauna with visual displays. Situated in Les Mielles, which is a mini national park and protected area. Rte 12A.

St. Ouen's Manor, St. Ouen. The Manor, which takes precedence over all others in Jersey in recognition of services to the Crown, is the family seat of the de Carteret family. Rte 8, 9.

Battle of Flowers Museum, St. Ouen. The museum houses award winning exhibits and floats used in Jersey's annual Battle of Flowers. Rte 8, 12A.

The Living Legend, St. Peter. Purpose-built centre with excellent displays and audiovisual presentation recalling Jersey's myths and history. Rte 8A, 8B.

Le Moulin de Quetivel, St. Peter. This National Trust property is a working mill with wheel and machinery still in situ. There has been a watermill here since 1309. Rte 8.

Parish of St. Helier

Today St. Helier (25,700 inhab.) is the principal town on the island of Jersey. This was not always the case. In the past, when defensive castles were essential to the survival of island communities, Mont Orgueil was, before the development of gunpowder weaponry, the island's headquarters. Then later, St. Aubin with its excellent harbour became the more important community centre. St. Helier only became the town proper for the island in the early 19C, when trading entrepreneurs, privateers, and wealthy fishermen started to build their houses here. In this way St. Helier grew from a market town to the administrative centre and capital of the island. So, although archaeologists have found remnants of earlier habitation in this region, and the parish church, Elizabeth Castle and a few other buildings date back to earlier centuries, most of today's architecture is Regency, Victorian and modern.

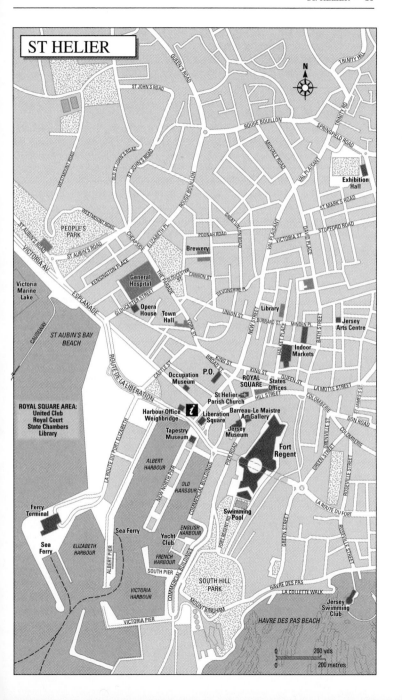

ST HELIER

QUEEN'S ROAD
TRINITY HILL
ST JOHN'S ROAD
N
ROUGE BOUILLON
SPRINGFIELD ROAD
MIDVALE ROAD
VAL PLAISANT
WESTMOUNT ROAD
OLD ST JOHN'S ROAD
ST JOHN'S ROAD
ROUGE BOUILLON
Exhibition
Hall
ST MARK'S ROAD
WESTMOUNT ROAD
GREAT UNION ROAD
VICTORIA DAV.
STOPFORD ROAD
ST AUBIN'S ROAD
PEOPLE'S
PARK
POONAH ROAD
VAL PLAISANT
DAVID PLACE
VICTORIA AV.
CHEAPSIDE
ST AUBIN'S ROAD
KENSINGTON PLACE
ELIZABETH PL.
THE PARADE
Brewery
CANNON ST.
Victoria
Marine
Lake
General
Hospital
DEVONSHIRE PL.
ESPLANADE
GLOUCESTER STREET
Opera
House
UNION ST.
Library
NEW STREET
BURRARD ST.
MINDEN PL.
HELVE PLACE
BATH STREET
Jersey
Arts Centre
CAUSEWAY
ST AUBIN'S BAY
BEACH
Town
Hall
YORK ST.
BROAD ST.
KING ST.
Indoor
Markets
CASTLE ST.
KING ST.
QUEEN ST.
LA MOTTE STREET
ROUTE DE LA LIBERATION
Occupation
Museum
P.O.
ROYAL
SQUARE
States
Offices
COLOMBERIE
ST JAMES ST.
ROYAL SQUARE AREA:
United Club
Royal Court
State Chambers
Library
St Helier
Parish Church
HILL STREET
DON ROAD
Harbour Office
Weighbridge
i
Liberation
Square
Barreau-Le Maistre
Art Gallery
GREEN GRENVILLE ST.
COLOMBERIE
LA ROUTE DU PORT ELIZABETH
Tapestry
Museum
Jersey
Museum
Fort
Regent
GREEN STREET
ROSEVILLE STREET
LA ROUTE DU FORT
ALBERT HARBOUR
NEW NORTH PIER
OLD HARBOUR
COMMERCIAL BUILDINGS
PIER ROAD
Ferry
Terminal
Swimming
Pool
Sea
Ferry
ELIZABETH
HARBOUR
Sea Ferry
Yacht
Club
ENGLISH
HARBOUR
PIER ROAD
ALBERT PIER
FRENCH
HARBOUR
SOUTH PIER
SOUTH HILL
PARK
Havre Des Pas
LA COLLETTE WALK
Jersey
Swimming
Club
VICTORIA
HARBOUR
MOUNT BINGHAM
VICTORIA PIER
HAVRE DES PAS BEACH

0   200 yds
0   200 metres

Elizabeth Castle

Elizabeth Castle is reached at low tide by a 1000m-long causeway from the east end of the Esplanade and, when this is covered, by amphibious craft from the shipway (fee). **Open** 09.30–18.00 (last entry 17.00) mid-March to early November; fee.)

History of Elizabeth Castle

The original site of the fortifications was known as St. Helier's Islet. St. Helier, son of a Belgian noble, arrived in Jersey during the 6C and took up residence as a hermit. Beheaded by pirates, he is said to have picked up his head and walked away from his murderers, much to their fear and consternation. His death led many pilgrims to visit this isolated place, and a substantial monastic settlement was established here by William Fitz-Hamon, an official of Henry II's court, in 1155.

As the commercial port of St. Helier gained importance it became clear that it needed greater military protection and in 1594 proper work began on the fortification of the islet under the military engineer Paul Ivy, author of *The Practice of Fortification*, who had already fortified Falmouth, and Kinsale in Ireland. By 1601 he had completed the Upper Ward. The first extension, completed by 1603, took in the curtain walls and bastions of the Upper Ward, enclosed the path down to Elizabeth Gate, and the construction of a new entrance at Iron Gate. The main purpose of the extension was to establish a cannon platform overlooking the harbour at an extra fortified level, now called Raleigh's Yard. An eight-bay Governor's House was built, Sir Walter Raleigh took up residence as first governor and christened the fortifications after Elizabeth I. The second extension was mainly carried out by de Carteret in 1626–36. The area where the Priory stood was enclosed and became the Lower Ward with its barracks and other military buildings. The third extension, in 1647, removed one outcrop where an invader could hide from the castle guns and fortified another with Fort Charles. The fourth extension in 1668 linked Fort Charles to the main fortification with the construction of curtain walls and cannon emplacements. The new area became known as the Outer Ward, containing the green and a fortified windmill within the castle boundaries.

At the end of the causeway is Fort Charles, constructed in 1646. Walk up the slope to enter the Landward Gate.

In a belfry above the gate is the **Castle Bell** (1797) which used to ring half an hour before the tide starts to cover the causeway. The first guard house, up a short flight of steps on the left after the ticket office, has an introductory exhibition which explains the early history of the islet as the site of the abbey, the reasons for its fortification and the development of the fortifications from 1600 to 1945. Illustrated panels provide brief information about the birds and plants which can be seen at the castle.

The main path leads up to **King William's Gate**. On the **West Bastion** is a 19C Armstrong-Frazer rifle muzzle loader, placed here against the threat of French attack from Louis Napoleon. It weighs 6½ tons, has a 7-inch bore and is of the Mark 3 type introduced in the mid 19C. The Germans re-fortified the castle during their occupation and at the north end of the green is a bomb-proof

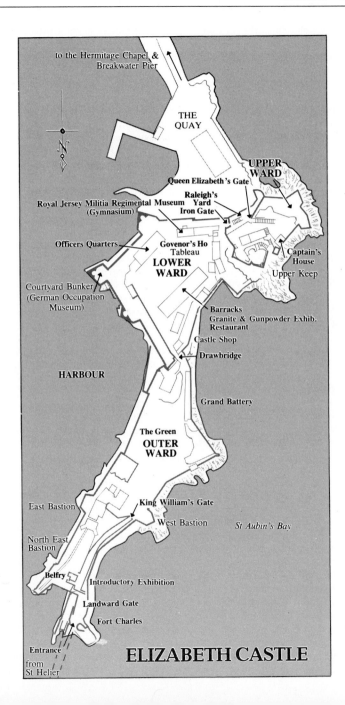

to the Hermitage Chapel &
Breakwater Pier

THE
QUAY

**UPPER
WARD**

Queen Elizabeth's Gate

**Raleigh's
Yard**
Iron Gate

Royal Jersey Militia Regimental Museum
(Gymnasium)

Officers Quarters

Govenor's Ho
Tableau
**LOWER
WARD**

**Captain's
House**

Upper Keep

Courtyard Bunker
(German Occupation
Museum)

Barracks
Granite & Gunpowder Exhib.
Restaurant

Castle Shop

Drawbridge

HARBOUR

Grand Battery

The Green
**OUTER
WARD**

East Bastion

King William's Gate

West Bastion

St Aubin's Bay

North East
Bastion

Belfry

Introductory Exhibition

Landward Gate

Fort Charles

Entrance
from
St Helier

ELIZABETH CASTLE

shelter. Adjacent, at the beginning of the Grand Battery, in another bunker, are to be found 110mm French guns taken from the Maginot Line, which was built to protect France from Germany in World War II, and was later overrun. Adjoining is a searchlight emplacement. A row of 24-pounder Carronades, once popular naval cannons, now line the Grand Battery.

Cross over the drawbridge, which once withdrew on rollers, and enter the **Lower Ward**. Continue up the slope to the main courtyard with a Cross marking the site of the Abbey of St. Helier, built in 1155. Surrounding the main courtyard are the **officers' quarters, gymnasium and barracks**. The officers' quarters houses an exhibition with sound effects, tableaux and some 'live' participants. The barracks also houses an audiovisual exhibition.

The gymnasium houses the **Royal Jersey Militia Regimental Museum**. The room on the left contains uniforms, medals, rifles, swords and regimental colours of the militia through the ages. Upstairs is a display of the regimental silver and drum major maces and a collection of officers' swagger sticks. The barracks on the west side of the main courtyard of the Lower Ward have recently been converted to house an interpretive exhibition, 'Granite and Gunpowder'. On display is a fragment of the bomb which destroyed the abbey on this site in 1651, when Parliamentary forces besieged the castle which was held by Royalists under Sir George Carteret. Examples of guns, from a falconet of c 1550 to an anti-tank gun used by the German occupying forces, have been used to demonstrate the relationship between fortifications and the arms used both to defend and to attack them. An audiovisual programme in the same building demonstrates the development of firepower throughout the ages and its influence on defences and modes of battle. It also provides an outline of the history of fortifications in the Channel Islands. In the officers' quarters on the opposite side of the courtyard is an exhibition telling the story of Elizabeth Castle 'in war and peace'.

Prior to 1651, and the attack of the Parliamentary forces upon the Royalists inside the castle, this ward housed the Priory. But on 9 November 1651 a mortar came through the roof, hit the ammunition dump in the crypt and destroyed the Priory and several other buildings, and now the only reminder is the Cross. The east German bunker shows the cramped conditions in which German Forces lived during the Occupation. It is now a small museum.

Through the **Iron Gate**, steps lead to **Raleigh's Yard**. The final gate, named after Queen Elizabeth, bears her coat of arms and that of Sir Anthony Paulet, Governor from 1590 to 1600. More steps lead to a courtyard with barbette emplacements on the left, the **Captain's House** ahead and on the right, the Governor's House. Inside the **Governor's House** are historical tableaux of famous people, in costume, who were connected with the castle. They include Sir Walter Raleigh, architect Paul Ivy, Charles II, the Duke of York (later James II), the Earl of Clarendon, and Sir George and Lady Carteret. The visuals are supported with sound recordings of famous events which took place in Jersey.

The Mount itself is now surmounted by a circular German control tower with an anti-aircraft position on its roof, but all the sophisticated equipment was removed in 1945.

In 1887 a 150m granite breakwater designed by Walter Knipple was extended from the castle to enlarge the harbour. Before this, **Hermitage Rock** was cut off from the islet at high tide. The saint lived at the top of the 27m outcrop where he slept in a natural rock cavity called St. Helier's Bed. This can still be seen in the 12C chapel built on the site. The oratory bears resemblance to monastic buildings of similar date in Ireland. Two of Jersey's most famous landmarks, Mont Orgueil and Elizabeth Castle were handed to the islanders in 1996, after centuries of British ownership. The castles were once Britain's defence against invaders from the Continent but since so many decades of peace have now intervened, the Queen recently decided to give the historic fortresses to the island, since the threat of attack is considered to be remote.

Liberation Square

The main coastal site of St Helier is now Liberation Square and its centrepiece is Philip Jackson's sculpture commissioned by the Jersey Public Sculpture Trust to celebrate the Liberation of Jersey from the German Occupation on 9 May 1945 and 50 years of subsequent freedom. It was unveiled by the Prince of Wales on 9 May 1995. The sculpture, with its seven over life-size figures and billowing flag symbolically held aloft, forms a triumphal arch through which people may walk while viewing the sculpture at close quarters. The figures are placed in two groups with, between them, the figure representing the liberator. The islanders, portrayed in diverse ages, have been sculpted to represent the farming, fishing, marine and business communities, and the family. The whole sculpture is five metres tall and four metres across and stands on a circular plinth surrounded by a waterfilled 'moat' signifying Jersey's island status. Divided into four sections, each part of the moat has three jets of water, 12 in all, symbolising the 12 parishes of Jersey. The celebratory site is well chosen because it is overlooked by the balcony of the Pomme d'Or Hotel, where in 1945 the liberation party foregathered on the day of victory. The hotel at that time was the German naval headquarters.

Occupation Tapestry Gallery

The highly acclaimed Occupation Tapestry, unveiled by the Prince of Wales during the Liberation Day celebrations in 1995 now has its home in a converted 19C warehouse on the New North Quay, adjacent to Liberation Square. This magnum opus consists of 12 two-metre panels and tells the story of the Occupation of Jersey during World War II. In 1989 the Tapestry Committee was set up, and in 1991 work began. **Open** daily, all year round. Summer 10.00–16.00. Fee.

Each of the 12 parishes took the responsibility for stitching one panel, and altogether there was a regular team of 300 stitchers. However, each parish had an open day when any islander was invited to stitch, so that the actual number of stitchers ran into thousands. An interesting problem which arose in the creating of this tapestry was that all reference material, dated back to the Occupation and was, of course in black and white. As the tapestry was to be in colour much depended on the stitchers' memory and imagination of past events. The end result is both creative and inspired, and is worth seeing. There is also an audiovisual presentation, and a display of 'Occupation Art'.

St. Helier's parish church

The church, which lies east of Bond Street and west of Royal Square, is one of the 12 parish churches on the island. Known as Chapelle de Saint Helier, the original church is recorded as receiving tithes before 1066 on behalf of William, Duke of Normandy. The present church, of reddish granite, is mainly 14C, with the chancel probably representing the remains of an 11C chantry. Chapels to north and south and the transept belong to the 12C.

Massive restoration took place (1864–68) when the south transept, vestry and porch were added and the nave lengthened. During the Hundred Years War with France, the church bell would ring, warning of an enemy attack, and the citizens would barricade themselves inside. By law, criminals inside the church were safe from arrest.

Much of the silver which is on display is over 300 years old and includes one alms dish 38cm in diameter (1704) another of 1731 (30cm), and cups and flagons of the same century. Queen Elizabeth the Queen Mother presented a crucifix and candlesticks as a thanks offering for the Liberation and for the faithful witness of laity and clergy during the German Occupation.

Royal Square

Royal Square, the original market place of the town until 1803, was dubbed by 19C writers the centre of 'business and gossip' and 'the resort only of the male lounger'. It is an attractive square with plenty of benches shaded with horse-chestnut trees. In the centre is a gilded statue of the Hanoverian King George II dressed as a Roman Emperor with a crown of laurel on his head but still wearing the Order of the Garter. He has been thus immortalised for providing a £200 donation in 1751 to improve the harbour. His statue is also the point from which mileage distances are measured from St. Helier to other towns throughout the island. The United Club at one end of the square once contained an arcaded corn market on the ground floor.

On the south side of the square are several State buildings including, in the centre, the Italianate **Royal Court**, completed in 1866. Several interesting pictures are to be found here including a portrait of General Conway by Gainsborough, a portrait of George III by Philip Jean, a Jerseyman, a portrait of Sir William Vernon and the Assize Court of Heritage (1897) by Lander.

At the Assize d'Heritage seigneurs renew their oaths; this takes place twice yearly. There is also a picture of the present Queen and a replica of Copley's *Death of Major Peirson*. The original of this hangs in the Tate Gallery, London. It is said that the baby in the far left of the picture is the great-randmother of Lillie Langtry.

Visitors may attend when the court is in session and sit in the Public Gallery. Set before the Bailiff is a silver gilt mace presented by Charles II 'as a proof of his royal affection towards the Island of Jersey, in which he had been twice received in safety when excluded from the remainder of his dominions'. The rivalry which exists between Jersey and Guernsey may date back to the Civil War when Jersey was pro-Royalist and Guernsey pro-Parliamentarian. The Royal Court House has occupied this site for centuries and as far back as 1309 it is recorded that the House where the King's Pleas were held was restored. Today, two entrances lead from the Square to the Royal Court, one (the Bailiff's entrance) bears the coat of arms of George VI and the other (the public entrance) those of

George II. The **Salles des Etats**, or **State Chambers**, are on the left-hand side of the Royal Court and are designed in pleasing Jacobean style with wall panels of embossed leather. The Bailiff's chair is several inches higher than that of the Lieutenant-Governor, signifying the importance of civil over military administration. Two galleries are provided, one for distinguished visitors and the other for the general public.

On the west side of the Royal Court is the **Public Library**, erected in 1886. The library has some 93,600 books including 16C to 18C volumes donated by the founder of the original Public Library in 1736. There is an imposing gallery, around the base of which names of Jersey authors are inscribed in gold lettering. Visitors may take out books provided they pay a returnable £5 deposit. Alternatively, if from the UK they may use one of their borough library tickets.

The market

In 1800 market stalls were forbidden in Royal Square and a new venue had to be found. The States erected a market, on the design of one existing in Bath, at the junction of Halkett Place and Beresford Street. The expansion of the amount of produce for sale caused more and more congestion so that in 1882 this market was pulled down and another erected in its place. The **New Market** in Halkett Place has a roof largely of glass, supported by iron pillars and outer walls of dressed granite with broad openings containing iron railings and radial grilles which divide it from Beresford St. The gates and railings at the Market Street and Hilgrove Lane entrance are from the previous market of 1803 and incorporate cast iron and polychromed grapes, cornucopiae and the heads of a great variety of animals and birds. These were designed by Phillipe Le Sueur, States Architect, and made by the local iron-founder, George Le Feuvre. Internally the space is light and airy and a circular fountain designed by Abraham Viel makes a lovely centre-piece.

Jersey knitting

'Jersey' is now a trade name for sweaters originally made from the wool of native sheep. The manufacture of jerseys had, by the end of the 16C, become such a thriving industry that by 1608, to ease manning problems in other industries, an edict was put out to forbid all people over 15 years old carrying out any knitting during seed time, harvest gathering and the collecting of seaweed. Very little Jersey knitting today is carried out in private houses; most is manufactured at the Summerland factory in Rouge Bouillon Road. Visitors may purchase, during special sales, direct from the factory.

Jersey Museum and Barreau-Le Maistre Art Gallery

The Jersey Museum is at 9 Pier Road which leads south from Bond Street past Fort Regent. The museum collections are owned by the Société Jersiaise, founded in 1873 for the study and preservation of Jersey's history, antiquities and natural history. The headquarters of the Jersey Museums Service is housed here.

■ **Open** summer Mon–Sat 10.00–17.00, Sun 13.00–17.00. Winter Mon–Sat 10.00–16.00, Sun 13.00–16.00. Closed Christmas period and New Year.

The British Guild of Travel Writers voted this museum 'the most outstanding tourist attraction to open in the British Isles' in 1992 and it won the National Heritage IBM Museum of the Year award 1993–94. The adjacent restaurant by the ground floor entrance has been awarded the Gulbenkian 'Best Museum Restaurant' title. Also by the entrance is an excellent bookshop. You should start your tour of the museum by watching the short audiovisual in the theatre which provides an introduction to the history of Jersey. A simultaneous translation is also available in French. Close by the theatre is a 'Question and Answer' interactive video, where visitors love to test their knowledge of the island and its history.

The **Ground Floor** houses the treadmill—a model of this punishment machine (1836) where up to twelve prisoners were kept at work while their efforts drove a pepper mill.

Another area on the Ground Floor is devoted to items associated with the famous beauty Lillie Langtry who was born in Jersey. The magnificent silver gilt travelling case (1842) fitted with all manner of containers for cosmetics is particularly interesting, and was no doubt a useful adjunct to her make-up when she trod the boards of the Jersey Opera House in the opening play *The Degenerates*. When she came to London she was acclaimed the loveliest woman of her generation. Oscar Wilde composed a poem comparing her to Helen of Troy, and among the many artists who painted her were Burne-Jones, Leighton, Millais, Poynter, Watts and Whistler. She was widely seen at the Court of St. James, where she became a favourite companion of the Prince of Wales, later King Edward VII.

The exhibition area on the **Ground Floor** features much interesting detail concerning the island's military history, her special relationship with the English Crown, and the German Occupation, discussed in the archaeology and history section at the beginning of this book. Still in living memory are events connected with the interesting exhibition of civilian life under German rule in World War II, with examples of the ingenuity demonstrated by the islanders in inventing simple machines for processing alternative foods when everything was in short supply. A room reconstruction shows the intrusion of German forces into a domestic interior and the dangers of listening to BBC broadcasts on forbidden crystal wireless sets.

The Ground Floor also has a graphic reconstruction of what hunting was like in the Ice Ages when the earliest inhabitants of Jersey had to hunt mammoth and woolly rhinoceros for their supper. This splendid natural history piece catches the attention of children and adults alike. On the next floor up the museum goes into more detail on this subject. Although no human remains have been found relating to this age, animal remains and flint tools indicate that these early men lived and hunted in a mild climate. On display are important relics from La Cotte Cave in St. Brelade, including a perfect example of a small oval hand axe and a tooth from an earlier species of elephant than the mammoth. The upper habitation level has revealed 13 adult human teeth characteristic of Neanderthal man, bones of reindeer, woolly mammoth, woolly rhinoceros and flint tools which place occupation around 70,000 years ago at the beginning of the last glacial period. Old Stone Age Man was thinly spread about the world and existed by hunting. The finds here show that in two different periods there was a permanent colony. The mammoth remains prove that Jersey was connected to the mainland of Europe and becomes separated from time to time through a change in sea-level. If the level were to fall 8m it would again be joined to the Continent.

Most of the **First Floor** is devoted to the history of Jersey using old photographs, artists' impressions and scenic displays describing the various industries that developed through the ages such as fishing, which was a major source of income in the Middle Ages, when salted conger were shipped in large quantities to the Continent. Then knitting became a major industry, and the trade name 'Jersey' became synonymous with the wool sweater. This work was so profitable that both men and children became involved and sometimes as many as 10,000 pairs of knitted stockings were exported each week. Cider-making became such a big export business that in 1682 a gentleman by the name of Poingdestre warned that 'the whole islands was in danger of becoming a continual orchard'. During the American War of Independence and the Napoleonic Wars Jersey sea folk sought 'lettres of marque' and took to privateering to make their fortune. At one stage during this period there were 150 French prizes moored up in St. Aubin's Bay.

A particular treasure of the museum is the **Golden Torque** made of solid gold and dug up in Lewis Street, St. Helier, in 1839. It is a twisted piece of pure gold, nearly 1.5m long by 2cm in diameter. The torque would have been worn over one shoulder as a sword belt by chiefs of distinction and warriors of the first rank.

On the **Second Floor** is the Art Gallery, named after two families, Barreau and Le Maistre. In 1924 Emmeline Augusta Barreau presented an art gallery to the Société Jersiaise in memory of her artist nephew, Arthur Hamptonne Barreau (1879–1922). Her gift also included an endowment with which to buy pictures, as well as to give support to Jersey students studying art. The original Barreau Art Gallery was demolished to make way for the present building. F.W.S. Le Maistre (1859–1940) also left a handsome legacy to the island, in addition to an art collection which included many of his own works, paintings of Jersey landscapes and local dignitaries, and prints by important British artists. The realisation of the Le Maistre bequest has made a major contribution to the establishment of the present gallery, which now displays works collected by the Jersey Heritage Trust, the Société Jersiaise and the States of Jersey, as well as works on loan from other institutions and individuals. The works chiefly depict Jersey subjects and are chosen from a collection of some 4000 objects.

In the 18C many artists started to paint the scenery of Jersey, and the people who influenced her changing history. Portraits include people who held high office on the island, caricatures, miniature portraits, military figures and families. The portrait by Millais of Jersey Lily (Lillie Langtry) shows her with a flower in her hand (which is actually a Guernsey lily).The portrait of Major Peirson famous for his gallant bravery in battle is by Walter Ouless. The most famous image of Major Peirson, is in the *Death of Major Peirson* by John Singleton Copley (1738–1815) painted in 1783, now in the Tate Gallery in London. It is notable for being among the first large pictures of contemporary history, and the States of Jersey owns a copy of this painting, by Holyoake. Marine painting and still life are well represented in the work on show, as well as abstract and non-objective work.

Seascapes have been an enduring source of inspiration for many artists connected with the Channel Islands, and because island ships traded all over the world, many ship owners wanted their ships to be recorded for posterity. Among these P.J. Ouless (1817–85) was highly successful because he was able to

Artists in Jersey
Lucy Schwob/Claude Cahun (1894–1954) and Suzanne Malherbe/Marcel Moore (1892–1972).

Two women artists living in Jersey provided a link between the Island and the Surrealist movement flourishing in Europe at the time. They used male pseudonyms, and were stepsisters. In 1916 Suzanne Malherbe was an established graphic artist working in Paris in the fashion world, at a time when France saw fashion export as part of the war effort. Lucy Schwob was well known as a writer and photographer when she met André Breton, the 'father' of the Surrealist movement. The artistic, literary and political ideas of the movement were to inform Lucy Schwob's work for the next 30 years. In 1937 the sisters, who had spent holidays in Jersey as children bought a house close to St. Brelade's parish church, overlooking the bay and lived here throughout the Occupation, apart from the time when they were imprisoned by the Germans. Their aim was to spread gloom and despondancy among the German troops, and some of their activities showed what can only be described as a Surrealist sense of humour, as when they hung a banner over the altar of St. Brelade's carrying the message: 'Jesus is great but Hitler is greater, for Jesus died for men whereas men die for Hitler'. When they were arrested in 1944 they were charged with listening to the radio, which carried a sentence of six years imprisonment, and inciting the troops to rebellion, which carried the death penalty. When sentence was passed Lucy Schwob is reported to have asked which sentence they should serve first. In the event they were imprisoned. Their house was requisitioned, and the works of art it housed either confiscated or destroyed, including works by Max Ernst and Joan Miró. Lucy Schwob's spirit did not fail but her health did and she died at the age of 60 in 1954. Suzanne Malherbe moved to a house in Beaumont where she lived until 1972. After her death a collector acquired many of the photographs and objects which she left and recently there has been a revival of interest in the work of Lucy Schwob/Claude Cahun, with exhibitions in Paris and New York as well as a biography published in 1992.

Malcolm Arbuthnot (1877–1967) was born in Cobham, Surrey. As a young man he was interested in painting, drawing, boating and cycling, and was apprenticed to the landscape and cat painter C.A. Brindley. On his 21st birthday his grandmother gave him a Kodak box camera and this began his life-long love affair with the camera. He exhibited for the first time with the Royal Photographic Society in 1902 and soon after began to lecture widely on photography. In 1913 he was living in Liverpool and together with Roger Fry organised a seminal exhibition of Post Impressionist Painting. It was not until 1933 that he was to make his first visit to Jersey, but from 1935 onwards he was to exhibit there many times, particularly at the Barreau-Le Maistre Gallery. In 1946 he moved to live in Jersey permanently. He encouraged young artists and became an active member of many art groups. Malcolm Arbuthnot was in the vanguard of abstract photographic art. His imagery moved from a romantic landscape mode to a style which evolved into photographs which were almost completely abstract. In 1967 he died in St Aubin at the age of 90.

Edmund Blampied (1886–1966) was born in St. Martin, five days after the death of his father. Like his friend Lander (see below) he visited Millais in his studio and was confirmed in his great desire to make his way as an artist. Although Blampied is generally described as an etcher, his work was mainly as a dry pointist, which involves drawing with a hard steel needle onto a copper plate. When Blampied returned to Jersey in 1916 and joined the Royal Jersey Militia he had left his materials in London, but he continued to produce work, using a sharpened six inch nail. His wit as a political satirist shared the same sharpness, as can be seen in a folio of his comic drawings published in New York in 1934 as *Hot Dogs*. In the course of his career he worked as an artist on the then *Daily Chronicle*, and as a freelance book illustrator, and later as an artist for *The Sphere*. He settled in Jersey with his wife in 1938 and stayed on the Island throughout the Occupation. Artists' supplies ran out in due course but Blampied kept working, and many of his friends received gifts from him executed with a needle on a cigarette case or tobacco tin. In 1942 he designed a set of postage stamps for the States of Jersey.

John Helier Lander (1868–1944) was advised by Millais not to try to make a career as an artist, but he was not deterred and studied first in Paris and then at the Royal Academy Schools in London. Over the years he formed firm friendships with Millais and two other Jersery artists who lived in London at the time, Walter Ouless an established portrait painter and the young Edmund Blampied, who was 18 years younger than Lander. When he returned to the Islands in the 1880s he began on an ambitious work, a painting of the Assize d'Heritage, a project which took four years to complete and which earned him £400. As his career progressed he was very much in demand for military portrtaits and later for portraits of the Royal Family. In 1923 he painted an unusually informal portrait of the Prince of Wales in polo kit, which delighted the prince and won the medal at that year's Paris Salon. Later he collaborated with Blampied on a portrait of King George VI in his coronation robes, which was featured in a special Coronation edition of the *London Illustrated News*.

Sir John Everett Millais (1829–1896). The best-known portrait painter of 19C was a child prodigy. He entered the RA schools in 1840. In 1848, together with Holman Hunt and Dante Gabriel Rossetti he founded the influential Pre-Raphaelite Brotherhood. One of his most important paintings, *Christ in the House of His Parents* (1840) had the dubious honour of being castigated by Charles Dickens. However, Ruskin defended the work and such was his reputation that this helped to establish Millais in the public estimation as one of those who, as Ruskin said was: 'laying in our England the foundations of a school of art nobler than the world has seen for three hundred years'. As Millais' career progressed he developed into a fashionable and technically brilliant academic painter of portraits, costume history and genre pieces, and gradually forsook his original theories on which he had founded the PRB. He was made a baronet in 1885 and became President of the Royal Academy in 1896.

produce portraits which were attractive works of art, as well as accurate records of his subjects. His picture of *The Rambler* demonstrates a very skilful observation of one of the main conventions of ship painting. which is the depiction of two views of the ship at once, not two ships as might at first be assumed. Some of the ship portraits here incorporate as many as three views: broadside on, port tack and starboard tack.

The silver on exhibition offers interesting insights into the historical reasons for the great skill in this craft which developed in 18C Jersey. Of particular interest is the *Prix Militaire* spoon awarded to the Royal Jersey Militia. From time to time the gallery offers a comprehensive overview of Channel Islands silverwork in special exhibitions.

In the still life section we see *Still Life with Game* by C.H. Poingdestre, on loan from a private collection. Poingdestre was born in Jersey and became President of the British Academy in Rome for 20 years. It is believed that this is the painting, exhibited at the Royal Academy in 1888 under the title *Christmas Presents in the Abbey*. It is freqently reproduced as a Christmas card.

In the Subject Painting section the picture of Liberation Square is an excellent example of the way in which artists use symbols and metaphors for different aspects of human emotion and experience. Several works by Edmund Blampied present scenes of rural Jersey life. Both *Race Meeting* at Grouville, and *Laying the Foundation Stone* are typically Victorian, showing all the strata of contemporary society.

The decorative arts are well represented in the collection.There is an ornate mirror of metal, glass and wood, left to the museum by Lillie Langtry, as well as a grandfather clock made by Thomas de Gruchy c 1832 and an exquisite carved cabinet by Le Feuvre.

There are wildlife inspired fine bronze bird sculptures by Malcolm Arbuthnot and the charming *Early Owl* by Martin McDowell. A major landscape by James Webb, was purchased with the aid of a grant from the National Art Collections Fund.

The **Third Floor** reflects two aspects of Jersey's history, the Merchant's House, No 9 Pier Road, built c 1820, is gradually being restored to its condition when in 1861 it was a wealthy merchant's house. We see Anne Nicolle's bedroom c 1865 as well as a night nursey and school room. The school room has a cupboard with children's clothes of the period which young visitors are encouraged to try on. Also available for 'hands on' experience are three hobby horses. On the landing is a magnificent dolls' house which Captain Dunlop, a founder member of the Société Jersiaise had made for his god-daughter in 1914. Children are asked to consider what the house might tell us about the little girl who owned it. Through the viewing window is seen the first signal station on Jersey and explanations of what the flags mean that were flown on Fort Regent are given.

Fort Regent

Fort Regent stands on Mont de la Ville overlooking the town and harbour from the east. Built almost in the shape of a coffin, it has walls—some of them 6m thick—and bastions running along the spine of the hill. These extensive fortifications were built to the design of Lt-Gen. John Humfrey of the Royal Engineers during the Napoleonic scare. They were started in 1806 and completed in 1814, one year before Napoleon was defeated at Waterloo. The costs were enormous. The well which had been sunk through 75m of solid rock took over two years to bore. Once completed, the garrison headquarters within the inner wall were supplied with 6000 gallons of water a day. During the Occupation German soldiers were housed here. In 1958 Fort Regent was sold back to the States of Jersey for only £14,500, the price for which the land was originally purchased. Since then it has been transformed into a comprehensive sports, entertainment and leisure complex with a concert hall, swimming-pools, roller-skating rink, squash courts, aquarium, funfair entertainments, restaurants, discotheque and many other amenities. **Open** 10.00–17.30. Many attractions remain open later.

Major new developments in the way of entertainment have been opened in the piazza and funfair areas. They include such as the Haunted House; Cine 180, in which the onlooker is surrounded by a giant screen, and Humfreys Magical Musical Hall, with a life-size puppet show. The history of Fort Regent is given in an imaginative and well presented audiovisual show. A recent addition is the exhibition of replicated terracotta warriors, similar to the life-size figures made in Xiang, China, with costumes, armour and other items from the Qin Dynasty. The discovery of the original terracotta warriors was one of the most important archaeological discoveries of our time, and this exhibition gives a valuable insight into an empire which lasted from 221BC until 1912.

Lunchtime in the piazza offers live entertainment, where an audience of all ages can have lunch and sing along to hits of the 50s and 60s, and watch an energetic stage show, with comedy sketches, singing and dancing. These and many other forms of entertainment, plus use of the enormous terraced swimming-pool, are included in the entrance price. Booking the use of other sports facilities and indoor bowls is extra; most equipment can be hired. Fort Regent is also used for conferences and exhibitions.

The Union Jack on the west bastion is flown at half mast only when a Sovereign dies. The height of commercial buildings has been restricted according to the terms of their title deeds in order, in the past, to ensure a clear range of fire from the Fort.

Esplanade Occupation Museum

The Island Fortress Occupation Museum on the Esplanade has an extensive collection of German military equipment left over from the Occupation, including guns, uniforms, field equipment and authentic documents. A video cinema shows a 40-minute film of the Occupation. **Open** daily mid-March to Nov 09.00–22.30 and from Nov to mid-March 10.00–16.00. Fee.

Town harbour and marinas

St. Helier's harbour is in a rocky bay where the tide recedes a great distance and heavy investment has been necessary to establish a viable haven. The oldest part is the Old South Pier, begun in 1700, and this was followed by successive additions including the Old North Pier started in 1790. Widened a century later, it now incorporates the New North Quay.

Between 1841–46 the Victoria Pier was built (and opened by the Sovereign) and between 1847–53 the Albert Pier was constructed, adding the outer harbours of Victoria and Albert to the Old Harbour, French Harbour and English Harbour. The Castle Breakwater, completed in 1887, acts as a protection to the harbour during south-west gales.

Much of St. Helier was built in the 19C, including the stonework of the inner harbour. Particularly fine is the workmanship of the steps and the curving corner of the landing-place at Victoria Pier (1887).

St. Helier marina

Yachtsmen approaching St. Helier harbour will find the St. Helier marina is conveniently situated in the upper harbour, only a few minutes from the town centre. The marina provides permanent berthing for some 180 local craft; additionally 200 visiting craft can be accommodated. The approaches to St. Helier are described in detail in the Channel Pilot and Admiralty Charts 3655; 1137 and 3278 refer. As the marina is situated within the commercial port of St. Helier, traffic through the area—particularly at peak shipping times—has to be closely controlled. Visiting craft fitted with VHF are advised to keep a listening watch on Channel 14 when approaching St. Helier. Pierhead Control maintains a 24-hour watch on this channel and is in direct contact with the marina and yacht basin. It can advise approaching craft on the availability of space, the intended movement of commercial vehicles and other port information.

The coast

Jersey naturally divides into two aspects—the coastline and the interior. As Jersey is a popular place for families, with excellent beaches, we will begin with the former, dividing it into five sections. The first section of coastline runs from St. Helier along the south coast to La Roque Point, and then half-way up the east coast to Gorey Castle. The second section runs from Gorey Castle up the east coast via Fliquet Bay and turns west along the north coast to Bouley Bay, which lies due north of the capital in a more or less straight line. Section three runs west along the south coastline from St. Helier to La Pulente. Section four runs up the west coast taking in St. Ouen's Bay, the longest sandy beach in the Channel Islands, before turning east along the north coastline to Grève de Lecq. Section five takes in the north coast from Grève de Lecq to Bouley Bay, which as mentioned earlier lies due north of St. Helier. The perimeter of the island brings you in contact with many bathing beaches, historical coastal defences, fishing facilities and water-sport centres.

Between St. Helier and Gorey

Total distance: 12km.

Swimming and water-sport activities

The beach facilities in this area include Havre des Pas with sea water swimming-pool. The surf, dive and ski school based here provides complete hire service of equipment. Grève d'Azette to the Dicq has good sand at low tide and rocky outcrops, Green Island has attractive sand and rocks around La Motte. Le Hocq is popular with wading birds. Beware of fast incoming tides. Royal Bay of Grouville has a sandy beach and is popular with windsurfers. Instruction is available.

Just outside St. Helier on the east side lies **Havre des Pas**. On the right the Jersey Swimming Club projects onto the beach.

The club is open to the public and provides swimming regardless of the state of the tide. At **Dicq Corner** (2km from Liberation Square) on a rock called Le Rocher des Procrits is an inscription commemorating Victor Hugo's exile in Jersey.

When the tide is out, the beach at **Grève d'Azette** (from the Breton, meaning a resting-place) through to St. Clement's Bay offers a fine walk. The sandy beach which is named after the saint is studded with treacherous rocks which have been ironically christened Bancs des Viollettes. One is left wondering if the originator of such a title was some seigneur benefiting from the 'right of wreck'.

In common with most of the rocks around Jersey these rocks have clumps of seaweed or 'vraic' adhering to them. Vraic is a Norman word and the seaweed has been important to Jersey farmers for generations. It is used as fertiliser. Many squabbles used to arise between the seigneur and his tenants over this product; the former used to insist that anything washed ashore was his by 'right of wreck'; therefore all vraic belonged to him. The matter was finally settled in 1607 by a Royal Commission which decreed certain days for the public cutting of vraic. There are two seasons for cutting vraic: the first begins at the first spring tide after Candlemas and lasts a month, and the second stretches from Midsummer to the middle of August. The law was that it could only be cut between sunrise and sunset. Vraic, strangely enough, was also used in cables and, when coal was scarce it was used as a substitute fuel, and the remainder was then used as fertiliser.

The oldest public 9-hole golf course on the island, stands in the Recreation Grounds at Grève d'Azette, St. Clement. It is popular with both local people and visitors, and is comparatively inexpensive. Green fees are £10 per round, £13 all day at the time of going to press. To hire clubs is £5 (deposit required) and trolleys £1.50. Other facilities include tennis and bowls. Restaurant open 09.00–22.30. ☎ 01534 21938.

Just past La Rue de Samarès is an entrance on the right to a house called Rocque Berg. Half-way up this private drive is a huge granite outcrop several metres high, known as Witches Rock. In several places small footprints can be seen and these were believed to belong to dancing witches who were said to hold their Sabbath here at the the full moon.

St. Clement's Bay, the first part of which is called Havres des Fontaines, could be said to be divided in two by Le Hocq Point which in the old days must have been a burial place because 'Hoc' (from the masculine form of Hougue)

French invasion (1781)

La Platte Rocque marks the east end of St. Clement's Bay and it is here that Baron de Rullecourt landed his 600 troops on 6 January 1781, with the help of a Jerseyman who piloted them safely. His force was defeated at St. Helier by Major Peirson. From the little harbour of La Rocque the land curves north to La Rocque Point and from here the Royal Bay of Grouville stretches north to Gorey Harbour, a distance of 4km. Between are five Martello towers and two 18C fortifications, Fort William and Fort Henry.

means burial mound. The bay stretches 3km from Havres des Fontaines to Plat Rocque Point and the tide runs out even further than that to La Conchière, a notorious graveyard for ships which have been victims of strong tides and fierce storms. There are several Martello towers in the area, some by the edge of the furthest reefs like Icho and Seymour and several on the east coastline which have now been converted into dwellings.

Royal Jersey Golf Club

The Royal prefix was granted by Queen Victoria in 1859 to sandy Groville Bay which is bordered by the links of the Royal Jersey Golf Course. The club was founded in 1878 and visitors who are members of an established club are welcome. Clubs and trolleys can be hired. Eighteen holes cover 5657m; par is 70. Green fees at the time of going to press are £35 per round and £40 per round on weekends and holidays. ☎ 01534 854416. This club's most famous member was Harry Vardon, six times winner of the British Open. Address: Grouville, Jersey.

Gorey

Nestled in the northern corner of Grouville Bay is the picturesque village of Gorey. The high hill on which Mont Orgueil stands gives the whole an immensely dramatic setting. Old houses line the ancient quay and the pier was extended in 1826, to protect the shipbuilding industry and the oyster beds. Nowadays, the harbour is given over to yachtsmen and other boat lovers. A ferry from the continent calls at the pier regularly during the summer with day visitors, and the village has earned a reputation for good food. Just behind the main section of the village which lies to the west of Gorey Castle is the **Jersey Pottery**, a flourishing industry (**open** Monday to Saturday 09.00–17.30; free). Visitors can see potters at work and purchase from a wide range of articles on display in the spacious showrooms. Additional facilities include a restaurant serving light lunches. There is a free car park.

Mont Orgueil ~ Gorey Castle

■ **Open** daily 09.00–18.00; last admission 17.00.

History of the Castle

The red granite headland on which the castle of Mont Orgueil stands has been occupied since remote times. In the clay which covers the rock the flint tooks and weapons of Palaeolithic men, who lived here during the inter-glacial period, have been discovered, Stone implements and pottery belonging to the Neolithic and Bronze Ages indicate continuous habitation. And excavations during the last decade have shown that the mount was defended by at least one rampart following the contour of the hill during the Iron Age. Roman coins found in and around the promontory indicate trading with Imperial Rome whose soldiers reached north-west Gaul in 56 BC.

Around the first decade of the 13C, when the Channel Islands became the last fragment of Normandy remaining in English hands, Gorey Castle was built as an English stronghold. For the next three centuries whoever

Mont Orgueil Castle, Gorey, Jersey

held this castle held Jersey. No conquest of the island could be complete if Gorey held out. Towards the end of the 15C improved cannon fire threatened the strategic importance of the castle which became vulnerable from attack from the mighty hill overlooking the fortress. Somerset Tower and Great Rampier were constructed so that gunfire from the castle could render this hill untenable. However, the tactical centre of Jersey now shifted to its south and St. Helier's Islet with Elizabeth Castle becoming the premier stronghold. After the Civil War, Gorey Castle slowly fell into disrepair, being partially reconditioned during the last French wars and re-fortified during the German Occupation.

Mont Orgueil received its name from Thomas, Duke of Clarence, a brother of Henry V who was so impressed with the castle's unique position and dominating powerfulness that he called it Mount Pride, an apt title which has been passed down through the ages. The castle divides into four wards: the Outer, Lower and Inner Wards and then the Keep. In each case the inner bailey dominates the outer bailey and the curtain walls enclosing them have mainly rock foundations. The walls are flanked by small bastions, along the top of which ran a covered way. The outer side was crenellated and loopholed for bowmen.

The approach to the castle lies through what was the King's Warren; the tower commanding the main entrance overlooking the ditch is **Harliston Tower** built in 1470. The **Outer Ward** contains an area of about 1500sq m. Passing through the Second Gateway we enter the **Lower Ward**, a pleasant courtyard where gardens stretch up to the walls of the **Middle Ward**. The medieval Lower Ward was full of houses and other buildings maintained by the islanders as refuges during attack. The Second Gateway has an open gorge, the object of which is to deny the attacker cover from missiles shot from this next line of defence. The southern tower was modified in the 18C to receive a traversing gun. Looking back towards the Keeper's Lodge and down towards the little harbour, a companion tower is visible. These towers ringed the medieval castle and were an essential part of the defensive system.

The wall of the collapsed Lower Ward ran between these two towers and the existing one has been built further back. The Machicolated Bastion was built in

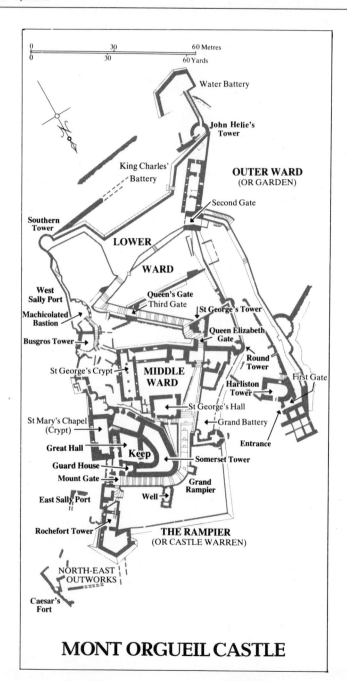

0   30   60 Metres
0   30   60 Yards

Water Battery

John Helie's Tower

King Charles' Battery

OUTER WARD (OR GARDEN)

Second Gate

Southern Tower

LOWER WARD

West Sally Port

Queen's Gate
Third Gate

St George's Tower

Machicolated Bastion

Busgros Tower

Queen Elizabeth Gate

Round Tower

St George's Crypt

MIDDLE WARD

First Gate

Harliston Tower

St George's Hall

St Mary's Chapel (Crypt)

Grand Battery

Great Hall

Keep

Guard House

Entrance

Mount Gate

Somerset Tower

East Sally Port

Well

Grand Rampier

Rochefort Tower

THE RAMPIER (OR CASTLE WARREN)

NORTH-EAST OUTWORKS

Caesar's Fort

MONT ORGUEIL CASTLE

the 14C, the original cross arrow slits and machicoulis are still intact and further embrasures were later added for the use of cannon.

Mont Orgueil was built on the concentric principle, employing a series of defences each independent of the other and their strength grows more apparent as the visitor begins his ascent through the Middle Ward to the Keep. The third gateway, built by Sir George Carteret in 1648, was defended by a drawbar as well as by the portcullis. This gate was renamed Queen's Gate following Queen Victoria's visit in 1846.

Continuing up the steps the Fourth or Queen Elizabeth's Gateway and the entrance to the Middle Ward are reached. The medieval **Middle Ward** contained about 2000sq m, most of which became built over. The gate, heavily protected by drawbridge and portcullis, straddles the cross-wall which runs from the Busgros Tower seawards to St. George's Tower and on to the Round Tower high above the entrance to the castle. Most of the buildings in the area are in ruins. In the large building known as **St. George's Crypt**, Governor Thomas Overay was buried in 1500 and Governor Sir Anthony Ughtred in 1532. The massive **Somerset Tower** was built to bring effective cannon fire against Mont Saint Nicholas but when in 1680 this updating of defences against possible enemy artillery was completed there was only room for four demi-culverins, two of which faced the hill and two St. Catherine's Bay.

Walk upwards around Somerset Tower to the Grand Rampier and the Mount Gate. Passing the castle well, at the top of the steps is (left) the **Rampier**. From here it is apparent why the importance of the castle declined when cannon replaced the bow. The towers which ring the castle are too lightly constructed to withstand shot and any attacker could position cannon to pound the fortress into submission from the heights of Mont St. Nicholas.

The north-east **outworks** and **Rochefort Tower** were constructed by John de Roches in the 14C when he was Keeper of the Castle. On the ground floor of the tower is the **East Sally Port** leading to **Caesar's Fort** which overlooks the small bay of Petit Portelet.

Before entering the **Keep** note a moulding enriched with figures of the chase and, above the arch, a tablet commemorating the building of Somerset Tower by Edward Seymour, afterwards Duke of Somerset, can be seen on Mount Gate. Modifications to the gate took place when this tower was built and the portcullis which protects it is unusual for a keep. To the right is the guard house and adjoining it the shell of the great hall and kitchen. On the left of the Long Gallery is the 12C Chapel of St. Mary, around which it is thought the castle grew.

You now arrive at the tableaux rooms. The first tableau portrays the defenders of Mont Orgueil in 1373 during the attack of Bertrand du Guesclin. The second tableau, in the Governor's dining room, depicts the Poulett family who governed the island from Mont Orgeuil for many years. Passing into the Governor's kitchen, we find a tableau of famous prisoners who have lived in the castle. A staircase leads past Prynne's cell to the Governor's ante-room where Admiral Philippe D'Auvergne held court. He is represented seated on his Chair of Office in what came to be called the **Throne Room**.

During World War II the Germans re-established the castle as a defence post with observation towers, gun emplacements, dugouts and trenches. A flame thrower was placed at the top of the steps leading to the Keep and the north-east outworks were heavily concreted as the **Battle Headquarters**.

Between Gorey Castle and Bouley Bay

Total distance: 8km.

Swimming and water-sport activities

The beach facilities in this area include Anne Port Bay, close to the coast road—easily accessible. Archirondel Bay is very popular. It has a pebbly beach with very clear water. St. Catherine's Bay has a pebbly foreshore with access by slipway at the lifeboat station. South of the breakwater is a popular shore dive with the best visibility around highwater, Flicquet Bay has a rocky inlet with slip, and La Coupe is sand and shingle, as is Saie Harbour. Rozel Bay has a picturesque harbour and quay sheltered from tidal currents popular with shore divers. So too does Bouley Bay with a steeply shelving shingle beach and diving school centre. Here the Jersey Underwater Centre has boats available for single dives or full day trips around Jersey and Sark.

North of Gorey Castle is Petit Portelet Bay, accessible by footpath from the coast road (B29). This secluded cove is popular in the morning when it is a sun trap.

Jeffrey's Leap

Where the road turns into Anne Port Bay there is a rocky headland known as Jeffrey's Leap. From here, villains were forced as punishment to jump onto the rocks below. One Jeffrey, so condemned, survived unhurt the first time and was thus by law a free man. Bravado caused him to try it again and he became a dead man.

Dolmen de Faldouet

A lane leads up the hill behind, just after Jeffrey's Leap to the Dolmen de Faldouet. At the top of the lane there is a left turn at the T-junction, then a sharp right and left turn where a signpost points to the dolmen. A path arched with trees leads to a well-reserved passage grave. It is 15m long with a chamber 6m wide, roofed with a capstone weighing 24 tons, which was brought from an outcrop of non-porphyritic rhyolite 500m away. This is believed to have lain under a mound, retained by two concentric rubble walls. Between these ran a kerb of stones, some of which are still on view to the south of the entrance. Today the outer wall turns inwards at the entrance, but the excavators thought that the mound was once completely encircled. Excavated in 1839, interments of adults and children were found in the cists. Also discovered were pottery vessels, segmented stone pendants and polished axes now on display at the Jersey Museum.

Anne Port, is an attractive village with hotel and tea-rooms. The bay itself affords good bathing from its pebbly beach at high tide, and at low tide plenty of sand.

Havre de Fer runs from La Crete Point to **Archirondel Tower** (1794). The design of this tower is unique to Jersey. In 1779 General Conway, the Governor, proposed that 32 'Towers of masonry with corresponding batteries' should be constructed. Twenty-three were built at a cost of £156 each, ringing all but the north coast. The specifications for the towers were that they were to be 10 to 14m high, 500m apart and solid for 3 to 4m from the bottom. The walls were to be pierced with loopholes for musketing in two stages and at the top. Only Archirondel and La Rocco Towers have surrounding curtain walls. The granite of this tower is in marked contrast to the rhyolite of the peninsula on which it stands. The tower was to be the south arm of a great harbour for naval ships in St. Catherine's Bay, an answer to the French naval base at Cherbourg 56km away, at a time when the imminent threat of French invasion governed British military thinking. However, when the St. Catherine's Breakwater at the north end of the bay was completed in 1855 the project was abandoned. The Jersey States took over the breakwater 1km north and built a lighthouse at the end of it. Today the bay is a popular beach and the breakwater provides a safe, protected and calm stretch of water. It also provides a good base for offshore anglers.

From **Verclut Point** there is an attractive stroll from the bottom of the break-water to **Flicquet Bay**. A lane follows the coast round to the white Martello tower. It is also possible to take the main road to the right, signposted to Rozel. Climb a steep hill to a T-junction, also signposted to the right for Rozel. From here there is a magnificent view over St. Catherine's Breakwater. The road continues round, and there is a right turn at the Rue de Flicquet which leads down to the white Martello tower overlooking the rocks of Flicquet Bay. The road now turns inland again and where it joins the main road (B91) there is a sharp right turn down a twisted narrow road that leads to both **La Coupe Point** and **Saie harbour**.

Offshore islets and reefs

The road for La Coupe Point turns off to the right and twists steeply towards the parking area overlooking **Les Ecréhous**, a reef of islets and rocks, some 8km out to sea.

When World War II ended France laid claim to these reefs which are situated halfway between the island and French mainland. France also laid claim to the Minquiers, referred to by the Islanders as the 'Minkies'—a reef of islets and rocks covering a large area to the south of St. Helier just under halfway between Jersey and France. The dispute had to be settled by the International Tribunal at the Hague, which in 1953 ruled in favour of Britain, but reserved the traditional fishing rights in the surrounding waters to the French. About a century before Victor Hugo aptly described the Channel Islands as 'Morceaux de France tombés à la mer et ramassés par l'Angleterre' (Pieces of France fallen into the sea and gathered up by England).

Les Ecréhous are part of the parish of St. Martin and have three main islets: **Blanc Ile**, **Maître Ile** and **Marmotière**. These have been inhabited since prehistoric times. One of the most colourful characters to take up residence was Philip Pinel who fled here to escape from his nagging wife. He was nicknamed the 'King of the Ecréhou' and was presented with a blue quilted jacket by Queen Victoria during her visit in 1857, which he no doubt found very useful during the winter gales. There are several houses on these three islands, nowadays mainly used by Jersey residents as holiday homes. On Maître Ile are the ruins of a chapel which belonged to a Norman Cistercian Abbey. To the right is a lane leading to the sandy section of Flicquet Bay which is mainly rocky and suitable only for offshore fishing.

The road for **Saie harbour** is straight ahead from here and ends with a grass verge where there is room for half a dozen cars. A lane off to the right leads, after 50m, to the harbour itself, a rocky bay. To the left another path leads up to the rocky headland, Le Couperon, 100m away which has a view over the next inlet, Douet de la Mer. The rocks all around from Saie Bay to Douet are good for offshore fishing.

By a small hut just back from the headland is the **Long Cist of Le Couperon**. This Long Cist has its entrance to the south-east and is enclosed with two parallel lines of stones. It was poorly restored in the last century. In 1919 efforts were unsuccessfully made to replace the septal slab to its most likely position inside the cist, dividing it into two chambers. It now lies across its entrance.

The B91 continues west along the Rue des Pelles, to **Rozel Bay**. From a right turn at the T-junction onto the B38 Rozel Hill curves round into the bay. Rozel is derived from the French 'rousseau', meaning reed. Nestled at the bottom of wooded hills, the bay is a good choice when the wind is from the south and a short pier shelters a few pleasure and fishing boats.

The road (C93) leads west out of Rozel Bay to Bouley Bay, where it is joined by another incoming road from the east. At 500m from the shorefront, on the right, is **Le Catel Earthwork**. An Iron Age defence, 200m long, 10m wide and 6m high, it was referred to locally as Caesar's Wall. Gaul coinage has been discovered here and it is thought that the defence works were operational as late as Roman and even Viking times.

At Pot du Rocher the C95 turns west towards **Bouley Bay**. At the end of this road is a T-junction. Off to the right and keeping straight on the road runs down Bouley Bay Hill to the jetty. This is the venue for the RAC National Hill Climb Championship, organised by the Jersey Motor-Cycle and Light Car Club. Near the jetty is a slip good for launching dinghies. It is also popular as a place for scuba diving because of the fish, crab and lobster in this area, especially around the outlying rock, Tour de Rozel. The surrounding cliffs are high, the beach shelves steeply and swimmers should take care.

Between St. Helier and La Pulente

Total distance 12km

Swimming and water-sport activities

Talisman, a 31-foot charter boat fully equipped for diving purposes, operates out of St. Helier and offers trips to various wreck and reef sites around the island. In Roseville Street, St. Helier, Aquanaut has a full range of diving equipment for sale or hire and specialises in giving diving courses. A boat charter service is available. The beach facilities in this area include St. Aubin's Bay—West Park to Bel Royal with shelving beach. A guard is stationed at West Park. St. Aubin's Bay—Bel Royal to Beaumont has a shelving beach with Steve's Ski Hire at Sugar Basin Slip at Beaumont. St. Aubin's Bay—Beaumont to St. Aubin has the Jersey Sea Sports Centre, strongly concentrating on water-skiing, at La Haule Slip, St. Aubin. Belcroute Bay has an unspoilt shingle beach. Popular Portelet Bay is a sandy sheltered bay accessed by steep climb.

L'Ouaisne has an attractive setting. St. Brelade's Bay is a favourite family beach with pleasure books for hire, windsurfing and sailing school at Wayside Slip. Beauport Bay is a quiet sandy bay with a steep climb to the car park.

The coastline west out of St. Helier starts from Liberation Square and proceeds along the Esplanade. On the left is the causeway known as the Bridge to Elizabeth Castle (1km). Nearby the route along this coastline divides. Victoria Avenue (A2) keeps to the actual coastline and St. Aubin's Road (A1) runs parallel but goes slightly inland. Both converge at Bel Royal. Victoria Avenue has on its left a marine promenade which overlooks the sands when the tide is out. St. Aubin's Road skirts the pine covered slopes of Westmount—a walk up here offers good views over this fine crescent-shaped bay, and then passes through a suburb known as the First Tower, named after a Martello tower which was built in the vicinity.

On the right in First Tower Park is St. Andrew's Church, built in 1926 of granite. The park was an area of sand dunes on the fief of Mélèches, until urbanisation. Within it are two megalithic monuments at the foot of Mont Cochon. To the south is a long parallel-sided cist (12m) with seven remaining capstones. Evidence indicates that the cist once extended further east and had two side chambers. A few steps north of the long cist is a circle of stones 6m in diameter surrounding a smaller cist. On these sites were discovered Bell beakers and Carinate pots. When the site was excavated in 1869 groups of fine large cinerary urns of the late Bronze Age were discovered in the sand, indicating a cremation cemetery typical of this period.

Church of St. Matthew

On the left by Coronation Park is the Church of St. Matthew, sometimes referred to as the Glass Church. Decorated as a memorial to Sir Jesse Boot, founder of the Boot's chain of chemist shops, the glass work is by René Lalique. The 5m-high luminous cross composed of glass lilies above the altar is supported on each side by glass pillars, all of which can be illuminated. The work was commissioned by Lady Trent in 1930 in memory of her husband. The font, altar rail, doors, windows, pillars and screen are all made of the same opaque glass. They are serenely set off against a background of white walls and deep blue hangings. The unifying theme of the lily motif lends a particular charm and distinction to the interior, blending as it does one of the best known conventional attributes of the Virgin with the well-loved symbol of the Jersey lily.

The Lady Chapel, and many other embellishments are also made of this special glass.

Note on the gable of the house known as Bel Royal (4km) and facing St. Aubin's Road, the sundial dated 1794. At Beaumont (5km) where the A12 comes down to the coast one can view a few metres up Beaumont Hill, a bronze gun just over 2m long, mounted under a thatch canopy; the inscription reads: 'Jhon Owen (of Houndsditch) made this pese anno dni 1551 for the paryshe of Saynt Peter in Jersse'.

Golf

Also just off Beaumont Hill, is Wheatlands 9 hole par 3 golf course set in 30 acres of parkland. Green fees are Mon–Fri £16.50 for a day ticket. Nine holes on weekdays is £9, and weekends £10.50. Eighteen holes are £13.50 and £15.00 respectively. Club hire is £4.00, trolleys £2.00. Restaurant, and also hot and cold snacks, available on Garden Terrace. ☎ 01534 888844.

The coastline continues west leaving the third Martello tower on the left (the second one, which was near St. Peter's Rd junction, was destroyed in 1943 by the Germans). The coastal road passes the Forester Arms, a landmark on the right, and close by is the property called Merman, the site of a cottage where Lillie Langtry once lived. She called it Merman after her horse of that name which in 1897 won the Cesarewitch and £39,000.

St. Aubin and its harbour

St. Aubin (6km) during the 18C surpassed St. Helier in importance. Although never the capital of the island, its importance was due to its excellent harbour built between 1754 and 1819. During the 18C some 150 captured French vessels were anchored in the harbour under the command of Sir George Carteret. In a land foray privateers from here even captured the washing of the curé of Caen, plus his two washerwomen. Much of the spoils of privateering at that time were used to finance the maintenance of the Royal Castles. Today the harbour is filled with small yachts and cruisers and is a popular holiday venue for those who like to be away from the main tourist centre. The **Royal Channel Islands Yacht Club** was the sixth to receive the Royal Charter and its first lady member was Lillie Langtry.

St. Aubin is named after a 6C Breton saint who was a former Bishop of Angers, and to whom the community turned for protection against pirates and invaders. In spite of this devotion there is no evidence that a church dedicated to him was built here. It is believed that there may have been a small dedicatory chapel to him built on the offshore St. Aubin's Fort. St. Aubin's Church constructed in 1892 is Victorian Gothic. In the Lady Chapel is an attractive stained-glass window designed by Edward Burne-Jones the pre-Raphaelite painter, and was produced in the William Morris workshop.

The town has half a dozen thoroughfares including the quaint High Street lined with an attractive medley of old buildings. There are hanging baskets and growing flowers in profusion. The bustling tidal harbour is enclosed by two jetties and a few hundred metres offshore is St. Aubin's Fort, constructed to protect the town from sea raids during Henry VIII's reign. Rebuilt in 1742, it was abandoned as a fort in 1840 and then re-fortified during the German Occupation. Care should be taken when visiting it not to be caught by the fast incoming tide. There is a good view from the ramparts of the sweeping shoreline around to Elizabeth Castle. St. Aubin was linked to St. Helier by railway in 1870. Up the side of the valley the site of the old railway track to Corbière has been converted into a delightful walk by the planting of flowers and shrubs.

From St. Aubin the A13 inland completes two sides of a triangle before the B57 Route de Noirmont branches off to the left at 8km. Crossroads occur 1km further on. The left turning descends to a tree-sheltered lane past Noirmont Manor where Lillie Langtry spent her honeymoon and left her initials on a window pane which she cut with her engagement ring. The original house was erected in 1695, and was rebuilt in the early 19C, since when it has been much modernised. It is not open to the public. **Belcroute Bay** was at one time a mooring for ships in quarantine. At low tide this is a good beach for digging bait. Straight on, at the crossroads the road comes to **Noirmont Point**, a public property and an excellent place for rambling and picking blackberries in the autumn. The headland of the Black Height was purchased in 1946 by the State as a memorial to the islanders who lost their lives in the last war. Binoculars set into the German fortifications give close-up views of the south coast. The German observation dome and naval direction tower are maintained by the Jersey Occupation Society. At the end of World War Two the islanders wished to remove all traces of the German occupation. However, some of the fortifications were too massive, and nowadays they are regarded by the islanders as an important part of their history and heritage. There are several well placed benches along the headland.

Just above the sea, at the south tip of Noirmont Point, is a rock crowned with the Tower—La Tour de Vinde—built at a cost of £3,645 in 1810 to defend the westerly approach to St. Helier. Over on the west side is the islet Percée which can be reached at low tide. In the middle of Portelet Bay, reached by footpath, is the Ile de Guerdain crowned with part of a Martello tower. It is still referred to locally as **Janvrin's Tomb**.

> In 1721 Captain Phillipe Janvrin's ship returned from Nantes with the plague on board. It lay offshore in Belcroute Bay in quarantine, and when the captain died the magistrates forbade his coffin to come ashore. The rector of St. Brelade held the service on the mainland and by signal the coffin was lowered into a grave on this island. Later his bones were reinterred at St. Brelade's cemetery, at his widow's request.

By the right turn at the crossroads (see above) and then the right fork, descend to **Ouaisné Bay**, a popular venue for swimming and sunbathing. Deckchairs, mattresses and windbreakers can be hired. The beachside restaurant here serves fresh fish to gourmet standard and in the evening as the sun sets the view is beautiful.

Beyond the quarry at the south end of the bay, steps lead up to La Cotte Cave. Discovered in 1881, this cave has been the subject of considerable research and excavation by members of the Société Jersiaise. The cave was created when the sea level was 18m higher than it is today, and two distinct periods of occupation have been determined. Palaeontology has revealed that the lower habitation level dates back approximately 150,000 years to the second half of the Saale or Riss glaciation, the last Ice Age but one. No human remains have been found relating to this age, but the animal remains and flint tools indicate that these early men lived and hunted in a mild climate. The cave is no longer open to the public (see the La Cotte display in the museum in St. Helier p. 50).

St. Brelade's Bay

St. Brelade's Bay is a short walk along the beach from Quaisné. To get there by car return to the main road (A13), turn left, take the next left and follow the Mont Sohier (B66) which runs along the sea front.

Situated at the west end of the bay near the slipway and sheltered by a cluster of trees is St. Brelade's church.

St. Brelade's church

St. Brelade's church, has a saddle-back tower and Celtic turret, and some historians believe that the Irish saint, 'Brendan the Voyager', built a chapel here in the 6C. Brendan was born in Ireland, and in one of his many journeys he is believed to have sailed from Brittany searching for the 'Isles of the Blest' and was driven by a great storm to seek shelter here. Thus he gave his name to the parish, which was later altered to St. Brelade. Other historians take the view that the name St. Brelade arose from the dedication of the church to St. Branwallader, another Celtic saint who came here with St. Sampson. The church was built from huge granite boulders taken from the sea shore. Crushed seashells and sand boiled in sea water were used to make mortar, and whole limpet shells can still be seen embedded in the granite.

Outside the church each gable carries a Greek Cross which is characterised by having each section the same length. There are twelve of these if we count those on the **Fisherman's Chapel**, the building to the right of the church. The church has a single bell (1883) which weighs 835kg (16½cwt). Records show that in 1550 the church possessed no less than five bells, but in common with all the other parish churches, all except one bell was removed, to help supply the raw materials for the fortification of Elizabeth Castle and Mont Orgueil. There is a story, certainly apocryphal in part, which tells how the ship transporting the bells sank in a storm, and that at certain times the bells can be heard still tolling, from their watery graveyard.

The nave and chancel are the most ancient parts of the church. Traces of ancient windows and arches can be seen in several places, particularly in the wall around the window behind the organ console. In the 12C the church was cruciform in design, with a chancel, nave and two transepts. In the following century a chancel aisle and nave aisle were added. In the 14C the roof was raised nearly a metre to a Gothic pitch. Note the double piscina by the high altar. A double piscina is almost unique in church furnishings. They were reserved for washing the sacred vessels and the priest's hands before the consecration of the host during Mass. The altar is one huge rock weighing c 760kg (15cwt). The five crosses cut into the stone at the time of consecration represent the five wounds of Christ. The pews, pulpit, rood screen and most of the oak furniture in the church is Victorian. The granite walls were originally plastered, and when this was removed in the 19th century, pointing work was carried out around every single block of granite. The stained glass windows in the church are 19th century. Seven are by the Jersey artist H.T. Bosdet (1857–1934) and display a strong pre-Raphaelite influence.

Although he studied painting at the Royal Academy, Bosdet was better known as a stained-glass designer, and examples of his work are to be found in churches, chapels, and manor houses in Jersey, France, and England. Some of the originals of his windows are on display in the Jersey Museum.

The four windows on the south wall of St. Brelade's show Christ after the forty days in the wilderness; the crucifixion, with the Virgin, Mary Magdalene and St. John; the parable of the sower, and the parable of the yeast; and an illustration of the 23rd psalm. Note the characteristic and traditional use of the figure of St. George, who embodies England. The name comes from the Latin georgic and means the farmer or ploughman. St. George has been perceived in art, literature, parable and fable as the ploughman who ploughs the earth of England itself, which will bring forth the fruit and harvest of salvation.

The nearby Fisherman's Chapel is a rare example of Celtic art and was built with similar materials to the church. It is only 13.25m long and 6m wide; the walls are 3m high and 1m thick. The walls are 6C and the stone roof, which was raised, belongs to the 14C. In 1818, after a severe storm, colour was seen on the ceiling which led to the discovery of several frescoes (it is necessary to turn on the light to appreciate them). The first fresco was a picture of the *Assumption*, in

Restored German bunkers

Several German bunkers have been restored by the Channel Islands Occupation Society, in order to show how Hitler's Atlantic Wall operated (see p,129).

The Underground Command Bunker, Noirmont Point, St. Brelade extends down for 40 feet on two floors. This bunker is **open** every Thursday evening during June, July and August from 19.00–21.30. Also most Mondays from 10, 00–12.00 until end of September. Not on a bus route, no toilets, large free car park. Adults fee, accompanied children free.

The Coastal Artillery Observation Tower, Noirmont Point, St. Brelade is **open** most Tuesday mornings 10.00–12.00 during June, July and August. Fee, free car park.

The 10.5cm Coastal Defence Gun casemate at La Corbière, St. Brelade is adjacent to the road leading down to the Lighthouse and is well signposted. Visitors can view the bunker's original gun, with other interesting relics. It is **open** every Saturday in July and August between 10.30 and 13.30. Bus Rte 12, free car park.

The Coastal Defence Gun and anti-tank casemates at La Carrée Point, St. Ouen's Bay. This twin bunker complex is adjacent to Five Mile Road between La Pulente and Le Braye. It houses some of the large Occupation relics including a railway truck, a tank turret, and a searchlight. **Open** from 12.00–16.30 on 10, 17 and 31 May; 14 and 28 June; 12 and 26 July; 9, 23 August; and 6 and 20 September. Bus Rte 12A, car park.

The Heavy Machine Gun Turret Bunker at Val de la Mare, St. Peter has steel cupolas up to ten inches thick. Bunkers like these were once common along the Atlantic Wall, but over the years scrap merchants have dismantled and moved many of them, so this one is quite rare. **Open** 15.30–18.00 on 26 April; 24 May; 7, 21 June; 5 and 19 July; 2, 16, 30 August; and 13 September. Free car park, not on bus route.

The Gun Emplacements and Underground Bunkers at Les Landes, St Ouen. This is a well-restored coastal artillery battery with many underground bunkers and lengthy passageways. Also on display is a 15.5cm coastal defence gun recovered from the foot of the cliffs in 1991. **Open** from 13.00–17.00 on 26 April; 9 and 24 May, 7 and 15 June; 5 and 19 July; 2, 16 and 30 August; 13 September. Adults fee, accompanied children free, Bus Rte 8, free car park nearby.

The anti-tank Gun Casemate at Millbrook, opposite La Rue de Galet. This bunker is very well preserved, and houses a rare Czechoslovakian anti-tank gun. **Open** Thursday 19.30–21.30 from 1 May–18 September except Battle of Flowers Day. Fee, free car park.

poor condition. Underneath the plaster was found another painting, an *Annunciation* of c 1315. At the foot of this painting are 14 figures, believed to be members of an old Jersey family. Another picture of the Annunciation is on the south wall behind the arch. A short distance west is the Blessed Virgin's hand clasped on a book resting on a lectern. Nearby is the head of a Magus, with the name 'Melchior' above it, and close by another of the Wise Men bearing the inscription '*Les Mages*'. Between the Wise Men, the body and legs of a chain-mailed soldier is quite distinct.

On the west wall are the *Resurrection* and *Last Judgement*. Over the north door is a picture of King Herod and close by *The Scourging of Christ*. On the north ceiling over the door is a picture of our Lord '*Riding upon an Ass*'; close by is a picture of a Roman soldier.

It is said that the murals show themselves better in certain atmospheric conditions—hence the local belief that they forecast the weather for fishermen who come to pray here before going out to harvest the sea. It remains the oldest place of worship on the island.

Bouilly Port, Beau Port, Flicquet Bay

These three bays are to the south-west of St. Brelade's church. On the cliffs near Bouilly Port is the grave of Lord Trent, formerly Sir Jesse Boot, founder of Boot's the Chemists. Beau Port can be reached by car by a small road west called Mont-és-Croix. From the car park there is a steep climb down through the bracken, not easy for the elderly, to a lovely little sandy bay. The second Lord Trent presented to the States of Jersey the land adjacent to Beau Port which is now called Joyce Trent Park, which is open to the public. Flicquet Bay is rocky; nearby, above it, are the Beauport and La Moye dolmens.

La Moye Golf Club

La Moye Golf Club overlooks the wide sweep of St. Ouen's Bay. By turning inland of Mont Sohier the A13 is reached at the crossroads. Turn left along Route Orange and you will see the driveway leading up to the club house with its golf shop, restaurant, driving range, and putting green. The 18-hole golf course, par 72, is now the popular venue for the Jersey Seniors open, part of the PGA European Seniors Tour. To play as a visitor, men have to have a handicap of 24 and below, and women golfers 30 and below, and belong to a recognised golf club who can give proof of handicap.

At the time of going to press Green fees are £40 per round, £45 weekends, £60 per day including lunch. Per week is £185.00. Clubs £5 per day, trolleys £1.50 and electric trolleys £5 per round. Balls for driving range £1 per basket. Standards of dress say that jeans are not permissible, and if wearing shorts, long socks must be worn. Address: La Moye, St. Brelade, Jersey ☎ 01534 43401.

Corbière Point

is reached by following a loop road off the A13. which later becomes the B44. The origin of Corbière is probably Celtic, meaning projecting point of the sea bird, from the Breton 'Corf' or Irish

Corbière lighthouse

'Corp' and Breton 'ar' meaning bird. It is more usually translated as 'place of the raven' and ravens are still seen flying around the nearby cliffs. The lighthouse, the first made of concrete in the British Isles, was built in 1874, is 500m offshore and can be reached by the causeway between half-ebb and half-flood tides. It should be noted that once the tide starts to come in it does so very rapidly.

At the start of the causeway is a memorial to 'Peter Edwin Larbelestier, Assistant Keeper at the lighthouse, who on 28th May 1946 gave his life in attempting to rescue a visitor cut off by the tide'. An electrically operated siren now warns the public of the incoming tide.

The tower is 36.5m above high water and in clear weather the light can be seen for 27km. On the headland a former German Observation Tower has now become Jersey Radio Station. Steps by the side of the Highlands Hotel on the main road lead down to La Rosiére with its Smugglers' Cave and Pirates' Cave.

La Pulente, the northern part of the loop back to the A13 passes the little bay of Petit Port which is rocky and not very suitable for swimming.

Just above this bay on the northern headland is La Sergenté, the remains of a Neolithic round hut tomb c 3500 BC, probably the earliest remaining dolmen in Jersey.

Soon after, where the B44 rejoins the A13, a left turn down the B35 leads to the Mont de La Pulente. The approach to La Pulente presents a panoramic view of St. Ouen's Bay. La Pulente beach is popular for gathering shells, and for keep fit enthusiasts, who can be seen jogging around the bay.

Between La Pulente and Grève de Lecq

From La Pulente, Grand Route des Mielles, Five Mile Road skirts the largest sandy bay in the Channel Islands, St. Ouen's Bay which straddles the west coast of the parishes of St. Brelade, St. Peter and St. Ouen.

Swimming and water-sport activities

St. Ouen's Bay runs almost the whole length of the west coast to a length of 6km and is a widely exposed sandy beach when the tide is out. It is a mecca for both swimming and water-sports. Windsurfing is very popular here depending on the wind direction, as is surfing. Surfing is only permitted between markers for safety reasons. The **Atlantic Waves School of Surfing** ☎ 01534 865492 can advise surfers which is the best bay to use on the day according to the direction of the wind. Likewise the **Jersey Surfing School** (☎ 01534 484005). Grève au Lancon is the largest north facing beach with sand, 1km wide at low tide and km deep, protected by rocks but subject on occasion to a heavy swell. The beach is covered at high tide.

Bathing is safe for the experienced and careful swimmer in St. Ouen's Bay, a red and yellow flag denoting safe bathing areas. A red cone is flown when bathing is dangerous. The exposure of the bay to wind and tide makes it a good area for surfing and the breakers can be a fair size. There are several surfing centres which hire Malibu surf boards, windsurfers, surf canoes and wetsuits. The Motor Cycle and Light Car Club regularly stages sand race meetings (small admission charge).

Les Mielles Golf and Country Club

On the inland side of the coastal road is Les Mielles Golf and Country Club. This 18-hole course has an American style parkland layout, with bent grass green, dwarf rye fairways and burns. Green fees are inexpensive at £18 for 18 holes during the week, and £20 at weekends. Nine holes are £12.50 and £13.00 respectively, and day tickets are £25 weekdays and £27.50 at weekends. Clubs, carts and buggies can be hired at £8.00, £1.50 and £12.50 respectively.

Defensive towers

There are a number of defensive towers along this coastline. The most southerly is La Rocco Tower, about 800m offshore, erected in 1800. La Tour Carrée, Kempt Tower and Lewis are onshore. They were all built between 1778 and 1835. Kempt Tower, now a visitors' centre provides information on the region's natural history and environment.

At the north end of the bay, an old German bunker has become a vivier, where a great variety of local shellfish is held in tanks of sea water ready for purchase. **Open** Tues–Sat 08.00–17.00.

Jersey coastal towers

Today 24 Jersey coastal towers remain out of the original 31 built. The first four were erected between 1778 and 1779 and in 1781, after the Battle of Jersey, building went on apace. The original design for the towers was probably by Henry Seymour Conway, Governor of Jersey at that time, as he had certainly studied drawing and fortifications as a young officer. The towers are circular, with equal strength all round. This is different from the Martello tower design, which is cam-shaped. The Jersey tower is approximately 35 feet in diameter at the base, narrowing to 29 feet at the top. Inside, the ground floor would have been used as a magazine, and store-room, and the upper room would have accommodated an officer and ten men. A bomb-proof arch covered the living quarters, and held up the gun platform on the top of the tower. A platform and central pivot on the roof gave a 360 degree range of fire.

In 1794 the Martello tower made its appearance around the Jersey coastline, when the British witnessed the successful defence of Pointe Mortello in Corsica when a small French tower with its single gun held off two British naval ships, without sustaining any injury from their heavy gunfire. In all, eight of these towers were built around the island during the 19C, of which Kempt Tower in St. Ouen's, now a visitors' centre, is a prime example. It was built 40 years after the Corsican incident, and now displays comprehensive information on Jersey coastal towers.

Les Blanches Banques and Les Monts Grantez

Just south of the B43 are the Great Menhir, the Little Menhir and the Broken Menhir at Les Blanches Banques. They are set into the ground below the present blown sand. The peat beds beneath the beach indicate ancient forest land which existed when the sea was lower than it is today. A sherd of red pottery, a flint thumb scraper and a stone rubber were found at the base of the Little Menhir.

To find the **Passage Grave of Les Monts Grantez**, take the C106 to the right after St. Ouen's Pond (before Kempt Tower), turn right then left at the junction and continue in the same direction (east). At the T-junction turn right and follow Mont Mathieu round to the crossroads. Then turn left and leave the Old Mill on the left and continue north to Le Chemin des Mont which runs west. Continue along this road for 500m and just south (the signpost is at the gate of a field) is the passage grave.

Excavation took place in 1912. The mound is 18m long and 6m wide. The entrance passage opens into an oval chamber which in turn gives way to an irregularly shaped side chamber. Seven adult and one child skeletons were found in the main chamber along with pottery and stone instruments. The grave lies mainly buried in the remains of its mound to the top of the uprights with only the capstones exposed.

Midway up the bay on the right is St. Ouen's Pond, rich in carp. Referred to formally as La Mare au Seigneur, it was the sporting preserve of the Seigneur of St. Ouen. It is now administered by the National Trust for Jersey. At the north end is a bird observatory, which records many of the rarer species passing through the ringing traps and studies the breeding habits of local birds. In winter duck and snipe find refuge here.

For generations the sweeping beach of St. Ouen has been a main source of vraic (seaweed), collected by the cartload and used as fertiliser. It was also here that Admiral Black disembarked the Parliamentary soldiers who in 1651 forced the Royalists to surrender.

Battle of Flowers Museum

■ **Open** from mid-March–end of November daily 10.00–17.00; fee.

To visit the Battle of Flowers Museum continue inland at the junction with the B64 for 400m and turn next left. This small museum which houses award-winning exhibits from past Battles of Flowers, has a charm and innocence about it which makes it irresistible. It is situated in the converted outbuildings of the Bechelet family farm. Florence Bechelet first saw an exhibit on its way to the Battle of Flowers when she was just a child. This inspired her to enter a float in 1934, and from then on for the next 60 years she created an annual exhibit whenever there has been a Battle of Flowers parade. During this period she has won 80 awards, and upon retirement in 1994 she was made a life member of the Battle of Flowers Association. Originally her entries, like those of the majority, were covered in hydrangeas, but later she entered in the Wild Flower Class. These floats are covered in harestails and marram grass which grow wild on some sand dunes. They are dyed to suit the subject portrayed. However, in these days of ecological correctness most plants have to be specially grown, and Florence Bechelet started to plant and grow what she needed for each of her exhibits. Except for the five large panels all from prize-winning floats, all the work in the museum is Miss Bechelet's own. She used to start in the spring, sawing and hammering to make the wooden armature which she covered in wire netting, using glue if a smooth finish was required. The great variety of subjects which she chose to create for figures for the Battle of the Flowers floats show an amazing talent for this style of sculpture. The animal kingdom is particularly well represented in the museum.

As you enter there are no fewer than 101 dalmations, a charming evocation of the Walt Disney film. Elsewhere there are 40 flamingoes; an American Indian on horseback, and four-life size buffalo; Cinderella with her coach and horses en route to the Prince's ball; an eskimo and his team of huskies; a tapestry of King Arthur and his knights; a tapestry of Queen Elizabeth II and a host of other subjects. Miss Bechelet says that the Jersey calf exhibit involved her in the most painstaking research because it would be viewed by so many expert breeders. She used a 4-month-old calf as her life-size model. On several occasions Florence Bechelet rode in the parade herself. In 1992 she donned the flowing cloak, now on the model, as she represented Boudicca in her chariot, to loud cheers from the crowd as she drove past. On another occasion she was Santa Claus with a sleigh drawn by flower-sculpted reindeer. The pink flamingoes were made in 1978 to celebrate the Queen's visit to Jersey, and were exhibited in Howard Davis Park to give the royal visitors an idea of how the floats would look in the open-air parade. A photograph shows Miss Bechelet being presented to the Queen.

Grosnez, Portinfer and Plémont

Soon after the north end of St. Ouen's Bay the B55 runs north to Grosnez, and then veers east towards Portinfer and Plémont. Adjacent to the north-west coast lies the heath, Les Landes, exposed to Atlantic winds. There is also a path from Grande Etaquerel to Plémont over the headland which provides a 4.5km walk through gorse and heather. **Pinnacle Rock**, on the left, is a mass of granite rising vertically from the ocean to a height of 62m. The col which joins the rock to the mainland was inhabited during the Neolithic, Bronze, Iron and Gallo-Roman eras. Two ramparts which guarded the site and used to extend further to the north and south are seen by the rock. They lie in the same stratum and belong to the Late Neolithic and Bronze Age. The outline of a double-walled rectangular building to the east marks the foundations of a small Romano-Celtic temple probably built in the 1C AD.

> The earliest Neolithic settlement was extensive and excavations of hearth, querns and middens containing the bones of ox, pig and sheep indicate a farming community. Associated discoveries include pottery, stone axes, hammers and arrowheads. The building of the inner rampart is attributed to later Neolithic occupation where finds included a copper axe, plain or cordoned pottery, sherds of bell beaker ware, long points of Grand Pressigny flint (from the mines and workshops of that name in the Loire) and barbed arrowheads. It is thought that farming took place on open ground which became covered by the sea and led to the abandonment of the col. Blown sand covered the area and it is in this that all later activity is recorded. Although bronze was scarce, finds include a basal-loop bronze spearhead. While no permanent Iron Age structure has been found, among the remains left behind during the 1C BC were an Armorican coin and pottery fragments of vessels belonging to the La Téne III period. In the Romano-Celtic temple wheel-made pottery was found and a coin of Commodus.

In the northern section of Les Landes is the one-mile-round race course, where the Jersey Race Club hold eight events a year. The first meet is at Easter and the last in August, and there are five races during each afternoon.

Passing a German lookout tower the path comes to the north-west tip of the island. Here **Grosnez Castle** stands at the top of sheer black cliffs; far below can be seen the lobster pots of fishermen. The castle today has an entrance gateway, where you can just walk in, with projecting bastions and a ditch in front. A drawbridge across the ditch and cliff on three sides made this castle a temporary refuge for the local populace from marauders. The castle is believed to have been built in the early 14C after the French had massacred some 1500 islanders during a raid in 1294. The granite walls, 2m thick, surround an area 70m by 20m. Grosnez was captured in 1373 by the French and subsequently must have been destroyed because on maps produced in 1542 it was marked as a ruin. Steps and a short path lead to the lighthouse on Grosnez Point. From here Guernsey, Herm, Sark, Alderney and the Paternosters can be seen on a clear day.

From the castle the walk east along the north cliffs leads to **Cotte à la Chèvre**, a Palaeolithic cave dwelling. To reach it there is a descent of 62m and it is advisable to be accompanied by someone familiar with the path. The flints and hand axe discovered here correspond with the period of the lower Palaeolithic level at St. Brelade (see above).

By road, Plémont Point is reached by a left turn north off the B55 on to the C105. At the end is a small parking area just above the attractive bay of Grève au Lanflon. It is 1km long with a sandy beach at low tide and five caves on the landward side. Swimmers must be careful of the incoming tide which cuts off part of the beach very quickly.

Douet de la Mer

Douet de la Mer is reached by a left turn off the B55 by the manor Vinchelez de Bas down La Rue de Géonnais. Where this road ceases and becomes a private road you can walk straight down to the headland.

Here there are a number of cliff paths. One turns off to the east which is overgrown with bracken and leads all the way down to Douet de la Mer with its attractive little waterfall. To the west better cliff paths lead along Grand Becquet, Petit Becquet, Creux Gabourel and Creux Gros. Along these cliff paths are a great many wild flowers, including foxglove, michaelmas daisy and wild gorse. The trees at the back of the headland are bent over from the westerly winter gales that frequent these parts, and overhead seagulls call to one another as they swoop up and down on turbulent winds.

The Dolmen de Géonnais marked on maps is no longer visible. Enquiries made to local people produce no further information regarding its whereabouts.

East of Douet de la Mer (.75km) is Grève de Lecq, home of the most popular beach resort on the north coast.

Between Grève de Lecq and Bouley Bay

Total distance 12km

Swimming and water-sport activities

Grève de Lecq is a sandy beach with outcrops of rock and is 500m across. At both ends of this popular little bay are cafés and shops and the north coast visitors' centre is to be found in the old barracks. Bonne Nuit Bay is the home of a quaint little harbour surrounded by high cliffs carpeted with heather in the summer. The beach is part shingle and part sand. The north and north-west coasts are the most wild and savage of Jersey's 80km of shoreline. High cliffs provide long sloping headlands which in places give access to deep water marks ideal for shoreline fishing. Piers in Grève de Lecq Bay, Bonne Nuit Bay, Bouley Bay and Rozel Bay are popular sites among local anglers.

Grève de Lecq with its attractive Martello landmark straddles the boundary of St. Ouen and St. Mary. The stream that runs through the valley from Le Rondu and pours into the sea here divides two parishes. On the east side on a high hill stands an Iron Age fortification. These extensive earthwork entrenchments known as the **Câtel-de-Lecq** were originally constructed to protect Iron Age inhabitants from invasion. But they may well have been in use as late as the early 14C and referred to as one of the 'five fortified castles' at the time.

Off the B40 coastal road to the east of Grève de Lecq are a number of minor roads which lead to attractive walks by footpaths across the cliffs. One route leads left at La Verte Rue where the B40 joins the B33. Further on (100m) is a school. A left turn here goes up to a T-junction, where immediately right, at the end of this road are signposts, one of which points back to Grève de Lecq, the other to Devil's Hole. Nearby the L'Ane headland where bridle and footpaths lead east with splendid views of Crabbé and the little islet of Agois. It is believed locally that an earlier civilisation dwelt on this island on a site yet to be discovered. The headland, Col de la Rocque belongs to the National Trust for Jersey. On a clear day not only Sark and Guernsey but also the coast of France can be seen.

Low water, La Rocque

If you want to keep your shoes dry, stick to the footpaths rather than the bridle paths.

A walk of 3km ending in a concrete path from the nearby hotel leads down to the **Devil's Hole** or **Le Creux de Vis**, a great opening behind the cliff which has been eroded by the sea. Vis is probably a corruption of the Norse word 'vik' or 'vick' meaning creek, and it is thought that the name Devil's Hole may have arisen because a Viking ship which seemed to the local people to have a prow shaped like a devil was wrecked at the cave's entrance. An effigy of the devil has been kept near this natural blow hole for the last 130 years, the first one being converted from a ship's figurehead.

By road these destinations can be reached by going to the end of the C103, forking left for Devil's Hole and right for Mourier Valley. Mourier is derived from the French 'murier', mulberry.

Near the Devil's Hole at Elm Farm are La Mare Vineyards (**open** May–September Mon–Sat 10.00–17.30; fee). There are interpretative exhibitions on wine- and cider-making.

Past a carnation nursery and near the valley is a reservoir with a waterworks building with parking facilities. Further on (200m) by the shoreline is a tiny waterfall. A walk along the cliff path east leads to Sorel Point.

A man-made pool called the **Lavoir des Dames** (Fairies' Bath) rests just under the headland. This 7.5sq m rock-pool with a depth of 4.5m is exposed at half tide; the water left behind is exceptionally clear. A quarry lies between Sorel and the next headland, **Ronez Point**. 'Sorrel' is the name of the pinkish granite found in the neighbourhood and 'Ronez' is the Old Norse word for rocky waste.

From Ronez Point the Route du Nord sweeps round on top of the cliffs, passing high above Mourier Bay and St. John's Bay. This marine drive was constructed by the States during the war to give work to Jerseymen who might otherwise have been employed by the Germans. Passing under the shadow of the ITA TV mast near the east end of the Route du Nord, turn left for Wolf Caves (sign-posted). A large car park, bar and coffee shop stand at the cliff edge by Frémont Point. Steps descend from here some 135m to Wolf Caves and Venus's Bath, a clear rock pool which can be seen at low tide. Wolf Caves is linked with the Norse raiders who were known as 'Les Loups de la Mers'. The descent is steep and occasional landslides remove the steps at the bottom end.

From the car park the first left and then the next left and the C99 road lead down to Bonne Nuit Bay with its stone jetty, pleasant little harbour and La Crète Fort at the east end. Fishermen used to circumnavigate the rock in the bay known as Le Cheval Guillaume on Midsummer Day to ensure that the next year's fishing would prove favourable.

From the picturesque bay and harbour in Bonne Nuit, with **La Crète Fort** (1835) at the east end, the road climbs to the highest part of Jersey. The ascending road, La Rue des Platons, continues to Les Platons, some 140m above sea level. In the area is a flotilla of masts belonging to BBC Radio, States of Jersey and the Decca Navigator Radio Transmitting Station. By branching left down the Rue D'Egypte and leaving the car at the end it is possible to walk north to Belle Hougue Point and with difficulty zigzag east through wooded terrain down to Petit Port. The Rue des Platons continues east until it joins the C102, a winding road to Bouley Bay.

Inland Jersey

The interesting features of inland Jersey and where they are to be found are listed under the different parish headings. This text, along with information appearing in the relevant coastal routes, referred to in each inland parish section, provides a full picture of what to see in each parish. The only exception to this formula are St. Helier, the capital, which is complete in itself, and St. Brelade, which because of its geographical position, most of its interesting features are placed along the coastline and therefore does not warrant an inland section on its own.

Parish of St. Clement

See also Between St. Helier and Gorey (p. 56)

The parish of St. Clement lies due east of the capital of St. Helier and stretches along a good section of the southern coastline. It is bordered by the parishes of St. Saviour and Grouville.

Green Lanes

A network of minor roads in Jersey have been designated 'Green Lanes' where pedestrians, cyclists and horse-riders take precedence over the motorist. These road lanes cover 72km and have a maximum speed limit of 15mph to discourage cars from using them, except for access.

More Green Lanes are being designated as they are proving popular with both local inhabitants and visitors. These are mapped on an official publication called *Discover the 'real' Jersey*. For example Green Lanes wander through the parish of St. Lawrence, enabling the visitor to explore superb countryside and traditional buildings such as Hamptonne—Jersey's Country Life Museum. In St. Peter's Valley, they meander beside woodland near Le Moulin de Quetivel, a stone built 18C watermill now restored to full working order by the National Trust of Jersey. Green Lanes are to be found all over the island, often leading to fascinating historic sites.

The benefit to the environment, the maintenance of tranquillity and olde world ambience created by this imaginative project has resulted in the British Guild of Travel Writers presenting Jersey with the coveted Silver Unicorn Award for this scheme.

St. Clement's church is close by the junction of the A5 and B49 roads. Early documents refer to Ecclesia Sancti Clementis de Petravilla in Gersuis—the church of St. Clement on the estate of Peter in Jersey. It is thought that an early wooden church existed here before the Norman period. Half the tithes of St. Clement were granted before 1066 to the Abbey of Montvilliers. In 1090 a charter was drawn up to pass the parish church into the ownership of the Abbey of St. Saviour le Vicomte in Normandy. It remained the property of this abbey until the Reformation. The nave formed part of the original chapel which was a small Norman building. In the 15C the church was enlarged with the addition of a chancel and transepts.

In 1880 restoration was carried out which revealed frescoes under the plaster. The best preserved is that of *St. Michael and the Dragon* on the north wall of the nave. On the west wall of the south transept are the remains of a fresco of a hunting scene with an inscription:

Helas saincte Marie et quelle
ces trois mors qui sot cy hideulx
mont fait meplre en gnt tristesse
de las vois aunxi piteulx

['Alas St. Mary! Who are these hideous corpses? It breaks my heart to see them thus piteous']. It comes from the legend of the *Three Living and the Three Dead*, told in an old French poem in which three young princes out hunting see three horrible corpses who warn them of the danger of living only for worldly success.

Other mural remains in the north transept portray *St. Barbara of Heliopolis in Egypt*, beheaded for her faith, and *St. Margaret and the Dragon*. The frescoes are believed to be 15C. The church possesses an interesting collection of silver plate including six chalices of which the oldest bears the date 1594. The font which stands in the south transept is 14C and a fine example of sculptured granite. It was unearthed following its removal during the Reformation when the church was being restored in the 9C.

During the late 17C one of the rectors, François Valpy, prosecuted the Seigneur of Samarès for altering a manor pew without his permission. Unfortunately for the rector, he had to pass through another manor pew in order to reach the pulpit, which the seigneur now filled with his servants. The rector was forced to bring a further lawsuit in the Royal Court in order to establish his right of way. In the end François Valpy retreated to the Rectory of St. Mary.

> Victor Hugo's republican sympathies, loudly asserted in public and private, led to his exile in Jersey in 1852. He and his family landed here on 5 August, 1852, where he was welcomed by an enthusiastic crowd of Jerseymen, Englishmen and French exiles. A guide book of the period describes how Jersey looked at that time—like a huge pleasure ground studded with trees. Hugo's daughter Adèle described it as 'a bunch of flowers dipped in the ocean, a bunch which has the fragrance of the rose, and the bitterness of the waves'. Hugo himself wrote to a friend: 'I am in the midst of poetry, among rocks and meadows, roses, clouds and the sea ... Poems rise up of their own accord from all this splendid nature.' He set up house in St. Clement. On 22 September 1855 Hugo defended a group of the French exiles who had made a virulent attack in the newspaper *L'Homme* on Queen Victoria because of her meeting with Napoleon III. They accused her of being amongst other things a perjuror and conspirator. The Jersey officials were appalled and Hugo challenged the officals to expel him. The challenge was pasted up all over St. Helier, so the Jersey officials took him at his word and on 27 October he was escorted to the harbour by the Constable of St. Clement. With his papers in the tin trunk which travelled with him everywhere he departed for Guernsey. History would agree no doubt that St. Clement's loss was Guernsey's gain.

Dolmen de Mont Ubé and Samarès Manor

One kilometre north of the crossroads on the A5 and just off the minor road of La Bliner is a signposted path, right leading up a steep and slippery slope to the Dolmen de Mont Ubé. A hedge surrounds the passage grave, which consists of 33 upright granite stones placed in typical bottle shape. The outer circle of stones, paving and capstones, although recorded, are all lost. During excavation several pottery vessels were retrieved including a Neolithic Jersey Bowl distinctive to the island. This is the only large communal grave where both burnt and unburnt bones have been discovered side by side. Cremation and some pottery of a later date are indicative that secondary burials took place here in the Bronze Age. This site was excavated in 1848 and is estimated to be 4000 years old.

Looking back down the hill, across the road behind the trees **Samarès Manor** is visible. A round tower covered in ivy is the remains of an 11C dovecote. Samarès is a contraction of 'Salse Marais', meaning salt-water marsh. The old way of making salt in these parts was to let the sea flow into the low-lying land, block the channel and allow the sun to evaporate the water, leaving the salt to be collected. The low ground of the manor was ideal for this purpose and salt was a valuable source of income to the seigneur.

The tenants who lived on land owned by the manor had fairly heavy duties to fulfil, including cleaning out the dovecote, cutting and fetching wood, hay-making and transporting the seigneur to Norman ports when required. Even the parish rector of St. Clements had his duties which included bringing the lady of the manor to church on a white charger for the customary service of thanks-giving following the birth of her child.

Parish of Grouville

See also Between St. Helier and Gorey (p. 56)

The parish of Grouville is bordered by the parish of St. Clement in the south, St. Saviour on the west and north, and St. Martin in the north as well. Her coastline rests along the east shoreline and a small section of the south. Pilgrims as far back as pre-Christian times have come here to worship at La Hougue Bie. Today Grouville is the centre of worship for parishioners.

Church of St. Martin de Grouville

The church of St. Martin de Grouville is at the junction of the A3 and B37. The first mention of the church is in a charter by Duke Robert of Normandy in 1035 when it was already a parish church. In 1149 Godfroi de Buisson made a grant of this church with its tithes and alms to the Abbey of the Holy Trinity at Lessay. This patronage was frequently interrupted by war, it was then exercised by the 'Seigneur des Iles'; and institution was given to the parish priest by the bishop of Coutances whose jurisdiction continued until 1568, though the Channel Islands had already been transferred by Papal Bull first to Salisbury and then to Winchester.

The chancel and south chapel are 14C. The south-west wall of the chapel has traces of paintings which probably at one time covered most of the walls. The orig-inal belfry was a square tower on which a steeple was built later which became a landmark for ships. Fishermen still refer to it as 'le pointu de Grouville'. When the weather cock was lowered for repairs after a minor earthquake in 1926 the following inscription was found on it: 'This cock after being stationary for about 50 years, was made revolve May 1908, H.A. Bertram, V.J. Bailache, Churchwardens'.

The 16C north chapel is said to have been built by Raulin Amy, a priest of an old Grouville family, who when caught in a tempest vowed to build a chapel onto the parish church if he landed safely. The octagonal font is medieval, made of Chausey granite, and each side is carved with a different design. The north wall of the nave of St. Martin de Grouville was built nearly 1000 years ago of stones from the seashore. The most recent addition is the 16C 'Chapelle des Amis'. An armoury was maintained here until the 19C. Plate includes 17C communion cups and a silver alms dish, a silver ewer and an 18C baptism dish.

La Hougue Bie

La Hougue Bie is 1.5km east of Five Oaks, and is by the junction of the B28 and B46 roads. Here there is an impressive mound some 13m high crowned with two medieval chapels. Below is a passage grave. It was discovered in 1924 and is one of the finest to be excavated.

The tomb divides into three sections for purposes of description. From the splayed entrance it is 3.5m to the start of the passage (B) and then just over 10m

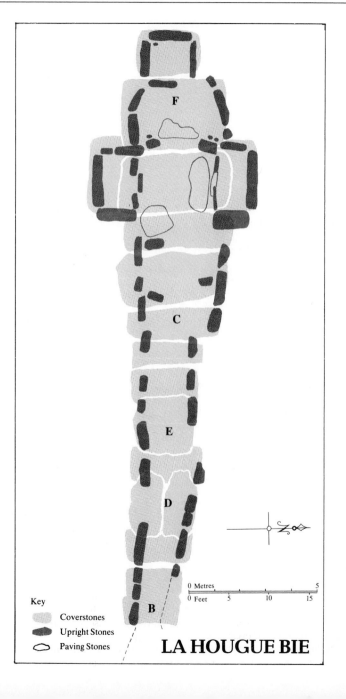

Key

Coverstones

Upright Stones

Paving Stones

LA HOUGUE BIE

to the Great Chamber. This is the first section. The width varies from 1m to 1.5m. The height varies from 1.5m, where you have to stoop, to just over 2m (D and E) where you can stand.

The second section is the oval **Great Chamber** (from C to F), approximately 9m long and 3m across. Five immense stone slabs, the largest of which weighs 25 tons, form the roof of the chamber, partly supported by uprights and partly by side walls. Headroom is over 2m.

Finally there are side cells, north and south cists and a third cist on the west side which is thought to have served as a sepulchre. The last is unique and has no counterpart in other Jersey megalithic structures. It is particularly well constructed, the stones having been carefully selected and the dry-walling in the interstices is of the finest workmanship.

The tomb had been pillaged prior to the 1924 excavation. Nevertheless some new finds of stone implements and weapons, pottery, beads, shells and human bones were made. Of most interest were miniature menhirs, which averaged 30cm in height and were probably memorials to the dead. Also of interest were the cupmarks. Cupmarks, like menhirs, are found all over the world and their use or meaning remains a mystery. The cup-shaped depressions on monumental stones mainly occur in groups, sometimes in geometric designs and sometimes haphazardly.

There are two chapels on the crown of La Hougue Bie mound. Although now sheltered by one roof, they were built centuries apart. The west chapel is **Notre Dame de La Clarté** (12C–13C). It is 6.25m long and 3.5m wide. Legend has it that this chapel was originally an oratory where masses were said for the repose of the soul of the murdered Lord of Hambye. The story goes that a certain Baron of Hambye, near Coutances, in Normandy, set out to slay a dragon who was ravaging the countryside. He came to Jersey, where he encountered the dragon and killed it. Afterwards, he was murdered by his servant, who then returned and told the Lady of Hambye that the monster had mortally wounded her husband but that he (the servant) had destroyed the dragon. He added that his lordship's dying wish was that she should be betrothed to his faithful servant. In his wedding bed the imposter talked in his sleep, disclosing the murder and betrayal of his master and in due course, he was hanged. The author of the *Chroniques de Jersey* adds to the legend by informing us that the Lady of Hambye erected a mound in a prominent position the better to see where her husband was buried and that she also built a small chapel in his memory.

The word Hougue derives from the Old Norse 'Haugr' which means eminence and was probably bestowed on the mound by Vikings. It is thought that Lords of Hambye owned land in Jersey and that originally the full name Hougue Bie may have been Hougue Hambye.

Early in the 16C Dean Mabon built a second chapel on the summit shortly after his return from a pilgrimage to the Holy Land, in honour of the Passion; its crypt containing a representation of the Holy Sepulchre. Major-Gen. James D'Auvergne bought La Hougue Bie in 1759. He built a tower over the two chapels, which for safety's sake had to be demolished in 1924. During that year the roof of the two chapels was covered with old tiles brought over from Sées in France. Then, on 3 September, a horizontal cutting into the mound was commenced at ground level which led in ten days' time to the discovery of this message tomb, one of the finest in western Europe.

On La Hougue Bie site there are several interesting museum displays. **Open** every day 24 March–2 November 10.00–17.00; fee. Wednesdays at 14:30 there is a guided tour of the mound.

On the left as you enter is the Geology Section, there are cases with specimens of shale, the oldest rock in Jersey (700 million years); volcanic rock (600–700 million years); granites and diorites (500–600 million years) along with a graphic description of how Jersey geologically broke away from the continent. Two cases are devoted to mineral samples and there is a geological map of Jersey.

In the Archaeology Section are bound papers on the Palaeolithic Period by Dr Ian Cornwall and on the Neolithic, Bronze Age, Iron Age and Roman Periods by David E. Johnston. Many cases display weapons, instruments, pottery and bones of animals from the Palaeolithic and Neolithic periods. Instruments and weapons range from a flint lore, used as a crude hand axe of the Palaeolithic period (c 150,000 BC), to (Polished Ladette) axe heads of the Neolithic Period (4000–1000 BC). Another case has a spear, sword, axe and other remains of instruments in very good condition from a Bronze Age hoard. On display elsewhere are carved corbels from the castle of Grosnez, believed to be 14C, medieval pottery and Roman coins.

The **Occupation Museum**, also on the site, is divided into separate rooms, we see on display German armaments, machine guns, field equipment, and a picture of Hitler—and large photographs of the Germans' march in during 1940 and back out in 1945. There are also reconstructions of the Officers' Quarters and the Soldiers' Room in the bunker.

Parish of St. John

See also Grève de Lecq and Bouley Bay (p. 75)

St. John is bordered by the parish of St. Mary in the west, St. Lawrence in the south and Trinity in the east. From its spectacular northern coastline on a fine day the Channel Islands can be seen as well as the Contentin Peninsula, which provides a visual geographical layout of this archipelago.

Parish church of St. John

The parish church of St. John is 200m west of the point at which the A10 joins the B33, on the right-hand side. In 1150, Guillaume de Vauville gave St. John's church to the Abbey of St. Sauveur in Normandy, according to an early charter belonging to the abbey. The church was called St. Johannes de Quercubus (St. John of the Oaks), probably because it stood in an oak wood. A big fair used to be held here in medieval times on St. John the Baptist's day. The chancel belongs to the original church and the rest was built up around it over subsequent centuries in a fashion common to Jersey churches. The end of the 15C was an active period of enlargement when the tower, spire and large south aisles were built. The south chancel was added later. In the 19C the assembly wanted a large pillar removed in the south aisle, which blocked the view of the pulpit. Permission was sought through the rector and Ecclesiastical Court but fearing roof collapse permission was refused. When the new rector took over permission was again sought and refused. He later went on holiday to France and returned only to find the pillar in his garden and the church still standing. In 1934 major restoration led to the north chancel and nave, which had been neglected, becoming the main portion of the church.

The church bell used to be rung at 8 am on funeral days, summoning relatives to come and select the grave plot. Today the bell still rings at this time.

Parish of St. Lawrence

See also Between St. Helier and La Pulente (p. 64)

The central parish of St. Lawrence is bounded in a clockwise direction by the parishes of St. Peter, St. John, Trinity and St. Helier. Its southern coastline takes in a central section of St. Aubin's Bay.

The fertile valley of St. Lawrence is famous for its brooks, and one of the fastest flowing streams on the island drops 120 metres in less than 5kms. This natural stream which shares the name of the town was called Mill Brook, and was harnessed to turn the wheels of six windmills. When these watermills ceased to be used for grinding corn, sugar and paper-making, the water fed reservoirs and the Valley of St. Lawrence became known as Waterworks Valley.

St. Lawrence church

St. Lawrence Church is on the left, 2km north of the A1, on the A10 running south to north. It was the original site of an early Norman chapel. John, Lord of the Isles and younger brother of King Richard I, according to a charter of 1198 'did give the church of St. Lawrence in Jersey with all its appurtenances' to the Abbey Blanchelande in Normandy, and so it remained until the Reformation. Like all parish churches in Jersey, St. Lawrence grew from small origins. The nave was lengthened, a tower and two transepts added. In the 14C the old nave was replaced by one of superior length and height and in the 15C the present chancel was completed. The beautiful Hamptonne chapel was built by the rector of that name in 1524 and the date is inscribed on the north-east buttress. The mid-16C saw the englargement of the church to its present proportions with the construction of a chapel alongside the nave. The bell is the oldest on the island, dating back to 1592. Of particular interest in the church is a broken granite pillar with an elaborate three-cord plait with interlaced loops carved on it. This and the remains of Celtic lettering of AD 600 make this stone an interesting relic. It is probable that at one time it was used as a tombstone for a Celtic monk. The monks are thought to have brought Christianity to Jersey as early as 600 but most of the architecture of this highly developed culture was burnt and pillaged by the Vikings.

> A bride-to-be was left waiting for her suitor here and legend has it that when wedding bells ring she haunts the lanes in her wedding coach looking for him. The pathway opposite the church on the other side of the road is appropriately named Mont Misére.

Several interesting buildings are to be found north of St. Lawrence village. They include the 17C traditional farm, La Ferme Morel, with its giant stone cider press and apple crusher, which is still in use and driven by a horse at harvest time. The farm stands near the corner of Rue Rouge Cul and Rue de la Fontain St. Martain.

This is a National Trust for Jersey property, as is the 17C cottage Le Rat at La Route de l'Eglise.

Hamptonne Country Life Museum

The most distinguished house architecturally in the parish is Hamptonne. It is signposted from Three Oaks village on the A10 road north of St. Lawrence Parish Church. The property was purchased in 1633 by Laurens Hamptonne, the Vicomte, and has strong links with Charles II, who is rumoured to have stayed here. The square 'colombier', or dovecote, was built in 1674.

Today the house, which lies at the top of Waterworks Valley has become a country museum with animals, restaurant, and shop. **Hamptonne Country Life Museum** reflects the rural life of the island in bygone days. It is part of the Jersey Museum Service and was bought by the National Trust for Jersey and restored by the Société Jersiaise. **Open** daily mid-March–early November 10.00–17.00; free parking.

Originally the farm was owned by the Langlois family and in Richard Langlois's house animals and stores were kept downstairs and the humans lived upstairs, which was reached by an external staircase. This style of architecture was common in medieval Brittany.

Hamptonne House, which give its name to the entire complex has, over the centuries, undergone many transformations as fashions and times changed. In the early 18C the two-storey Dower wing extention was added. This house is now furnished in 17C/18C style, with many huge wooden chests where the family would have stored their clothes. There is a replica of a four-poster bed and truckle beds for the children, as well as other well-restored antique furniture. Downstairs over the open fire is the trepis or stockpot in which the family meals were cooked.

The **Syvret building**, also on the site, dates from the 1830s and has high ceilings which were common to the houses being built at this time in St Helier. Here a short video shows how rural life has changed over the last few decades.

On the tour of the museum visitors will also meet with the costumed 'good wyfe', who is a real comic turn. From her the ladies will learn many interesting facts about fashion and be shown how the 17C outer skirt which women wore, could be taken off when it rained and worn as a mantle, and how the bodice was laced at the back for those who could afford servants, and at the front for those without servants.

The north part of the site is a range of buildings, one of which contains an apple crusher, a twin-screw apple press and barrels, as well as other farm tools. In the **Cider Barn** during the month of October some 2 tonnes of apples are crushed between 10.30 and 15.30 to make cider. As in the past, a horse drives the crushing wheel, and when the job is finished the juice is stored in barrels and is drinkable in about 3 months. In olden times no chemicals or yeast were added, but sometimes beetroot was used to give colour. Apple crushing started at the end of the 16C and cider was exported to both England and France. Before World War II some 60 types of apple were grown on the island. At the end of the 19C there were 2600 farms and 4000 people were employed on the land. Today there are 433 farms and 2400 people employed.

On the estate there is also a colombier or dovecote. The first recorded colombier here was built by Richard Langlois and is one of only two square dovecotes on the island. Visitors who wish to picnic on site can choose their food from the restaurant, have it packed into a hamper and taken into the orchard to eat.

German Underground Hospital

The easiest way to locate this military hospital is to follow the B89 where it leaves the main A11; 500m further on is the entrance with car park opposite. **Open** 09.00–17.00; last admission 16.30; fee.

The German Underground Hospital is a grim reminder of the last war and what it could be like to live underground in the event of another. This damp dungeon is hewn out of solid rock, organised by Dr. Fritz Todt. It took 2½ years of slave labour by wartime prisoners to build and those who died in the frequent rock falls were buried where they fell, and many died of exhaustion and malnutrition. Altogether 14,000 tons of rock were removed. It was originally planned to have four parallel tunnels 100m long, traversed at right-angles by seven smaller tunnels. Today, the hospital is well restored, showing the operating theatre, dispensary, medical store, staff quarters and hospital ward. Also there are a great number of exhibition panels with photographs and memorabilia that record the history of this period as well as an interesting video. It is doubtful if any patient could have survived major surgery or a long sojourn in this grim place and in actual fact it was never used for the purpose for which it was built.

Parish of St. Martin

See also Between Gorey Castle and Bouley Bay (p. 62)

The parish of St. Martin is bordered by Trinity, St. Saviour's and Grouville and the north-east coastline. Its church was referred to even before the Norman Conquest as 'St. Martin the Old'.

St. Martin's church stands where the A6 road ends at the T-junction with the B30. Once the site of an early Norman chapel, this church is mentioned in 1042 when William Duke of Normandy granted to the Abbey of Cérisy 'the church of St. Martin-le-Vieux and a third part of its tithe of grain'. The chancel was the original chapel, then over the centuries the nave, two transepts, a south chancel and south aisle were added. Extensive restoration makes it difficult to date additions. There used to be a path by which those who sought sanctuary in the church could escape to the sea. It was last used successfully by Thomas Le Seeleur in 1546 when he fled the gallows and booked his passage to Normandy. The steeple of this church acted as a lighthouse to local ships during the threat from the Spanish Armada towards the end of the 16C.

Parish of St. Mary

See also Between Grève de Lecq and Bouley Bay (p. 75)

St. Mary's parish is on the north coast and is bordered in an anti-clockwise direction by the parishes of St. Ouen, St. Peter, St. Lawrence and St. John. It has the smallest population on the island.

Parish church of St. Mary

St. Mary's parish church is at the junction of the B54 and the B53. Like many Breton churches, the main steeple is surrounded by four smaller ones. In old documents the church is referred to as St. Mary of the Burnt Monastery, a name which may have been passed down from the days when, perhaps, a Viking raid rased to the ground a monastery on this site. William, Duke of Normandy, in 1042 granted a third of the church's tithes to the Abbey of Cérisy near Coutances. To the parish church was added a tower and spire. Later the nave was added and standing back from the church it is apparent that the nave is higher than the chancel and a separate building. In the mid-13C the north aisle was added, parallel to the original chancel, to give a double chancel. The next addition did not take place until 1840 when the south aisle was added. Inside, the standard of the Jersey regiment is inscribed 1781—the date of the Battle of Jersey.

John Wesley visited the island and this parish in 1787, and the bicentenary of this visit by the founder of Methodism was celebrated in Le Marais. The Methodist place of worship here is the church of Bethlehem on the Rue des Batles.

Butterfly Centre

The Butterfly Centre and Carnation Nursery at Haute Tombette is worth a visit. The Butterfly Centre is set among exotic flower beds and little waterfalls and the great variety of carnations on display in the nursery enables visitors to purchase, either taking flowers with them or having them posted home. There is a gift shop and a licensed café. **Open** daily May–Oct 09.00–18.00; fee.

Parish of St. Ouen

See also Between La Pulente and Grève de Lecq (p. 71)

St. Ouen is bordered by the parish of St. Peter in the south and St. Mary in the east. Its shoreline runs along a considerable section of the north and west coasts. Geographically it is the largest parish on the island. It is dedicated to St. Ouen (609–683AD) who became Bishop of Rouen in 639. No one is sure of the date of its original construction. It did, however, receive mention in a charter by Duke William before 1066 and the Battle of Hastings. The church was placed under the protection of the Abbey of Mont St. Michel in 1156 when Robert of Torigny, a kinsman of the de Carterets, was abbot. When the church came under the auspices of the abbey, it was enlarged and enriched.

The wall of the first chapel was pulled down and a second chapel with round Norman arches (13C) running from the chancel to the south aisle was constructed. Then a third chapel was added later which now contains the church organ. The Tudor coat of arms over one of the windows in the north aisle and the Tudor portcullis indicate that this aisle was most likely built during the reign of Henry VII. An interesting stone staircase leads from the centre of the church to the belfry, which was used by the clergy to take a quick look at the sea in case of wrecks or invasion. The stained glass is 19C and there is valuable silver plate including three early 17C cups, and several interesting brasses. Restoration was carried out in 1870 during which time the gallery for 'smokers only' was removed.

St. Ouen's Manor

The manor, on the left of the A12 going north just prior to the C117, takes precedence over all others in Jersey in recognition of the services rendered to the Crown. It is the family seat of the de Carterets, whose name is consistently linked with homage to the Dukes of Normandy. Two of the family fought with William the Conqueror at Hastings and Renaud de Carteret supported Duke Robert in a crusade. It seems likely, therefore, that a de Carteret was with Duke William I when he invaded Jersey in AD 933, and that the family received St. Ouen as part of the spoils. From historical records it is known that in 1135 a manor house stood here. When King John lost Normandy in 1204, those barons with lands there had to decide where their allegiance rested. The de Carterets chose to serve the English crown, and thenceforth the main family seat moved from Carteret in Normandy to St. Ouen in Jersey.

Today the oldest part of the present manor, the central hall and towers, is medieval. In 1483 Philip de Carteret sought to crenellate the manor, and permission was granted since, 'The propinquity of his house to the sea puts his goods and servants are in grave peril from malefactors and the King's enemies, we grant him leave to fortify his manor within and without with towers, battlements, bulwarks, moat, drawbridge, and artillery for the defence of himself and his household'. No doubt permission to fortify was welcome because a few years earlier in 1461, the French invaded Jersey and soon after tried to arrest the Seigneur of St. Ouen when he was out fishing. He managed to escape on his black charger, with a giant leap of 22 feet across a sunken road ditch, and made his way back to the manor. As a result of the exertion his horse fell dead beneath him. To commemorate the brave deed, a picture of this famous black horse hangs in the manor, and his burial place is marked by a tombstone in the garden

One relic of this romantic marriage is the 15C Italian bowl which rests beside the chapel. It bears both the de Carteret and the de Harliston coats-of-arms.

The 17C saw the Prince of Wales seeking refuge in the manor during his exile. For this loyalty and hospitality, the Prince, when he became Charles II presented Sir George de Carteret with lands in America, to which the Seigneur gave the name New Jersey. A vast kitchen and two wings were added to the house c 1676, which have since been converted into living rooms. There followed a long period of neglect, during which the de Carterets were most of the time at the king's court in Westminster. During the French wars the house became a barracks for French Royalist refugees.

The manor was redeemed and restored from dereliction in 1856 when Colonel Malet de Carteret inherited the property. The Colonel transformed the interior by creating a splendid great hall with staircase and gallery. Some medieval oak panels which had been stored in the cellars for centuries were rediscovered and used to enhance this splendid room.

The exterior of the house was improved by extending the two towers and adding a porch to the main entrance. He also restored the manorial chapel dedicated to St. Anne which had become a hayloft. It had served as a butcher's shop during the German occupation, but has since been re-consecrated to its original purpose. Also during the German occupation the house was again used as a military barracks, and the south wing was damaged by fire. Since then this wing has been renovated and the building returned to its rightful owner. It has been the home of the de Carterets for over 30 generations, and although the direct male line ceased with the Earl of Granville, descendants still own and occupy this private residence. It is occasionally open to the public.

There are five manors of which the Seigneurs are Tenants-in-Chief, holding direct from the Crown. They are St. Ouen, Mélèches, Rozel, Samarès and Trinity. St. Ouen has been in the possession of the same family for the longest.

A Jersey legend

There is a well-known Jersey legend regarding Philip de Carteret who lived in the manor during the 15C. A certain mean spirited governor, named Baker, committed perjury by forging a letter from de Carteret to certain nobles in which an offer was made to betray the island to the French. For this false evidence de Carteret was thrown into a dungeon at Mont Orgueil, while the Governor set sail for the mainland to show the forged document to the king. Fortunately, the nobleman's wife, Margaret de Harliston left her bed where she had recently given birth, and reached England in an open boat before the governor, and gave the true story to the king first. This resulted in de Carteret being sent to Westminster to be tried by the Privy Council. He was honourably acquitted, which in turn led to the disposal of the evil official. Had it not been for Margaret's quick action, leading to the fair trial of her husband, St. Ouen would have been returned to the Crown and the de Carteret line expunged from the hall of fame.

Parish of St. Peter

See also Between St. Helier and La Pulente and between La Pulente and Grève de Lecq (p. 71)

St. Peter's parish has two coastlines, one in the south and one in the west. It is bordered by four other parishes, St. Ouen, St. Mary, St. Lawrence and St. Brelade and is the site of Jersey Airport.

Parish church of St. Peter

This church lies at the junction of the A12 and B41. In ancient documents it is referred to as San Pietro in Deserto (St. Peter in the Desert) due to its proximity to the sandhills. A charter signed by William, Duke of Normandy, prior to his conquest of England, shows that this church had been promoted from a chapel to a parish church. The duke transferred half of the tithes being paid to the parish church to the Convent of the Holy Trinity at Caen. The walls of the original chapel, built of rough stones from the beach, can still be seen in the existing chancel. During the 12C the west wall of the chapel was demolished and a nave and transepts built, giving the building the shape of a cross. In the 14C two chapels were added, one of which was later pulled down, and in the 15C the south aisle was built. In the latter half of the 19C, part of the south transept was rebuilt and later the north aisle was added. The church has the tallest spire in the Channel Islands (37m) and because it is close to the airport it carries a red light. The sculptured altarpiece of the *Last Supper* is worthy of attention.

St. Peter's village

Here we find the **Jersey Motor Museum**. Open Mar–late Oct 10.00–17.00; fee.

Among the items of interest here are a Phantom III used in 1944 by Field Marshal Montgomery, a 1930 8-litre Bentley which used to be referred to as the fastest lorry on wheels, and by contrast a child's model Bentley (1937) with 125cc engine and coach work by Mulliner. There is also on display a carriage belonging to the former Jersey Railway and Tramways Ltd. It has first- and second-class sections as well as a guard's and luggage compartment.

The area of St. Peter's village is also accessible via the A12 road out of Beaumont. Sharing the same car park of the motor museum is the St. Peter's Bunker Museum (**open** daily Mar–Nov 10.00–22.00; fee). This bunker was a strong point guarding important crossroads leading to the airport in the west. Over 30 men slept in the bunker, which could be air and gas sealed in case of attack. There are seven rooms of displays and the emphasis is on radio equipment used by the Germans in the last war.

Watermills

There are several picturesque watermill sites in St. Peter's Valley which, going north, are Tesson, Quetivel, Gargate, La Hague and Gigoulande. In times past these mills played a vital part in the life of the community. Their most important role was grinding grain, but several were also engaged in grinding malt, crushing sugar and the production of paper from rags and bones. Each mill was originally the property of the king who would often grant it to a feudal seigneur or to an abbey or priory. Tenants of the fief were obliged to grind their corn at the mill and render service in the form of labour or materials for the upkeep. The mill enabled the tenants to obtain flour for their bread and was a source of revenue to the owner.

Quetivel Mill

Le Moulin de Quetivel lies on the A11 at the junction of the B58 almost at the southern tip of St. Peter's Valley. Some 40 watermills are thought to have been built between the 11C and 19C alongside streams and a few were revived during the Occupation. Today, with the exception of Le Moulin de Quetivel, none are operating and few have their wheel and machinery still in situ. There has been a watermill on the site of Quetivel since 1309. Quetivel derives from the old Norse name 'Ketill', a personal name, and 'Vellix' meaning fields. This mill was worked until the 19C and re-activated during the war. Later it was mainly destroyed by fire. Between 1971 and 1979 the National Trust of Jersey restored the mill and now visitors can see the mill producing stone-ground flour, which can also be purchased. **Open** May–Oct Tues–Thur 10.00–16.00; fee.

Parish of St. Saviour

See also Between St. Helier and Gorey (p. 56)

St. Saviour is bordered by St. Helier on the west and then in a clockwise direction by the parishes of Trinity, St. Martin, Grouville and St. Clement, as well as a very small section of the south coast. One of its main towns is Five Oaks. Oaks, in Jersey, are always in odd numbers; three oaks in St. Lawrence, five here, and seven in St. Brelade.

St. Saviour's parish church

Part of St. Saviour is almost a suburb of St. Helier. On the A7 leaving the capital, and where St. Saviour's Hill swings round to the left, you will see on the left the parish church. St. Saviour's Church was consecrated in 1154. The church began as four separate chapels, St. Saveur de l'Epine (east), La Ste Vierge Marie (west), St. Jean (north-east) and St. Martin (north-west). Each was owned by a different family and had its own priest. Connecting walls were built joining the east and west chapels to form a parish church sometime before 1145 when a Papal Bull first mentions 'the tithes of the Church of St. Saviour in Jersey'. In the 13C this church was lengthened and in the 14C a central tower was added. Later the St. Jean and St. Martin chapels were incorporated. In 1563, when the plague in St. Helier was at its height, the Royal Court foregathered in the church. At the turn of the 20C, thorough restoration was carried out. The father of Lillie Langtry, the actress and friend of Edward VII, Dean Le Breton was rector here. Lillie Langtry was twice married in this church and is buried in the churchyard under a marble bust of herself.

Longueville Manor Colombier

Longueville manor house, is now a hotel. Longueville Manor Colombier, or dove-cote, originally belonged to the manor and was given to the National Trust for Jersey in 1970. Although there is a right of way by permission of the present owner of the hotel, the best access is by an entrance at the east end of the manor grounds in La Rue St. Thomas. The path leads through a gate alongside the hotel. The colombier will be seen to the right. The earliest existing record of a colombier at the manor occurs in the Assize Roll of 1299. In 1692 it was rebuilt in Le Jardin de St. Thomas. It is now in good condition, although it would originally have had a conical roof. It has a cobbled floor and can accommodate 600 pairs of pigeons.

Parish of Trinity

> *See also* Between Gorey Castle and Bouley Bay *and* Between Grève de Lecq and Bouley Bay (pp. 62 & 75)

Trinity parish borders some of the north coast of Jersey, and in an anti-clockwise direction from St. John's parish on its west side, it is bordered by the parishes of St. Helier, St. Saviour and St. Martin. It is the home of Gerald Durrell's Jersey Zoo, now one of the most famous in the world.

Jersey Zoo and Wildlife Preservation Trust

■ **Opening times:** 09.30–18.00, dusk in winter; fee; free car park.

The Zoological Park of the Jersey Wildlife Preservation Trust, founded by the late Gerald Durrell, is one of the most interesting and well run small zoos anywhere in the world. It has a wide variety of animals, birds, and reptiles, that will provide a full day's viewing and entertainment. In summer there are talks organised by staff every day from 11.00–15.00, with a short break for lunch. These talks are given in conjunction with the feeding times of many of the animal groups, such as flamingoes, black macaques, orangutans, lemurs, tamarins, spectacled bears, gorillas and snakes. The times of the Keeper Talks, and where they are held is listed on the noticeboard near the zoo entrance.

Young animals, pregnant and nursing mothers, old and sick animals, often need special care and attention, especially in regard to their diet. Visitors learn about the secret lives of animal families from the people who look after them, and this is both entertaining and educational. The layout of the gardens is enhanced by imaginative tree planting, watercourses and landscaping.

Most entertaining places to see are the Gorilla Walk Play Area, and the Orang-utan Habitat and Play Area. Cat lovers will enjoy the cheetahs who lie right out in the open, but are likely to be disappointed when it comes to seeing the shy snow leopard. Multifarious birds of every description from pink flamingoes to white eared pheasants can be seen throughout the zoo. However, the dodo, the symbol of the Wildlife Trust, brought to extinction by man (hence the expression 'as dead as a dodo') can only be seen on posters. The dodo was a flightless and defenceless bird, native to the island of Mauritius. After it was first sighted it took man less than a century to kill it off. Hence the dodo is a suitable symbol for the Trust, whose main aim is to save rare species from extinction.

The greatest success that the Wildlife Trust has achieved is saving the pink pigeon, which like the dodo, was indigenous to Mauritius. At one time the pink pigeon numbered fewer than 20. Today there are over 220, and third-phase plans are in place to increase the population still further.

Many rare species of reptiles are cared for in the well-laid out Gaherty Reptile Breeding Centre, the warmest building in the zoo. Temperatures have to be maintained at 26 degrees centigrade at all times because reptiles require this temperature to function normally. Many of the reptile species are semi-aquatic, and can be seen swimming around. They include terrapins and lizards from different parts of the world. Tortoise-breeding projects to save species from extinction, which are killed by man for their beautiful shells and meat, enable visitors to see them mating and breeding in captivity. Much success had also been achieved in saving several species of Caribbean boas. In the reptile world parents are inclined to pay little attention to their young after birth, and the Jamaican boa can have up to 35 young at a time, and this requires a lot of atten-tion, and special breeding units.

In the new Princess Royal Pavilion, the remarkable multi-audiovisual presen-tation on the Wildlife Trust's work can be seen, which is discussed more fully on p. 93. This film should not be missed and has won many major awards in both Britain and North America. The show lasts 20 mins and runs every half hour from 10.00–17.00. The photography is superb.

Many different publications of the Trust's work, as well as Gerald Durrell's own entertaining books, are available here in the bookshop and reception area. Children can obtain a Wildlife Passport, which they can have stamped, as they visit animals from different parts of the world. Many children also decide to have their face painted by the zoo artists in the style of their favourite animal. The cheetah and snow leopard seem the most popular choices.

On the estate there is a self-service restaurant and souvenir shop.

The Jersey Wildlife Trust

In 1959, the late Gerald Durrell, author, animal collector, and naturalist, opened the Jersey Zoological Park. Les Augrès Manor by Trinity, became the headquarters which provided the fields, valley, and woods, which would be landscaped to become one of the world's most famous zoos and preservation centres for 'Saving Animals from Extinction' (SAFE).

From the beginning it was the founder's intention to build up breeding populations of endangered species, with the intention of returning them safely to their natural habitat. This was the first zoo to be founded on this ecological and far-seeing principle. To assure the future of his unique institution, Gerald Durrell became Honorary Director of the Jersey Wildlife Preservation Trust in 1963, when it was first called to order as a charitable association, incorporated by the Royal Court of Jersey. In 1972, the first world conference on the breeding of endangered species in captivity was held here, and the new Preservation Trust joined up with the Fauna Preservation Trust, forging a link between the zoological and nature conservation fraternities, which has grown in strength over the years, and in 1991 JWPT won the coveted international Peter Scott Merit Award, for leadership in conservation. In 1973, Gerald Durrell, responding to the growing support for his work from overseas, founded a sister organisation—the Wildlife Preservation Trust International in the United States, and 13 years later the Wildlife Preservation Trust of Canada was also launched.

In systematic harmony these three trusts are working to save nearly 100 endangered species worldwide, and among those which inhabit the Jersey Zoological Park, there are programmes for lowland gorillas from Africa, orangutans from Indonesia, lion tamarins from Brazil, lemurs from Madagascar, cheetahs from East Africa, snow leopards from Central Asia, wild pigs from South-East Africa, a great variety of birds from all over the world, such as kestrels from Mauritius, ducks from Madagascar, white-naped cranes that winter in China, parrots from the Windward Islands, and so on. Among the many reptiles with breeding programmes are iguanas of the Caribbean, tortoises from Madagascar and snakes from the West Indies.

Breeding to save certain animal species from extinction requires tremendous attention and observation, co-operation between governments and zoos and money. To give one example, let us look at the programme for the Rodrigues fruit bat. They live 406 miles east of Mauritius on a remote island in the path of regional cyclones. In 1976 the population had dwindled to 120, who clung to remnants of forest still suitable for feeding and roosting. The Trust started collecting bats to initiate breeding programmes in Jersey and Mauritius. Happily the breeding in captivity has successfully increased the population, which is now established in six collections in three countries, and on Rodrigues the habitat and restoration programme is well underway, so that the wild population has increased to over 1000 bats, and regarding the captive groups—'DNA' fingerprinting techniques are determining the paternity of the entire captive population in order to encourage mating, and to strengthen the gene pool.

Returning endangered species to the wild usually requires careful monitoring of re-introduced animals for months and possibly years. Hence one of the most important developments of the Trust has been the creation of the International Training Centre. The centre has already welcomed 900 students from over 80 countries, which include zoo directors, keepers, forest rangers, game wardens, and heads of national parks, and a host of other personnel. Sixty undergraduates arrive each year, and there is now a global network of graduates who exchange ideas and results of their research.

To breed animals in captivity calls for a strong back up of veterinary facilities to plan diets, to provide preventive medicine and to cure sick animals. The Veterinary Hospital has to have and use all the latest equipment for this purpose which includes an operating theatre, and a ward for in-patients, as well as sophisticated facilities for radiography, endoscopy and ultrasound examination.

Gerald Durrell was a man of destiny, and his message to homo sapiens was simple: 'The world is as delicate as a spider's web. If you touch one thread you send shudders running through all the other threads. We are not just touching the web, we are tearing holes in it. Now think of the web as a safety net; the thin strands of survival.'

Trinity parish church

The parish church is situated where the A8 meets the B51. Trinity church is first mentioned in a charter before 1172 by King Henry II in which he gives it to the Abbey of St. Helier. An original 'Chapelle de la Saint Trinité' rested on the site of the present chancel. Later, a nave and transepts were added to give the building the shape of a cross. This was followed by a spire and a Lady Chapel. When lightning struck the spire in 1629 a diarist recorded the event as a sign of the Almighty's wrath at 'the pontifical grandeur of the Dean'.

Trinity manor house

The manor house lies midway between the A9 and the A8, 400m south of the B51. The oldest part of the present manor house was built during the reign of Queen Elizabeth I. Charles II was a guest here during his stay in Jersey in 1646. There was an enormous restoration of the ruined manor between 1910 and 1913 by Mr Athelston Riley which gave the manor the appearance of a French château.

Trinity manor

Sir Francis Cook Gallery

On the A8 road, at the top of Trinity Hill, next door to the Oaklands Lodge Hotel, is the Sir Francis Cook Gallery (large car park). This old Methodist church was converted by the artist Sir Francis Cook into a private gallery to house over 1300 of his paintings, using the chapel, schoolroom and extensions to provide a number of galleries. In 1984 Brenda, Lady Cook, the artist's widow, presented the building and its contents to the Jersey Heritage Trust, to become a public art gallery for temporary exhibitions and to house the museum conservation and technical workshops. A programme of temporary exhibitions is arranged annually and advertised locally when the gallery is open. Some 50 paintings by Sir Francis Cook can be viewed at the same time. The gallery is also the base of the Jersey Museums conservation department.

Orchid Foundation

■ **Open** 10.00–16.00 Thurs, Fri, Sat year round including Bank Holidays. Closed Christmas Day.

The Eric Young Orchid Foundation, Victoria Village, Trinity is a living monument to one man's passion for exotic and beautiful orchids, and a centre for their breeding and cultivation. It is an absolute must for keen gardeners. The late Eric Young who founded this collection was a former chairman of the World Orchid Conference Committee, whose floral exhibits won the highest awards.

Today, under some 30,000 square feet of glasshouse is one of the world's finest collections of orchids, ranging from *Cymbidium* bred in Jersey, to the glorious red of the Peruvian *Cochlioda Noetzliana*. Altogether there are some 25,000 species of orchids worldwide, and hundreds of these are displayed at the Foundation complex to great advantage in a landscaped garden of tree trunks and miniature waterfalls. Many new hybrids are being cultivated all the time, and the founder is commemorated with a mainly yellow *Odontioda Eric Young*. The shop inside the exhibition has a large range of literature on the subject of orchids, including information on nurseries in the UK where different varieties are grown.

The Pallot Steam Museum

■ **Open** 1 Apr–31 Oct 10.00–17.00; fee. Steam train rides mid-June–mid-Sept, Tues and Thur.

The Steam Museum on the Rue de Bechet lies between the A8 and the A9 and is signposted off both. The founder, the late Lyndon Pallot spent his early life as a trainee engineer with the old Jersey Railway. Hence, by the side of his museum, which is an assortment of fascinating old equipment ranging from a gas engine to an intertype printing machine, is a specially built railway.

Inside the station is a selection of steam engines and carriages. For a small fee visitors can travel in some of the carriages drawn by a steam engine round the rail track. The iron staunchions in the station come from the old station of Snow Hill.

Jersey's railways

There were two railway lines in Jersey. JER operated a line from Snow Hill in St. Helier to Gorey Harbour, a distance of 10km. The line was opened in 1873 and extended to the harbour in 1891. Co-operation with the French Railways and a steamship link enabled JER to operate a service from St. Helier via Gorey to Paris. The route closed down in 1929 due to competition from road transport. The other railway line opened in 1870 and ran between St. Helier and St. Aubin. Today the tourism office is part of the original terminus at St. Helier, and St. Brelade's Parish Hall was once the Railway Hotel. The Jersey Railways Company Ltd, who opened the line, went into voluntary liquidation in 1895. The following year it was taken over by Jersey Railways and Tramways Ltd and in 1899 the line was extended to Corbière. In 1921 a first-class return cost 1/6d and a second-class return was 1/1d from St. Helier to Corbière. In 1924 and 1925 the line carried a million passengers a year. Then road transport began to take away passenger traffic and the line closed in 1936.

Bailiwick of Guernsey

Guernsey is the second largest of the Channel Islands, covering 63sq km. With its dependencies of Alderney, Herm, Jethou and Sark it forms the Bailiwick of Guernsey. The island is formed like a right-angled triangle, the horizontal being the south coast which runs from Pleinmont to Jerbourg. It has an excellent walking region along a cliff line roughly 10km long. The perpendicular is the east coast, running north from Jerbourg to Fort Doyle, a distance of 10km. On this coastline is the capital, St. Peter Port, and the old harbour town of St. Sampson. The hypotenuse, just over 15km, runs from Pleinmont to Fort Doyle and provides the more accessible swimming beaches. From the cliffs in the south the island slopes down to L'Ancresse Common at the northern end. Guernsey is 128km from the south coast of England and 48km from the French coast. The landscape is intriguing, with small walled fields, crossed by a mesh of narrow winding lanes and the occasional major road.

The following **bus routes** take the visitor to different points of interest on the island and back to St. Peter Port:

Rte B1:	St. Peter Port (Fountain St), Jerbourg, Saints, Icart Corner, St. Peter Port Terminus
Rte B2:	St. Peter Port (Fountain St), Icart Corner, Saints, Jerbourg, Fermain, St. Peter Port Terminus
Rte C1:	St. Peter Port, Airport, Torteval Church, Pleinmont, L'Erée, St. Peter Port
Rte C2:	St. Peter Port, Airport, L'Erée, Fort Grey, Torteval Church, St. Peter Port
Rte D:	St. Peter Port, P.E. Hospital, Bird Gardens, Strawberry Farm, L'Erée, Perelle, St. Peter Port
Rte E:	St. Peter Port, P.E. Hospital, Bailiff's Cross, Castel Church, L'Erée, Strawberry Farm, Underground Hospital, St. Peter Port
Rte F:	St. Peter Park, Rohais, Saumarez Park, Cobo, Vazon, St. Peter Port
Rte G:	St. Peter Port, Beau Sejour, Butterfly Centre, Saumarez Park, St. Peter Port
Rte F/G Sundays only:	St. Peter Port (the quay), Saumarez Park, Cobo Bay, Vazon Bay, Grandes Rocques, St. Peter Port
Rte G/F Sundays only:	St. Peter Port (the quay), Cobo Bay, Grandes Rocques, Vazon Bay, St. Peter Port Terminus
Rte H1 Monday to Saturday only:	St. Peter Port (the quay), Camp du Roi, L'Islet, Oatlands, Guernsey Candles, St. Peter Port Terminus

Rte H2 Monday to Saturday only:	St. Peter Port (the quay), La Passée Estate, Grandes Rocques, St. Peter Port
Rte H1/2 Sundays only:	St. Peter Port (the quay), Grandes Rocques, L'Islet, St. Peter Port Terminus
Rte J1:	St. Peter Port, St. Sampson's, L'Ancresse, Bordeaux, St. Peter Port
Rte J2:	St. Peter Port, St. Sampson's, Bordeaux, L'Ancresse, Bougy, St. Peter Port
Rte L1:	St. Peter Port, L'Islet, Houmet, La Passée, Oatlands, St. Peter Port
Rte L2: Monday to Saturday only:	St. Peter Port, L'Ancresse, Vale Church, Sandy Hook, Oatlands, St. Peter Port
Rte L2/1 Sundays only:	St. Peter Port, L'Ancresse, L'Islet, Oatlands, St. Peter Port

Bus fares

As well as the standard fares for the scheduled bus services there are special money saving offers in the form of **Rover Tickets** which can be purchased for 1, 3, 5, or 7 days. There are also monthly tickets and ten journey vouchers. These tickets and vouchers can all be bought from Guernseybus at the Terminus Kiosk and the Piquet House. They can also be bought on all Island Coachways buses. A Shuttle Bus operates between the island's busy centres of St. Peter Port and St. Martin's. A park'n'ride scheme operates at Footes Lane where the Shuttle service will take the visitor to the town centre. In addition high frequency services by **Express du Nord** operate between St. Peter Port and St. Sampson's. Buses can be boarded at any of the bus stops found on poles or painted in the road or a bus can be hailed anywhere within designated points.

Bus number to a selection of destinations:

Airport	C1, C2
Bailiffs Cross	D,E
Beau Sejour Centre	G
Bird Gardens	D,E,
Bruce Russell Silversmiths	D,E
Cobo Bay	F,G
Coppercraft	C1,C2,D
Doyle Monument	B1,B2
Fermain Bay	B1,B2,S3,S4
Folk Museum and Park	F
Friquet Butterfly Centre	F,G
Forest	C1,C2
German Occupation Museum	C1, C2
Golf Course (L'Ancresse)	J1,J2,L2
Grand Havre Bay	L1

Grandes Rocques Bay	G,H2
Guernsey Candles	Express du Nord H1,H2
Guernsey Pottery	Express du Nord H2,L1
Icart Corner	B1,B2
Jerbourg Point	B1,B2
L'Ancresse Bay	J1,J2,L2
Ladies Bay	K,L2
L'Erée Bay	C1,C2,D,E
Lihou Island	D,E
Little Chapel	D,E
Moulin Huet Bay	B1,B2
Oatlands Craft Centre	Express du Nord H1,L1,L2
Pembroke Bay	L2
Petit Bot Bay	C1,C2
Pleinmont Point	C1,C2
Port Soif Bay	H2
Rocquaine Bay	C1,C2
Rose Centre	D,E
St. Martin	B1,B2,C1
St. Peter-in-the-Wood	C1,C2
St. Sampson Express du Nord	J1,J2
Saints Bay	B1,B2
Saline Bay	H2
Sausmarez Manor	B1,B2,S3,S4
Saumarez Park	FG
Telephone Museum	F,G
Tortevel	C1,C2
Underground Hospital Museum	D,E
Vazon Bay	D,F
Woodcarvers	D,E
Yacht Marina	J1,J2

The parishes of Guernsey

Guernsey has ten parishes, all of which border the sea except St. Andrew. This is because the island is small and you are never further than 3.5km from the sea. Beginning in the north they are Vale, St. Sampson, Castel (sometimes spelt Câtel), St. Peter Port, with the capital of the same name, St. Saviour, St. Andrew, St. Peter-in-the-Wood, Torteval, Forest, and St. Martin. Following on from the description of St. Peter Port, the Blue Guide outlines travel and what to see around the coast on the northern half of the island from St. Peter Port to L'Erée, and then around the southern half from St. Peter Port to L'Erée, before finally introducing inland Guernsey. As everything in Guernsey is so close to the sea, you can reach nearby coastal areas in a few minutes after visiting an inland site. The island has many bays along its coastline that have interesting caves which can be visited, but because of the fast running tides extreme care must be taken if they are to be explored. Among the most interesting are Le Creux ès Faies on the north side of Vazon Bay, Le Creux Mahie around 20m across and 70m deep—the largest cave in Guernsey, and Le Grand Creux, with a hole open to the sky, some 27m deep at the southern end of Fermain Bay.

Highlights

St. Peter Port

Guernsey Museum and Art Gallery is in Candie Gardens. This award winning museum and gallery houses treasures from the past, illustrates the history of Guernsey, and offers a rare insight into the artistic work of those connected to the Bailiwick by birth and association.

Candie Gardens has a pretty bandstand, now a cafeteria, and forms part of the museum and art gallery complex. There is a statue of Victor Hugo who is striding out in a strong gale, while deep in thought, it seems, as well as two of the first Guernsey greenhouses, still in use by the States Parks and Gardens Department.

Castle Cornet, is an impressive repository of the history of Guernsey from Roman times forward. There are superb views and a range of museums.

Hauteville House is where Victor Hugo lived during his exile in Guernsey. It contains an eclectic collection put together by Hugo and family and includes furniture, tapestries and medieval woodcarving. On the top floor is Hugo's work room with views of the surrounding landscape.

Town Church of St Peter. The parish church of St. Peter Port was in use as a place of prayer and devotion as early as 1048. There is much to learn here of Guernsey's history through times of war and of peace.

Royal Court House, built 1799, houses the Greffe where public records are kept and the Royal Court Chamber, the venue of the States of Deliberation, which is the island's parliament.

War Memorial. Decorated with figures of St. George and the dragon, it stands between the Old Government Hotel and the Court House.

Market House. This market is interesting architecturally with elegant arches, roofs, stone-work and all that is most confident in Victorian buildings.

Guille-Allès Library. This is one of the most impressive buildings in Guernsey. It once housed the Assembly Rooms and was completely renovated in 1970.

Beau Séjour Centre. The island's modern centre for community activities and a good place to go on a rainy day. Facilities for tennis, indoor swimming, badminton, table-tennis, roller-skating and squash, as well as keep-fit classes, a cinema, solarium and concert hall.

Round the island

St. Sampson's church. Legend has it that St. Sampson brought Christianity to Guernsey, and that he built a chapel on the beach where he landed. The present church is certainly very ancient and sports a saddle-back tower, most of its original windows and the oldest church steeple on the island.

In **Vale Parish** is **Le Déhus dolmen**. There is a carving of a face cut into one of the capstones and side chambers worth examining.

Vale Church is one of the most ancient in Guernsey. There has been a place of worship here for something like 1000 years. Outside is a menhir, which was discovered in the churchyard in 1949. At some point it was given a 'Christian' aspect by the incision of a cross.

Sausmarez Manor in **St. Martin** is occasionally open to the public and even when not the setting is worth a visit. It is a Queen Anne house, with entrance gates bearing the arms of the island's most significant family for many centuries. On the estate there is also the Doll's House Collection in a Tudor Barn.

Moulin Huet Bay is probably the most beautiful bay on the island and its beauty has been celebrated by no less an artist than Renoir. The approach along the cliff from Petit Port is well worth the effort.

Forest is the home of the **German Occupation Museum** which contains fascinating memorabilia of a dramatic period in Guernsey history.

Forest Church is one of the many in Guernsey which bears testimony of the pragmatism of the early Christian missionaries who tended to build their churches close to menhirs and megaliths. In use for probably 1000 years it was the only church on the island closed during the Occupation—because it was so close to the airport.

The Little Chapel of Les Vauxbelets in **St. Andrew** was started in 1923. Composed of pieces of china, pottery and shells it is justifiably popular as a piece of genuine 'folk architecture.'

The Guernsey Folk Museum is in **Castel** on the Saumarez Park estate. It houses a collection of farm vehicles and tools, a cider press and a reconstructed Guernsey kitchen from olden times. Administered by the National Trust of Guernsey it is an attraction which should not be missed.

Parish of St. Peter Port

St. Peter Port (15,600 inhab.) is the capital of Guernsey.

History of St. Peter Port

Picturesque granite buildings, arcades, red roofs and narrow streets, many of them cobbled, built on the hillsides surrounding the harbour, make St. Peter Port an attractive seaside town. Offshore, Castle Cornet was built to protect this settlement in the 13C and by the 14C a market town had grown up. During this period St. Peter Port was used as an anchorage for ships bringing wine from Gascony to England and returning with dried fish and agricultural produce. Excavations in the Bordage (1976) led to the discovery of pottery from England, France, Holland, Germany and Spain from the 14C to 19C and have suggested the role Guernsey played as a useful anchorage for trading vessels. Most of the pre-17C material was Continental and most of the 18C and 19C was English, perhaps indicating the pattern of trade.

Guernsey was free from British import duties in the 18C and this led to St. Peter Port becoming a commercial centre where wine and brandy were stored before being shipped to England in smaller quantities, when the market was favourable. High import duties encouraged smuggling to become a profitable way of life for the islanders who, for purposes of respectability, referred to it as 'Free Trade'. Many fortunes were made. Privateering, licensed by the British Government, whereby the prize was shared between the crown, the owners of the vessel and the crew, wrought havoc to foreign ships in the English Channel and brought further wealth during the 18C to St. Peter Port. Many fine Georgian and Regency residences were built in the town from the profits of smuggling and privateering.

The harbour

The first reference we have to a harbour here dates back to 1060, in a document which referred to 'Sancti Petri de Portu'—St. Peter of the Port. In those days there was a rough breakwater that served to protect trading ships from inclement weather. This was destroyed in the 13C by the French. A south pier 100 metres long was built in 1580. Heylin, in *A Survey of Guernsey* (1629), states: 'The principal honour and glory of this island, I mean of Guernsey, is the large capaciousness of the harbour. It is able to contain the greatest navy that ever sailed the ocean, fenced from the fury of the winds by the islands of Guernsey, Serk and Erme'. A north pier was completed by the 1750s, and the quay protecting the houses in the High Street by the 1770s. A new harbour was built during the latter part of the 19C, and new piers were built on rocky outcrops—to the south on Castle Rock, and to the north on White Rock, and the town quay was broadened to take traffic.

By the turn of the 20C there was a regular passenger service of a dozen steamers out of Southampton and Weymouth, and for less than £1.50 passengers could buy a return excursion ticket. In 1925 a jetty was built for the mailboat, and in the 1970s roll-on roll-off car ferry facilities were installed.

Recently, the comparatively reasonable cost of berthing leisure boats in Guernsey has led to a demand for these facilities, which is now catered for by Albert, Victoria and Queen Elizabeth marinas.

Today the harbour, which was bounded to the north by St. Julian's Pier, which runs out to White Rock, has been extended to Salerie. This area incorporates the North Beach Marina, car parks and a 'ro-ro' area, and now also provides a 20-acre marina with pontoon moorings for 800 boats, together with ten deep-water berths for yacht renovation. Parking is available for 760 cars on the south quay, and for a further 300 to the north of the marina adjoining Salerie Battery. A large roundabout eases the flow of traffic at the Weighbridge.

The south end of the harbour is bounded by Castle Pier, from which Castle Cornet is reached. The Condor and Emeraude ferries berth alongside the new jetty by St. Julian's Pier and nearby, where this pier extends to become White Rock Pier, boats for Alderney and Sark depart. Where the pier joins the mainland visitors embark by fast launches for Herm.

St. Peter Port Marina has three pontoons capable of taking 150 yachts not longer than 14m, whose maximum draught is 1.80m. In the harbour pool yachts of greater length and draught can be accommodated.

Castle Cornet

The castle figures prominently in the history of the island. **Open** 10.30–17.30 April–October; fee.

The **Lower Barracks**, which is the first free-standing building as you enter the fortress, is a museum and exhibition dedicated to the history of the castle. These barracks were erected in 1745 to house garrison regiments when rela-

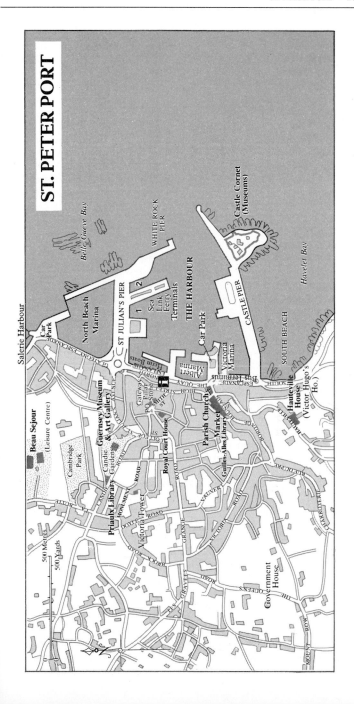

ST. PETER PORT

Salerie Harbour

Belle Gueve Bay

WHITE ROCK PIER

Castle Cornet (Museums)

Havelet Bay

Car Park

North Beach Marina

ST JULIAN'S PIER

2

1

Sea Link Ferry Terminals

THE HARBOUR

Car Park

CASTLE PIER

Victoria Marina

Albert Marina

Bus Terminus

SOUTH BEACH

THE QUAY

Beau Sejour (Leisure Centre)

Cambridge Park

Guernsey Museum & Art Gallery

Candie Gardens

Gateway Pillar
Post Office

HIGH STREET

SMITH ST

THE ESPLANADE

ST. JULIAN'S AVENUE

THE ESPLANADE SOUTH

Priaulx Library

Victoria Tower

Royal Court House

Parish Church

Market

Guilles Alles Library

Hauteville House (Victor Hugo's Ho.)

Government House

500 Metres
500 Yards

tions between England and France were on a warlike footing and the Channel Islands were of great strategic importance. This offshore castle acted as a main defence against any invader who attempted to attack St. Peter Port, and capture the island. This function lasted until 1812, when the more modern Fort George, built up on the hill, now replaced by a housing development, took over this role. The story of the lives of the garrison regiment, and the people who lived here during the threat of French invasion, introduces the main story line of Castle Cornet.

After this preliminary introduction, visuals describe how the rock on which the castle stands, **Castle Rock**, composed of ancient crystalline rocks, mostly granite, was formed in geological time. The rock known as **Cornet Reef** is triangular in shape, rises 30 metres above sea-level, and is half a mile offshore from the town of St. Peter Port, which grew around an area that is a natural haven for shipping. Sheltered from prevailing westerlies, and flanked by rock reefs, archaeological evidence shows that people have exploited Cornet Reef since the Bronze Age, long before a fortress was built upon it. Hence it was a natural development to build a castle there in order to guard this harbour.

In 1204, King Philip of France took back Normandy from King John, and two years later we get the first mention of a king's castle when a shipment from Sussex is listed as being 'for the King's castle in Guernsey.' This almost certainly refers to Château des Marais. Castle Cornet was built some years later and it is estimated that the castle was fully functional by c 1275 and able to guard Guernsey, which remained loyal to the English Crown, along with the rest of the Channel Islands. The original castle was accessible only by foot at low tide, and was entered along a rocky path on the east side of the islet. It consisted of a tower keep and a chapel, with two courtyards on the upper level of the outcrop. Some of the exhibits show a stonemason of the time and the building materials that were used. In 1338 Castle Cornet was captured by the French, and although Guernsey was re-taken by the English the castle remained in the hands of the invader until 1345 the year before the Battle of Crécy. During the Hundred Years War the French tried many times to capture the castle and Guernsey; the crisis did not end until the Pope declared the Channel Islands to be neutral territory in 1483.

The next phase of development took place during the Tudor and Stuart period. Warfare had changed with the advent of gunpowder and artillery. Following a Commission of Enquiry in 1567, modifications and an extention of the sea defences were augmented in line with the latest technology. The great outer walls with their bastions and bulwarks were mostly constructed under the governship of Sir Thomas Leighton, under the supervision of Paul Ivy and other eminent engineers of the day. Paul Ivy was the greatest authority of modern warfare and castle defence of his time. He was a Cambridge man, who was also heavily involved in building Elizabeth Castle in Jersey, as well as other fortifications in Falmouth, and Kinsale in Ireland. His book *The Practise of Fortification* became the bible on fortification defence as soon as it was published in 1589. Castle Cornet owes much of its present appearance to his work. Several panels show the changes required during this period because of the development of explosive weaponry.

During the Civil War in 1642, the castle remained stubbornly loyal to the Royalist cause and supplied by sea, it withstood a siege lasting eight years, before surrendering to a Parliamentarian fleet. Sir Peter Osborne, the Governor of the castle, was a staunch Royalist who barricaded himself inside the fortress. Three

Parliamentarian Jurats, who went to seize him were themselves enticed into the castle, and imprisoned in a dungeon. Castle Cornet was the last part of the British Isles to surrender to Cromwell. Displays summarise both the Royalist and the Parliamentarian causes. After the Restoration of the Monarchy and the return of Charles II to the throne, Castle Cornet was fully maintained as a fortress. However, 20 years later, in 1680, all the Channel Island castles came under the auspices of the Board of Ordnance, and Governors ceased to be responsible for the paying of their garrisons. From 1661 until 1670 the castle served as a prison for Major-General Sir John Lambert, considered by many to be a potential successor to Cromwell, as the Lord Protector. The general was a famous gardener, and his garden has recently been restored and replanted in the 17C style. Two other gardens besides this have been redesigned by Peter Thoday to show how the interior landscape looked during these times.

The medieval tower, which contained the powder magazine, was struck by lightning in 1672. Lord Hatton, the governor, was blown on to the battlements in his bed. His wife, mother and five other people were killed. The explosion destroyed the keep, the chapel and the governor's residence. Since then no governor has lived in the castle.

Castle Cornet was eventually repaired to meet the French threat during the rule of Napoleon Bonaparte. The married quarters and hospital were constructed in the mid-18C, but by the 1780s the castle was no longer suitable as a first line of defence. It was difficult to reach, overcrowded and easy to bombard from the main island. Nevertheless, it remained armed with 300 men and 70 guns, during the Napoleonic period, but by 1812, just prior to the Battle of Waterloo the British garrison moved its headquarters to the newly-constructed Fort George.

The role of the citadel now changed to become a major gun platform to protect the shipping lanes and east coast of Guernsey. The Guard Room with its cast-iron colonnade, was added in Victorian times, and the last garrison regiment was stationed in Guernsey in 1939.

With the fall of France in 1940 it was no longer possible to defend the Channel Islands, and they were left to be occupied by the Germans. Further work was undertaken by the Third Reich, during their occupation of the island in World War II, when it was made a stronghold for the defence of the harbour. They added concrete shelters and anti-aircraft gun emplacements. As a result, Castle Cornet is the only castle in the British Isles to suffer bombing by the Royal Air Force. On 9 May 1945 the British Liberation Force recaptured the island and returned it to Home Rule, and in 1947 King George VI presented Castle Cornet to the islanders for their loyalty in two world wars. It is now maintained by the Heritage Committee of the States of Guernsey.

Adjacent to the **Victorian Guard Room** is the **Saluting Battery**. It is here that a 21-gun salute takes place on Queen Elizabeth II's birthday, as well as on the occasion of a Royal visit. The seven cannons used for this purpose were cast in 1987 to replace those taken away by the Germans. They are a similar design to the 1601 Saker, found in the Tower of London, and are fired by members of the Guernsey branch of the Royal Artillary. This event is followed every year by celebrations, which often include Morris dancing, military displays and a banquet. It is a popular day out.

Martial music precedes the daily firing of the Noon Day Gun, by the Castle Keepers. This very large cannon bears the cipher of George III and was cast in

1799. It is to be found just round the corner from the Married Quarters at the harbour end of the castle.

On the **Mewtis Bulwark**, overlooking Havelet Bay, by the steps which lead down to the **Gunners' Tower** stands the castle's oldest cannon. It is the bronze six-pounder cannon, called the Guernsey Falcon, which was cast in 1550 by gun founder Thomas Owen, during the reign of Edward VI. It escaped being melted down for armaments by the occupying Germans as it was in Plymouth, Massachusetts, at the time of the Occupation.

In 1921 the Honourable Artillery Company of London gave it to the state of Massachusetts to commemorate the 300th anniversary of the Pilgrim Fathers' landing. After a 35-year effort to retrieve it, the cannon is now displayed in the very bulwark at the fortress it had been designed to protect. Reciprocal arrangements were made for a replica of a Saker cannon, a type known to have been carried on the *Mayflower*, to be given to the town of Plymouth in return for the Guernsey Falcon.

There is also an **RAF Museum** devoted to 201 Squadron which was officially affiliated to the island of Guernsey.

In recent years, different mainland theatrical companies have been staging open-air performances of Shakespeare's plays, during the summer in the courtyard by the **Spenser Room**. The castle is floodlit at night and is an enchanting setting for such occasions.

The castle contains several interesting museums. Prominent among these is **Maritime Guernsey**, housed in the 18C Married Quarters, which traces the maritime history of the island from Roman times to the present day. In the same building are the **Hatton Gallery**, and the **Castle Refectory**.

Julius Caeser conquered Brittany in 57BC, and the Channel Islands became important staging-posts for traders sailing between Gaul and the province of Brittania. Wine was an important export, and granite from Guernsey was found during the excavation of the Roman palace at Fishbourne in Sussex. The discovery of a wrecked trading vessel from Gaul at the entrance to St. Peter Port harbour in 1982, as well as the Plaiderie excavations are well recorded on audio-visual equipment and in display, at the start of the Maritime Museum. It is now known from island excavations that by AD 100, the leading citizens in the Channel Islands could read and write Latin, dressed in Roman fashion, and worshipped the Roman pantheon of gods.

Adjacent to the **Gallo-Roman Trade Room** is that informing visitors of medieval trade fishing. From the 13C to 15C, the Channel Islands were vulnerable to French raids until they were declared to be neutral in 1483, by the Pope. This neutrality held until the late 17C, and enabled the islanders to trade in reasonable safety. In a triangular trade, Guernsey ships carried stores to fisheries in Newfoundland; fish to the Mediterranean; and wine and spices to Guernsey and England, which led to growing prosperity for the island. This in turn led to essential improvements to St. Peter Port harbour, financed by a levy on visiting ships.

Other rooms on the ground floor describe the harbour, mentioned above, which includes a scale model, and the **Maritime Art Gallery**, with many oil paintings, which portray the weather conditions around the rocky shores of the Channel Islands, that were a great hazard to sailing ships. Note the restored Guernsey fishing boat—*Gem 11*.

Fishing boats in the Channel Islands were usually three-masted, having a black hull but painted green below the plimsole line and in the interior. They varied slightly in design from one island to another, for instance the jib and mainsails, generally a tan colour, were in Sark dyed a bright red, so that they could be recognised by the family of the fishermen when returning home in bad weather. The frames were of solid oak, the hulls were carvel-built with pine planking, and the sails were gaff rigged. These fishing boats were fast and seaworthy, which was essential in these dangerous waters. During the winter most fishermen wisely turned to farming.

In the Royal Navy room upstairs some of the activities of the senior service are recorded with particular attention given to two famous Guernsey naval officers. Firstly, Captain Philip de Sausmarez, who served in the fleet which captured the Spanish ship *Nuestra Senora del Cabadonga* in the mid-18C, said to be the wealthiest prize ever taken at sea (see also p. 126). And secondly, Admiral Lord James de Saumarez, Captain Philip's nephew, who saw action in the American War of Independence, and then in the French Revolutionary Wars, where he commanded the Channel Island Squadron (see also p. 132).

As can be seen in the adjacent **Privateering and Shipbuilding Room**, privateers in the Channel Islands were very active during this period. A privateer was a private merchant ship licenced to act as a man-of-war by the Crown of England with a 'letter of marque', which permitted it to attack the enemy trading vessels. The Channel Islanders were extremely successful at these escapades, due to their detailed knowledge of the reefs and rocky coastline, and they so disrupted the shipping business out of Bordeaux, La Rochelle and Nantes, that goods destined for the Americas, the Caribbean, and the three major ports in France went to St. Peter Port instead. From these acts of piracy, then a legitimate trade, there grew up alongside the illegitimate business of smuggling. From both activities the leading island families became extremely wealthy and the island prospered. But with the defeat of Napoleon at the Battle of Waterloo in 1815, peace was restored and privateering ended. Much of the money made from privateering and smuggling was invested in shipbuilding and by 1870 the merchant fleet of Guernsey ran to over 150 vessels.

Guernsey merchantmen traded as far afield as South America, India and China. Their ships carried products as diversified as coffee, rice, rum, wine, silk, coal and stone. Of the ships themselves, the *San Francisco Newspaper* on 22 January 1868 wrote this about the *Costa Rica Packet*, 'This ship is now lying at Volley's wharf: she was built at Guernsey, one of the Channel Islands, is constructed of teak and copper fastened throughout. She is without exception the best built ship that has ever entered this port.'

The largest and probably the most beautiful ship ever built in Guernsey was the *Golden Spur*, launched in 1864. She was 200 feet in length, carried over half an acre of canvas, weighed 656 tons, and was capable of carrying cargo up to 1400 tons, at a speed of 17 knots or over 350 miles a day, when a fair wind was blowing. She was built to compete in the lucrative China tea trade, where the first ship home was richly rewarded. With the coming of the steamship these beautiful boats ceased to be employed in carrying cargoes, and slowly they disappeared from service. The Guernsey shipping industry, as it was then, died. The only steamer to be built on the island was the *Commerce* in 1874. Among the many items on display in this section is a shipwright's shop showing the many kinds of tools that were used to build the splendid sailing vessels.

With the advent of steamships, cross-channel passenger travel service from the mainland was no longer dependent on wind and tide, and soon after the first paddle steamer, *Medina of Cowes*, visited the island in 1832. Henceforth a regular mainland service from Southampton came into being. The history of the packet boats and railway steamers from that year forward for nearly 150 years, is the subject of another top floor room, along with the aviation service that began from the UK in 1923 with flying boats. Designed by R.J. Mitchell, who later designed the Spitfire, these early single-engine bi-planes carried six passengers from Southampton to Guernsey for only £3.80 single fare.

The last room on the top floor deals with safety at sea, and the history of the St. Peter Port lifeboat service, which has a long and heroic record of rescue in terribe storms. It also tells the tale of harbour divers. Children are fascinated by the old heavyweight diving suit, with its great brass helmet, and the decompression chamber which saved men from the agony of the 'bends'.

From here the museum has an entrance to the **Hatton Gallery**, named after former governors, which contains early paintings of Castle Cornet, along with paintings of historic citizens who gave Guernsey its great heritage.

Visitors to the castle can eat at the attractively laid out refectory in the Maritime Museum.

The castle hospital built in 1746 contains, on the ground floor, the Spencer Collection of uniforms, badges, buttons, insignia, and medals, including some awarded to General Thomas de Saumarez (1760–1845), of the Channel Islands' Militias (open only on certain days).

The **Upper Floor**, whose entrance is up some steps behind the building, houses the **Royal Guernsey Militia Museum**. Here we see uniforms, swords, helmets, drums (National Sark Militia) dating back to 1743 and a list of Governors from 1177. Coats of arms of past Governors and Lieutenant Governors line the walls. The key exhibit is the Dundas Sword, 'Gift of the inhabitants of the island of Guernsey to Major General Thomas Dundas 1793'. The General was stationed in the Bailiwick of Guernsey for a number of years during the French Revolution. He had the foresight to strengthen the defences of Guernsey so that the island was in a state of readiness when France declared war on Great Britain in 1793. There is also an obelisk presented by the officers of the Guernsey Militia to Lieutenant General Sir John Doyle in 1814. This local force, in which nearly all the local male citizens have served, was disbanded in 1939.

St. Peter Port's parish church

The town church is by the south-east corner of the old harbour. This church, with its fine architecture has been referred to as 'the cathedral of the Islands'. William the Conqueror, Duke of Normandy, first referred to it in a charter (1048) when it passed with five other churches to the Benedictine Abbey of Marmoutier, near Tours. Some of the stones of this church may have echoed to the Te Deum at the last successful invasion of England in 1066. With the dissolution of the monasteries in 1414 it came under the patronage of the English Crown. For another 150 years until 1548 it was part of the See of Coutances (Normandy) and the Bishop of Coutances appointed the clergy and collected dues from the Island.

The church is built of granite and originally served as a fortress. The oldest part of the building is the 13C nave; the choir is 14C. The church has been extended over the years to accommodate the growing population. The guns of the militia were stored here until 1822 together with the town's fire engine. Careful restoration work was carried out between 1822 and 1826 and again in 1866. Extensive damage was done to the windows during an air raid in 1944 and many had to be replaced.

The 14C central tower is supported on four strong piers with elegant vaulting. The aisles of the choir were rebuilt in the 15C and the porch on the north side of the nave and the parvis above it were added in the early 16C. The square central tower with its fortifications is 15C but the present octagonal spire is 18C. During the Civil War the church was fired upon by the Royalists defending Castle Cornet and the fabric probably received a few hits. The colours of the Guernsey Militia hang in the chancel and the Lady Chapel. In 1973 major restoration work was carried out and three new windows, one commemorating the Queen's Silver Wedding, were unveiled.

The church has a peal of eight bells cast in Brittany in 1913. The Caen stone pulpit is modern. The position of the three altars is marked by carved piscinae; the carvings on the back row of the choir stalls represent the life of St. Peter. The window themes in the Lady Chapel are the Presentation of the Child Jesus and the Annunciation. The themes above the altar represent the Te Deum and those in the north transept show St. Peter walking on the water.

The Market

The Market (formerly the Rectory garden) at the back of the church developed over many decades. The old Market Hall, with the Assembly Rooms over it was built in 1780. The Doric Market Hall was added in 1822, soon to be followed by a grander south eastern addition and the ornate Victorian fish and meat markets. A visitor in 1847 wrote, 'Marketing seems here the grand object of the people's lives. Gentlemen twirl the fish dangling at their wrists, with the same dégagé air with which the Londoner would flourish his cane'. Some of the ambience remains, and there are still bargains to be found, as St. Peter Port has a series of markets of which French Halles, built in 1780, is the oldest. Six years later the neighbouring building was constructed to house the Queen's Weights. Opposite are the fish, vegetable and meat markets. The latter was erected in 1822 and the arcades in 1830.

A folly commemorates Queen Victoria's visit

Victoria Tower, reached from Monument Rd, east of the War Memorial, across College St, is a splendid folly built to celebrate a Royal visit in 1846. The brief to the builder was, 'A castellated tower to be erected to celebrate the landing of the sovereign, and to serve as a telegraph station for Alderney and as a lookout for royal and other flags.' The 100ft tower was built on the site of a menhir, La Pierre L'Hyvreuse, from money (£2000) raised from public subscription, and it still dominates the skyline of the town.

Priaulx Library and Candie Gardens are off Candie Rd which leaves the town centre to the north-west and runs parallel to Monument Rd. The Candie Estate was given in 1887 by Oswald Priaulx to the people of Guernsey. Candie

House became the Priaulx Library which houses some 25,000 volumes dating back to the 15C, which visitors may consult. (**Open** 09.30–17.30; closed on Sun and Bank Holidays.) In 1898 the States of Guernsey voted money to lay out the gardens with exotic trees and plants; of particular interest is the maidenhair tree. The museum informs us that this tree, from China, is a 'living fossil' found in rocks over 250 million years old.

The public library

The Guille-Alès Library is in the former Assembly Rooms in Market Street behind the Town Church, where John Wesley preached in 1787. The library is **open** daily, Mon–Sat from 09.10–17.00 except on Thurs when it closes at 12.30 (open until 17.30 on Saturdays). There are over 50,000 books and practically every publication about the Channel Islands is housed here. Local papers are on reference files. UK visitors may borrow books on their local borough library tickets. On the top floor is a museum devoted to the natural history of the island.

The Royal Court House

The Royal Court House is in Manor Place, near the War Memorial, 200m east of the North Esplanade. The original Royal Court House was in La Plaiderie (a barn belonging to the king), first mentioned in documents in 1248. It was sold into private ownership in 1803 and replaced by the present Royal Court House in La Rue du Manoir. In the Royal Court Room the sittings of the Royal Court are held, and States of Deliberation. The building also houses the Bailiff's Chambers, the Jurat's Room, the Law Library, the Office of the Greffier, the Public Registry and Magistrate's Court. After World War II the court house underwent extensive alterations. Visitors are admitted to both courts and may sit in the Public Gallery and may also visit the Greffe, which houses all the charters granted to the Island since 1394.

Early city defences

Gateway Pillar Stone. At one time it was decided to enclose St. Peter Port with a defensive wall and six granite blocks were set up to define the gateways. In Smith St by the post office one of these blocks still remains with the inscription written on a brass plaque, 'This stone is one of six stones erected by the order of the Royal Court in 1700 to mark the sites of the gates of the town when in the XIV century, St. Peter Port was walled in for defensive purposes.'

Guernsey Museum and Art Gallery

■ **Open** daily from Apr–Oct 10.00–17.00 and until 16.00 from Nov–Mar, except for a few days over Christmas. Fee. A joint ticket is available for Castle Cornet, Fort Grey and the Guernsey Museum.

The Guernsey Museum and Art Gallery stand just at the back of Victor Hugo's statue in Candie Gardens. This museum, opened in 1978, was purpose-built to house the collection previously on show in the Lukis and Island Museum. The museum tells the story of the island and its people. It is highly recommended. The modern buildings incorporate a most attractive glassed-in Victorian bandstand (refreshments). The museum itself is organised into a cluster of octagonal pavilions, the scale and form of which derive from the bandstand.

Attached to the museum is a wing which houses the headquarters of La Société Guernesiase and the museum's Education Service. This area is not open to the public, although the 70-seat lecture theatre is sometimes used for school classes and public lectures. The Société's archives are also housed in this building.

At the entrance to the museum is a display lobby where books, guides and leaflets can be bought. See the multi-visual programme in the theatre which introduces you to the island and museum. Well scripted and supported with excellent displays, the museum is made up of three octagonal rooms which take you through the geological formation of the islands in the Bailiwick, surrounding marine life, local fauna and flora with information on a number of Guernsey's naturalists, including Joshua Gosselin. Outlining the excellent work carried out by Frederick Corbin Lukis and his talented relatives in the field of archaeology during the last century, there is an introduction to prehistoric man, his buildings, statues, tools and utensils which have been found throughout the island.

Chronologically, the exhibition moves through Roman, Saxon and Norman times. It outlines the close links with England from 1066 up to the present day and, of course, includes the German Occupation during World War II. One section deals with famous Guernsey personalities, and another with historical industries, agricultural and dairy husbandry, fishing, knitting, quarrying, horti-culture and tourism. The museum has three interactive visual display screens which offer a vast amount of additional, and fascinating information.

A new **art gallery** was opened in 1997 where watercolours and sketches by the gifted local artists Peter Le Lievre (1812–78) and Paul Jacob Naftel (1817–91) are displayed with works such as Thomas Whitcombe's oil painting of a storm off Castle Cornet in 1796. Other interesting paintings include works by the Sark artist Ethel Cheeswright who died aged 102. Paintings will be changed from time to time, as the museum has a large stock of paintings in store from which to draw.

The old gallery houses a series of changing temporary exhibitions.

St. James, College Street

The former church of St. James in College Street, architecturally one of the most important buildings in St. Peter Port, is a fine concert and assembly hall. It was opened by the Duke of Kent in July 1985. The church of St. James the Less was consecrated in 1818, having been built to provide a place of refuge for the English-speaking community and the British garrison in Guernsey. It became redundant in 1970. It has now been restored to its original beauty and elegance by local craftsmen. It was constructed to a design by John Wilson by a local builder, Edward May, at a cost of 7000 guineas. It marks the start of Guernsey's movement away from the medieval town and towards the Regency 'new town'. Apart from Torteval Church, it was the first planned and designed public building on the island. The Greek Revival style is most pronounced on the west façade of the building which has fine Doric columns and entablature carrying a pediment. The composition is surmounted by a steeple in the Ionic style, with Classical balcony, pepper-pot dome, ball and weather-vane. The proportions and detailing of the building are perfectly derived from the Greek Classical period, yet it is completely original. The decoration of the interior, which has superb accoustics, is plain and reserved. Note the well-proportioned fluted columns

Artists
John Caprane (1856–1940)

Caprane was one of Guernsey's adopted sons. He was born in England and spent the first 40 years of his life there. Little is known of the work he did in England with the exception of his *Double Rainbow* (1895). This is a remarkable painting in its composition and its courageous use of colour, particularly the yellow and lilac. Like many great artists, he was not concerned with dating his work, and although he suffered from extreme penury, he was loathe to sell anything he produced. He identified so closely with his work that he could hardly bear to part with it. He shows some influence of Constable and Turner, perhaps most in his handling of the interaction between sea and sky. Although he cannot be called an Impressionist in the full meaning of that term, he was, like many Impressionists, constantly looking to Nature for his inspiration and his work was always informed by his desire to translate nature into art. One of his favourite subjects was the iris, a flower which was a constant source of inspiration for him. He loved, and was an expert on this fragile work of creation, and his love and knowledge of his subject is clear to see in the many paintings of them.

The painting which probably best sums up the totality of John Caprane's work is his large painting called *Bon Port Ravine*. It is his most complete evocation of his reverence for Nature. It is technically magnificent, but above all it captures at its most profound and enduring level all that is best about this artist's beloved adopted home, all that sums up Guernsey, the source of his inspiration.

Peter Le Lièvre (1812–1878)

Le Lièvre was born in St. Peter Port in 1812 and lived all his life in Hauteville. He had Victor Hugo as a near neighbour, who spent most of his exile here living in Hauteville Manor. When his father died in 1848, Peter Le Lièvre took over the family business, and became ever more involved with the public life of Guernsey. He never married, which may have been a contributory factor to his plunging himself into public life. He also found time to paint. He took particular interest in the upkeep of the town church and its organ and he was also instrumental in the planning of the town markets and the new harbour. He had a great deal of influence over the final choice of a design for the two lighthouses in the harbour.

Like all the men on Guernsey at that time, Peter Le Lièvre was a member of the Guernsey Militia, rising through the ranks to become Lieutenant-Colonel in command of the Artillery Regiment in 1868.

His favourite subjects were the people of Guernsey going about their daily tasks. He was able to catch a moment in time in the lives of these hard working people, sometimes indeed resting for a moment from their labours as in his picture of a man sitting with his faithful dog at his feet. A woman's work, he seems to maintain, is never done. Both the woman in the red cloak and the woman in the Sark cottage appear to be knitting. His delightful *Sleeping Cat* is reproduced on post cards which may be bought at the Candie Museum shop, but to experience the full impact of this deceptively simple little painting, which is a distillation of all sleeping cats that ever were, it is necessary to see the original in the gallery. He has also recorded the changing face of the rocky seashore of the island.

On the question of his work as an artist Le Lièvre was astonishingly modest and unassuming, and regarded his painting as a hobby. When there was an exhibition of 24 of his watercolour paintings in 1904, 26 years after his death, in the Guille-Allès Library, the catalogue revealed that, '...none but his intimate friends ever saw his pictures; he scarcely ever mentioned them in conversation ... as a consequence ... his name is quite unknown in the art circles of England and the Continent ...'.

Paul Jacob Naftel (1817–1891)

Paul Jacob Naftel was Guernsey's only locally born professional artist of his period. It is generally agreed that he was a self-taught artist. His early works were drawings of scenes from Guernsey and Sark. He also excelled in painting water, in particular the seas around the west coast of Guernsey in all seasons, either in the heat haze of a summer's day or in rough weather with the vraic gatherers struggling to bring in the seas' harvest while the oxen yoked to carts waited to take the load away from the beach. Naftel liked to produce his watercolours on long, narrow strips of paper. This was ideal for his panoramic coastal views. Some critics found fault with the very strong colours he used and occasionally catalogues referred to scenes of his as 'Mediterranean'–a clear implication that viewers found it hard that anywhere in this part of the world could produce such intense colours. Visitors to Guernsey could set this record straight. When he moved to London in the 1870s Naftel enjoyed great popularity with the Victorians. His pictures were, in fact, 'best sellers' and at a conservative estimate he produced 2000 pictures during his lifetime. *The Times* obituary had this to say, 'It will not be claimed for him that he was a man of great originality as an artist, but his landscapes, always good technically, were brilliant and refined studies of the places in which they were painted.'

Apart from his career as a successful artist, Paul Naftel was also a busy teacher. He had an enormous number of pupils in Guernsey and according to the fashion of the day it was not unusual for him to put the finishing touches to a pupils' piece. In some cases he would do no less than 80% of the watercolour, and for that reason attribution is often a difficult business. It was not unknown, during his lifetime for dealers to sell work by a pupil of Naftel's as the master's own. When Victorian art in general fell from favour, so did the work of Paul Naftel, and his work is rarely available for sale today. However, in the past 15 years there has been a renewal of interest and appreciation for this industrious and talented son of Guernsey. In 1991 a centenary exhibition was mounted in the Guernsey Museum and Art Gallery to celebrate his work and career.

Pierre Auguste Renoir (1841–1919)

Renoir, one of the greatest of the Impressionists, went to Guernsey for the first time in 1880 and visited the Channel Islands many times between then and 1883. He loved the islands for their charm and simplicity and they suited his simple tastes very well. He always proclaimed that his aim was for his pictures to be full of charm and delight, and Guernsey proved the perfect subject. The landscapes which he brought back from Guernsey are full of iridescent colours. They depict Guernsey as a happy, smiling island which we can imagine to be inhabited by Calypso and her nymphs. There is nothing in them which recalls the stern rock, ceaselessly battered by storms, of which Victor Hugo has given such frightening images. With fluency and skill Renoir set down his sheer delight in the sensuous beauty of the world in which he found himself. Pinks, greens, and blues predominate in the pictures, forms are dissolved by light touched by shade. Looking at such pictures as *Beach Scene*; *Seated Bather*; *The Bay of Moulin Huet through the Trees*; *Fog on Guernsey* and his large painting *Children on the Seashore*, it is hard to understand how for many years his work was scorned or ignored.

In the late summer of 1883 Renoir painted a number of pictures of Guernsey, all inspired by the bay and beach of Moulin Huet. They happened to be within easy walking distance of where he was staying: 4, George Road, St. Peter Port. Of Moulin Huet he wrote to a friend, 'Here I am on a very fine beach, utterly unlike the Normandy beaches ... We go bathing among the rocks, behind which we change, for want of anything better at hand. Nothing could be prettier than the sight of men and women huddled together on huge rocks. It's like stepping into a landscape of Watteau, rather than reality. This gives me a whole stock of lively, graceful themes on which to draw. Such delightful bathing suits! Here as in Athens the women haven't the slightest qualms about the presence of men-bathers beside them. What fun it is, slipping from boulder to boulder, to come upon the girls in the midst of changing their clothes. But even though English, they don't seem to mind'.

Renoir made no attempt to record images of the island's burgeoning agricultural and industrial life. Greenhouses were, in the 1880s, already making their appearance, to house the ubiquitous tomato, taking over from the island's previous principal crop of grapes. The island at this time also quarried granite and harvested seaweed. Renoir, however, chose to give his attention to the island as a lightly inhabited landscape, a peaceful retreat from the bustle of the modern world.

carrying the balcony and the simply decorated balcony front. Acanthus-leaf plaster frets can be seen in the corners of the ceiling.

Hauteville House

Victor Hugo purchased Hauteville House from William Ozanne in 1856. At a time when Guernsey shops were laden with the spoils of privateering, Hugo purchased fabulous antiques with which to furnish his new home. With considerable talent he dismantled sideboards, chests, cabinets and other pieces of outstanding craftsmanship, and cut up tapestries only to reassemble them to suit his unique taste in interior design. He said of himself 'J'ai manqué ma vocation, j'étais né pour être décorateur'.

Victor Hugo

What Victor Hugo found on his arrival in Guernsey was an island where magnolias flourished, fuchsias grew to be eight feet high and were still in flower in November. The impressive scenery was to have a profound effect on his writing. He had fallen foul of the authorities in Jersey because of his loudly expressed Republican opinions, but his ejection from Jersey had not cooled his ardour for politics, nor did he moderate his opinions in any way. He was visited by a series of thinkers of like mind. One guest was to record how Hugo would drink a toast after dinner to the future English republic, and to the United States of Europe, which he believed would be established shortly.

In May 1856, his recently published collection of poems *Les Contemplations*, having been successful both financially and artistically, Hugo acquired Hauteville House (he debated with himself whether or not to call it Liberty House). It is interesting to speculate on the irony of the situation in which this placed him. Hugo, who had fulminated against Queen Victora in Jersey and would refuse to stand when *God Save the Queen* was played was, by his purchase of Hauteville House, constrained to pay *droit de poulage*, a rent of two hens a year to the Queen.

Hugo was to spend the next 19 years of his life at Hauteville House, working from the 'look-out' which he built at the top of the house, working every day in all weathers, in winter and in summer. He stood, wrapped in a long red dressing gown leaning against his high oak desk, beside his porcelain stove, decorated with a statue of Venus, the goddess of love.

As regards his social life, however, he and his family did not really fit in in Guernsey. He did not attend church, so they thought he must be an atheist. He was French and he was a poet—these were also causes for mistrust and suspicion. Added to which he had brought with him into exile, as well as his lawful wife, his mistress, Juliette Drouet. She lived just a short distance from the Hugos, at 20 Hauteville Street, where Victor, ever the keen interior decorator, embedded plates over the mantelpiece and had the mantel carved with his initials, V. H. Juliette reinforced this proprietorial theme in the garden by planting flowers to the same design in the middle of the lawn.

In August 1859 an amnesty was granted to all republican exiles. Hugo immediately declared his intention on no account to return to France. His reasons must have had to do with pride, but also it must have had to do with his affection for the Channel Islands, and Guernsey in particular. On 4 October 1861 Hugo signed the contract for the publication of *Les Misérables*. This novel had been in his mind for the past 16 years and he had worked on it on and off. The publisher paid 240,000 francs for the first text and a further 60,000 for the translation rights. Hugo was a hard headed businessman. Correspondence shows that he was fully aware of the importance of good marketing of the product and when the proofs were sent to him for correction his publisher had to pay the postage.

In June 1853 he started work on *Les Travailleurs de la Mer*. He finished it in April 1864, writing in his 'glass room'.

Around the time of the publication of *Toilers to the Sea* observers began to collect Hugo's malapropisms: 'Bug-pipes' on which the hero played the 'lament' Bonny Dundee; the First-of-Fourth, ie, the Firth-of-Forth. The novel, set in the Channel Islands has at its heart the theme of the eternal triangle, with the sea as its tragic hero. It concerns the fate of Gilliatt, a man on the margins of society, who becomes a hero for love, who has much in common with Jean Valjean in *Les Misérables*. Although it owes something to his time in Sark, Hugo dedicated this great work to Guernsey: 'To the rock of hospitality and freedom, to this corner of old Norman territory inhabited by the noble small seafaring people, to the island of Guernsey, severe and sweet, my present asylum, my probable tomb.'

Victor Hugh did not die in the Channel Islands, he may have looked sometimes on his exile as a cage, but it was here that he produced his most magnificent and profound works of prose fiction and poetry.

The **Entrance Hall** displays Chinese paintings, medieval figurines and medallions of Victor Hugo and his daughter. The door opposite the entrance hall leads to the garden. Each side of this passage and the ceiling are decorated with china from Delft, Rouen and other famous factories. The decorations even include a Sèvres service presented to Hugo by Charles X of France. Double doors on the right lead into the **Billiards Room** which contains paintings by his wife and himself. Hugo was an artist as well as a writer and some 350 of his pictures are on view in the Maison de Victor Hugo in Paris. From the Billiards Room another door leads into a room where the walls and ceilings are covered with tapestry from Aubusson and Flanders, and the mantelpiece is sculptured from furniture of the Middle Ages, Renaissance and Louis XIII periods.

Off the Entrance Hall another door leads to the **Dining Room**. The walls above the panelling are covered with Delft tiles. The space between the windows is occupied by a wooden seat, designed by Victor Hugo, and known as the Chair of the Ancestors. On the back is the coat of arms of the Hugos of Lorraine. No-one was allowed to sit in it. The ceiling is covered with an 18C Gobelins tapestry. The intricate craftsmanship in this room took ten Guernsey craftsmen, under a master carpenter called Mauger, a year to complete. The dining room became known to the Hugo family as 'La Salle à Mauger'.

On the **First Floor** are the large Red and Blue Drawing Rooms, named for the colour of their silk upholstery. The ends of these spacious rooms have large mirrors to give an impression of added depth. Four life-size gilded figures taken from the Venetian Doge's barge, the 'Boucentaure', hold up a canopy. Other furniture in these rooms includes 17C bead tapestries from Portugal, 18C Chinese lacquered panels set in the double doors separating the two rooms, a Louis XIV firescreen with 'petit point', a marquetry table, Louis XV armchairs, a 'bergère', and chandeliers of Murano glass.

On the **Second Floor** are the Bedroom and Study which Victor Hugo intended to use but their lengthy completion led him to select the floor above. He invited Garibaldi to come and stay in the large four-poster bed with a canopy whose ceiling is made of sculptured wood taken from old chests. He did not come and the bed has never been used. Everywhere in these rooms is carved wood, benches, panels, cabinets, a mantelpiece with columns, three chairs inscribed

'Pater', 'Mater' and 'Filius' and a unique candelabra supporting at its top a Virgin designed and partly sculptured by Victor Hugo.

The **Third Floor**. A narrow staircase leads to the top floor. A passage with book shelves leads to a balcony completely covered with glass. Among Victor Hugo's books is a complete collection of the works of Charles Dickens, translated into French.

Hugo's glass-walled **Studio** at the top of the house has magnificent views overlooking the harbour and other islands in the Bailiwick and on a clear day the coastline of France is visible. Heat, when necessary, is provided by a small Dutch tiled stove. From the library a passage leads to the poet's spartan **Bedroom**, with one end of the room being taken up with a not too comfortable narrow bed. Portraits of the family decorate the walls and by the window are drawings by Hugo depicting the story of the Princess and the Knight.

Victor Hugo was extremely disciplined in his habits. He wrote on the panel in the drawing room:

Lever a VI Diner a X
Souper a V Coucher a X
Faict vivre l'homme X par X.

Every morning he started with a cold shower, and as he ate his early breakfast he drew. Then he would write for five hours in his 'lighthouse' study, standing up. In the afternoons he took long walks by the sea and through the countryside. Ideas often came to him at night, and he would wake up and jot down notes in a book he kept at his bedside before going back to sleep again. His first efforts in the morning were then to recall his moments of insight. 'I am the man,' he wrote, 'who pays special attention to his night life.' This round of contemplation, concentration and moments of insight led to the production of a prodigious amount of work during his 15 years at Hauteville House including *La Légende des Siècles* (1859), *Les Misérables* (1862), *William Shakespeare* (1860), *Les Chansons des Rues et des Bois* (1865), *Les Travailleurs de la Mer* (1866), *L'Hommes qui Rit* (1869) and other posthumously published works.

Beau Séjour Leisure Centre

Beau Séjour is Guernsey's main leisure centre. It provides many facilities such as a swimming-pool, roller skating, bowls, sauna, solarium, bars, restaurants and a cinema. Musicals, plays, pop concerts and disco dancing take place here and the entertainment pages of the local press list events.

The coast

St. Peter Port via the north to L'Erée

Configuration of Guernsey

Along the north and west coast of the island are many sandy beaches for children. They start at **L'Ancresse Bay** and run southwards to **Vazon Bay** and are often close to open common land where you can park and picnic. There are other good bays from west to east along the south coastline which stretches from Petit Port to

Moulin Huet Bay westwards and around the corner, so to speak, to **Portelet Bay**

The south coast has high cliffs from Jerbourg to Pleinmont, some 30km in length. Here fascinating cliff paths meander, overlooking the white foam flecked waves far below where the sea beats ceaselessly against the rocks. A considerable variety of nesting sea birds—gulls, gannets, guillemots and puffins, are also seen wafting in and around the cliff sides.

When the wind blows from the west there are several bays to select on the east coast, such as Fermain and Soldiers' Bay. Guernsey folk all have their favourite bays and niches, and are pleased to impart their knowledge. The azure sea, the unpolluted beaches, and the warm Gulf Stream led Victor Hugo to refer to Guernsey as a 'climate for leisure'.

North-east, north, and north-west coast

The coastal road north out of St. Peter Port leads to St. Sampson. At 3.25km it passes **Belle Grève** (right) which means 'fine bay' (*grève* is applied to some sandy beaches). The bay has granite outcrops and is of shingle and sand with a sweep of 2.5km and half-way round on the left down Victoria Avenue (1km) is **Château des Marais**, known locally as Ivy Castle.

Formerly surrounded by marshland, this medieval fortification has a wall enclosing a wide outer bailey and an inner wall and ditched mound which forms the inner bailey, the whole covering an area of 1.6 hectares. The castle was in a ruinous state in the 16C and was briefly re-fortified against possible French invasion during the 18C. Excavations sponsored in 1975 and 1977 by the Heritage Committee and with the help of La Société Guernesiaise revealed that the present ditch was recut in the 18C and again in the 19C to provide drainage. The medieval origin of the castle was proved by the excavation of 13C coins in what may have been a chapel under the existing stone wall. This links with documentary evidence referring to the appointment of a chaplain to 'Notre Dame des Marais' in 1244.

St. Sampson

The sea road continues past a Martello tower, to the south side of the pretty little harbour of St. Sampson (7000 inhab.). Here are facilities for unloading cargoes from Britain and the Continent and in former days this was an export centre for island granite. From the quayside sailing ships were towed out of the harbour to catch a fair wind for England.

A boom in privateering during the 18C encouraged growth in shipbuilding and yards were built along this coast from St. Peter Port to St. Sampson. Some 300 ships, barques, brigs, schooners and cutters were built in Guernsey yards during this period until wooden ships were phased out as sail gave way to steam. Meanwhile the export of granite to England began to dominate the scene and quarries in the vicinity of St. Sampson led to the building of new piers so that ships could handle the traffic more easily. The boom years of this industry were in the 19C when John Macadam introduced new methods of road building using crushed stone; exports rose from 12,000 tons in 1854 to 458,000 by the end of the century. The steps of St. Paul's, London, owe their origin to Guernsey. With the development of asphalt after World War One trade declined and today the harbour is mainly used for repairing small craft.

St. Sampson's harbour was begun in 1820 at the east end of a sea inlet which once divided Guernsey. Bridge Road is where the old bridge linked the two land masses. Inland along the quay from Bulwer Avenue, the second turning on the left leads to St. Sampson's church.

St. Sampson's church

St. Sampson, Guernsey's first Christian missionary, and now its patron saint, arrived in 556. He was a Welshman, who later became Bishop of Dol in Brittany. Where he landed he built a little oratory and from this the present church has grown. None of the original 6C church can now be seen. The present building is believed to date from the early 12C.

The oldest part of the church is either the east wall of the chancel or the north half, which resembles the parish church of Mont St. Michel, particularly in the saddle-back tower which rises from the middle of the north nave. The church has a nave and a chancel, on either side of which is a chapel.

The chancel is early Norman and built of local granite. The south side was built with granite from the west shore and has a reddish colour. The roof is vaulted with pebbles from the beach. The choir stalls are of oak, carved by modern craftsmen. There is a marble tablet over the priest's stall recording the death of a young lieutenant in 1799 when a 26lb cannon-ball lodged itself between two bones in his thigh. When the surgeon first examined him he did not notice it and it was only discovered after the unfortunate man's death. The regimental colours at each side of the altar are those of the old Guernsey North Regiment of Militia, placed there in 1887, during Queen Victoria's Jubilee.

Over the altar is a three-light window by Hardman, depicting the Resurrection. In the 14C south chapel the east window has some of its original granite tracery. The window, by Clayton and Bell, depicts St. Peter walking on the water. The two-light window in the south wall is of the Blessed Virgin and St. John; the former was used in the design of the postage stamp issued in 1972 to commemorate the silver wedding anniversary of the Queen and the Duke of Edinburgh. The west window depicts St. Sampson in his robes, carrying his pastoral staff.

In the earlier north chapel are three arches, each containing a tomb, one of which is deeply scored with a cross. They are the only ones of their kind on the island. Some church ornaments, probably secreted there during the Reformation, and only discovered when repairs were being carried out in the church, now form part of the furnishings of this and the baptistery in honour of St. Magloire, the cousin of St. Sampson, who lived on in the Channel Islands after the death of St. Sampson.

The church is rich in plate and valuable ornaments including a crucifix, candlesticks and a chalice, well known to antiquaries and authorities on church plate. It is silver gilt, probably French and of 14C origin. Renovated at a later date, it has underneath the inscription 'Sum ecclae Divi Sampsonis 1614'.

St. Sampson is a quaint harbour town and interesting to walk around, with plenty of boats, shops and cottage industries to see, such as Guernsey Candles (Les Petites Capelle), Guernsey Pottery and Glassworks (Les Gigands Road) and Oatlands Craft Centre (Braye Road).

Vale Castle stands on an escarpment guarding the entrance to the north side of the harbour. It was once the main entrance of the Clos du Valle before Lieutenant-Governor Doyle had it joined to the mainland. From the ramparts of this derelict ruin there is a good view of the east shoreline. Dating from Norman times and probably earlier, it has played an important role in the island's history. In 1372, during the raid of Ifan of Wales, Lieutenant-Governor Rose successfully defended Guernsey from here and Castle Cornet. During 1799 and 1800, in a little graveyard near the castle entrance, some of a contingent of 6000 Russian soldiers were buried. They had been quartered here after fighting with British troops in Holland. Many of them died of diseases contracted in the low Dutch marshland. The British ceased to use the castle as a barracks in the last century but it was refortified by the Germans during the Occupation.

One kilometre north of St. Sampson is **Bordeaux harbour**, a fishermen's cove with a great variety of marine life. At low tide there is sand with an intricate rock formation, and the cove provides good bathing at high tide. From the car park on the north side it is possible to walk along the coastline for 400m to the islet of Hommet Paradis, referred to in Victor Hugo's *Toilers of the Sea*. Hereabouts the hero Gilliat resided in his haunted house.

Seven hundred and fifty metres up the coastal road is a small signpost to the **Déhus Dolmen**. Turn right and immediately left into King's Road and at the top of the hill, behind some bushes, is the dolmen. The light switch is encased in the wall on the right after entering the gateway. From the low entrance visitors pass through a passage 3.4m long and 1m wide into a main chamber 6.15m long by 3.4m wide. This is one of the most impressive passage tombs in north-west Europe and the second largest in Guernsey.

Outside the main chamber, but accessible from it, are four side chambers. Seven capstones of enormous weight roof the tomb. The first capstone at the west end is 4.6m long, 2.3m wide and 1m thick and made of crystalline rock allied to granite. On the under surface of the second capstone a bearded figure is carved, possibly a pagan deity who acts as guardian of the tomb. To prevent the tomb from being broken up for building stone an enlightened Guernseyman, John de Havilland, bought the site in 1775 for £4.10s, and it was excavated in 1837 by F.C. Lukis. His original plan shows a circle of 30 stones. The name, Le Déhus, and its variants, come from the Germanic element *dus*, (old Norse *dys*, Danish *dysse*), meaning a cairn or barrow, and was given to an area of the Clos du Valle mentioned as early as 1307 in the Rent Rolls of the Priory of St. Michel du Valle.

The Channel Islands yacht marina

The marina is due south of Fort Doyle in the north-east corner of Guernsey. Pontoons are illuminated at night and there are ample water and electricity points. Limited repair facilities are available at the marina, major repairs and overhauls arranged in St. Sampson's Harbour or St. Peter Port. Fuel is available from a barge situated in the marina. Charges are calculated on overall length of craft. Permanent berths are rented on an annual basis. Besides marina offices, there is a restaurant and snack bar. Facilities include brokerage, car hire, chandlery, grocery and off-licence, showers, public telephone, local weather forecast and mail delivery service. Ample car parking is available close to the pontoons.

The main coastal road turns west at its northernmost point and runs along the south side of **L'Ancresse Common**. Turn right where the main road bears south (7.5km) to **L'Ancresse Bay**. Duke Robert, father of William the Conqueror, on his way to England to help his cousins Alfred and Edward against

Canute, is said to have met contrary winds and put his fleet into this northern bay for anchorage. L'Ancresse is probably a corruption of 'L'Ancrage'. L'Ancresse is also a Celtic term from the Breton 'ankelhier', meaning 'that which goes round', circular. Open to northerly winds but sheltered from easterlies, the bay has a large sandy beach with a café nearby, and chairs for hire.

Lanes across the grassy headlands lead to **Fort le Marchant** and **Fontenelle Bay**, with a sandy beach and excellent bathing. Available for hire are chairs and floats. The whole of this coastline was fortifed with forts and Martello towers during the Napoleonic threat and many are now popular picnic places.

Watch Tower No. 5,
Nid de l'Herbe, L'Ancresse, Vale

Golf

On L'Ancresse Common are the golf links. By a leaning loopholed tower in the north west corner are the Royal Guernsey Golf Club and L'Ancresse Golf Club. The former club received its Royal Warrant in 1891. Green fees are only issued to visitors who are members of a recognised golf club. Use of the course is not permitted before 17.00 on Sundays and no round shall commence after 12.00 on Thursday and between 12.00 and 17.00 on Saturday. Holders of green fee tickets are entitled to the use of the R.G.G.C. facilities. Clubs can be hired. The 18-hole course is 5619m and 70 is par.

In and around the golf links many prehistoric monuments have been discovered, including the single chamber megalithic tomb **L'Autel des Landes** by the sixth tee box, a megalithic complex 30m south of Martello tower No. 7 with a few uprights and a capstone, and, by the 17th green, **La Varde Dolmen**. The last is the largest megalithic structure in Guernsey, with an 11m long chamber, 4m at its widest point and 2.15m high. The tomb has six capstones, the largest nearly 5m long, 3.23m wide and 1m thick. There was originally a circle of small standing stones of 20m diameter surrounding the tomb. By the fifth green a burial chamber has been discovered in excellent condition.

From Chouet at the north-east section of the island **Grand Havre Bay** sweeps round to the loopholed tower on the south peninsula with many superb sandy beaches divided by rocky islets. In old charts Guernsey is shown as two islands, the north and very much smaller one being separated from the remainder at high water by a narrow channel, the east end of which was St. Sampson's harbour and the west end Grand Havre Bay, near Vale Church. This small island was known as Clos du Valle and that part of the quay at St. Sampson's, named The Bridge, was so called because at this point a bridge spanned the narrow channel. The congregation using the Vale Church on the main coastal road had to cross by boat. In 1805 the isthmus seen at low tide was filled in.

Vale church

Where the coastal route turns south down L'Ancresse Road (1km), on the right is the church of St. Michel du Valle (Vale church), built on an early Christian site. Christianity was brought to Guernsey from Brittany in the 6C by the Welsh saints Magloire and Sampson. The church was consecrated in 1117 and is believed to be on the site of a church connected with the priory of Mont St. Michel. In 1949 an early Christian monument (7C), was unearthed outside the west door, indicating the presence of a Christian community on this site.

There are traces of monastic work visible in the present church, especially in the mouldings and capitals and in the irregularity of its layout. No angles are square, no walls parallel and the main axis of the chancel is out of line with the main axle of the nave. This is attributed to the monks' wish to bear in mind Christ's body upon the cross. On the south wall can be seen a piscina, of which the church contains four. The head carved above the pulpit, usually taken to represent a lamb, is probably a mason's mark. The church is poor as regards ancient vessels. It was united with St. Sampson's for 200 years and, when a division was decided upon, the sacred vessels remained the property of the latter. The masonry of the windows on the north side as well as the doorways on the west form a type of hood moulding which can be seen from the outside of the building. The church tower is reached by an outside stairway. The three medieval bells which had been in service for at least 500 years were taken to London in 1891 for restoration and renovation.

Leaving the Vale church on the right, the coast road skirts the southernmost section of Grand Havre Bay along L'Islet Rd. To visit the Megalithic Tomb, Cist and Circles complex at **L'Islet** turn left down Sandy Lane and continue to L'Islet Methodist Church at the north end of Rue Carré. Walking along Sandy Hook Rd, take the first left fork, then the next left turn which is a cul-de-sac.

The complex, one of the most interesting prehistoric monuments, is sited at the far end on the right, behind a house. The main oval enclosure is at the south-east end, and outside it is a small circle of seven stones. Adjacent to it is another circle, 3m in diameter; within this is a cist 1.5m long, 3.5m wide and 0.5m deep. On the north side and outside the main circle is another circle of boulders 2.5m across, of which the south side forms part of the main oval circle. Adjacent to it is another small cist. Within the main enclosure is a rectangular megalithic tomb, 2m long and 0.75m wide. Its long axis lies east to west instead of the usual north to south. At the west end is a 2m sq antechamber with a south-facing entrance.

The L'Islet road bears to the right into the Route de Picquerel section, along the main coastal road (11km) to the bay of **Port Grat** (pleasant bay, from the Breton 'gratant', pleasing). The curving, sandy beach offers good bathing at high tide and has a restaurant nearby. This coastline has rocks and reefs of pink granite, unique to this area. The road next passes three small bays, starting with the Péqueries (11.5km). Portinfer (12km) has a pebbly foreshore with some sand as the tide falls. The name comes from the Breton 'porthfa', meaning harbour. Port Soif (12.5km) is a shallow circular bay, with rock headlands, sandy foreshore, and bathing at half and high tide. 'Soif' is probably a corruption of 'scorf', meaning an outlet from a pond; the form and appearance of the bay support the surmise that this may have been a pond in earlier times.

To the west of Port Soif is the **Grandes Rocques** peninsula surmounted by a

German fort, which as a lookout post provides panoramic views over much of the north-west coast. The fort marks the north end of Saline and Cobo bays and Fort Hommet marks the south end. At low tide the reefs on the sandy beaches divide the two bays. **Saline Bay** has good bathing and plenty of rock pools to explore at low tide. Amenities include restaurants, cafés, chairs, floats and toilets. At the end of Saline Bay on the left is Cobo Rd which leads inland and back to St. Peter Port.

The coastal road continues straight on and to the right is Cobo Bay. 'Caubo' is an ancient family name, from the Welsh 'Cau' or 'Co', meaning hollow or enclosed, and 'Bo' meaning bay. A long house, which used to accommodate both people and animals, was found in this area. In it was French pottery of the 10C and 12C. There is good bathing and often good windsurfing but certain areas are marked on the maps as having dangerous currents and it is wise to heed local warnings. At low tide there are wide stretches of sand and in the pools are often found colourful sea anemones.

Vazon Bay, the next along, has Fort Hommet at the north end and Fort Le Crocq at the south end. At certain times stock-car racing takes places on the sands of Vazon Bay. At one time much of the island was covered in a peat bog and part of a peat bed is sometimes uncovered by storms at Vazon. This bay, once a forest, is said to be haunted by a sow and her litter foraging for acorns that grew in the oaks long since submerged. The apparition is known locally as *La coche du Vazaon* (the Vazon sow). Vazon itself is of Norman French derivation meaning marsh, inundated place or place covered with mire. A section of the bay is marked with black and white chequered flags and car and motorcycle racing takes place on the sand fortnightly during the summer. There is a large, open expanse of sand and rocks with good bathing at the south-west end and surfing is also popular here.

Between Fort Richmond (8km), a disused fortress on the north headland, and Fort Saumarez (10km) on the south peninsula lies **Perelle Bay** (Perelle is the Celtic word for rock). The bay is protected by an enormous reef, good for shrimping and ormering.

Le Tricoteur Factory, where the traditional 'Guernsey' sweater is knitted, hand finished, and sold, is found by the centre of Perelle Bay. The sweaters are knitted in many colours and in sizes that will fit a small child to a giant.

On the peninsula between the end of Vazon and Perelle Bay stands the second largest of Guernsey's existing menhirs. **La Longue Pierre** (The Long Stone; La Pierre de L'Essart; the Witch's Finger) stands 8m above sea-level in line with a low overgrown wall bounding a field north of a driveway leading to a private house, near the end of the Point Le Crocq. The granite standing stone is 3m high, 1m wide at its broadest point and nearly 1m thick. At its base were found pottery and stone mullers. In a field north are the scattered remains of a megalithic tomb and 23m east of La Longue Pierre is the menhir at Le Crocq; this red granite tapering stone is just over 2m high.

Near the disused battery of Le Catioroc, midway between Fort Richmond and Fort Saumarez is a signpost to **Le Trepied Dolmen**. This stands on a flat-topped hillock at the end of Le Catioroc Point, 11m above sea-level and within 50m of the coast. F.C. Lukis began excavations here in 1839. The chamber is 6m long, 1.25m high and 2m across at its widest point.

This dolmen is prominent in folklore. Between 1550 and 1650 many witches

Le Trepied Megalithic tomb at La Catioroc

(so-called) were burned at the stake 'for practising the damnable art of sorcery'. Confessions from witches who held their sabbath on Friday nights testified that the devil in the form of a black goat called 'Baal Berit' or 'Barberic' sat on the centre of the three capstones at Le Trepied while witches, warlocks and fairies danced around in worship chanting 'Que hou hou, Marie Lihou' in mockery of the shrine of Notre Dame de Lihou on the nearby island of Lihou.

The third largest megalithic tomb in Guernsey, **Le Creux ès Faies**, is 20m above sea-level on a hillock in the middle of L'Erée promontory. Just south on the coastal road, take the last turning to the right before the L'Erée Hotel along the Rue du Braye; the tomb is 300m away, adjacent to the road. The entrance faces east and the tomb is partly buried in the hillock. The interior of the chamber is 5.5m long, 3m wide at the west end, 2m high and roofed with two giant capstones each 5m long and 3m across. Legend maintains that this was an entrance to fairyland and that fairies sallied forth on Friday night to join in the revels at Le Catioroc.

At the end of the peninsula is a car park with a memorial plaque to the crew of MV *Prosperity* which went down on La Conchée reef in 1974. On this dangerous coastline, it is possible to cross Lihou causeway to Lihou Island at low tide, but no crossing must take place during the rising tide, particularly if any part of the causeway is awash. *Lihou* is a Celtic word meaning sea mud.

The ormer

The ormer (the English name came from the French 'oreille de mer', sea ear) is a Guernsey delicacy. It is a Mediterranean species of mollusc and the Channel Islands are its northernmost limit. It may be taken only on four days of each year (on the day of the new moon and the succeeding day in both January and February) and must not be less than 8cm in diameter. Duncan's *History of Guernsey* records: 'An eye witness of the ormer fishing, on the 9 March 1841, it being a low tide, computed that, in the bay of La Perelle, there were at least 200 persons who, in 3 hours, caught each, on average, 100, making 20,000 ormers.' The colourful empty shells of the ormer were exported for inlay work and the making of imitation pearl buttons. They are still seen as decoration in garden walls on the island.

Lihou Island

Originally Lihou was a pagan sanctuary, and early Christian missionaries, rather than compete with old religious beliefs, sought to take over and adapt these sites of worship. In an area noted for the number of vessels coming to grief on the surrounding dangerous reefs, the monks claimed the 'right of wreck', which made them unpopular with the local fishermen and there was trouble about the tithe. The monks claimed that the fishermen did not hand over the just amount of their catch and only gave them coarse fish. When the religious insisted on accompanying fishing expeditions, the catch was always small. Hence the local superstition that a clergyman on a boat is unlucky and brings poor catches.

The priory of Notre Dame de la Roche, whose ruins were excavated in 1838, is believed to have been founded in 1114 and linked to the Vale Priory. Documentary evidence of the priory's existence is to be found in a Papal Bull issued in 1156, where it is listed among the properties of Mont St. Michel. The last recorded appointment of a Prior was in 1560 and in 1656 the priory was recorded as being in a ruinous state. There was also an iodine factory on the island. There are some attractive rock pools here, Venus's Bath and Nun's Bath; the former is big enough for bathing.

On the main coast road by the hamlet of L'Erée there is an inland road which returns to St. Peter Port.

St. Peter Port via the south to L'Erée

South-east, south and west coast

From St. Peter Port, by the South Esplanade, the road divides three ways. On the left the road leads round to the Dive Centre. The road straight on and up the hill along Le Val des Terres joins Fort Road at the top, which takes its name from Fort George. The fort was built between 1782 and 1812 to protect St. Peter Port from naval attack. It is now a residential development. Soldier's Bay, next to this estate, is within walking distance of the old military hospital and was used by generations of soldiers for bathing parade, hence the name.

Diving
Havelet Bay is home to Guernsey's largest Dive Centre. It has a charter boat service out to wrecks and reefs, PADI training centre, and a shop which hires and sells diving equipment at competitive prices. ☎ 714525.

Eight hundred metres down Fort Road, just after a post box built into the wall, is a road left to **Fermain Bay**. Fermain is Breton and means strong rock. The bay is situated at the bottom of a densely wooded glen 500m from the main road. It is an attractive place for bathing, with sand at low tide. At high tide care must be taken as the beach shelves steeply. There is a loop-holed tower on the green. No parking facilities exist. However there are other means of getting to the bay. There is an attractive and highly recommended cliff walk which is well signposted and runs from St. Peter Port to Pleinmont Point passing Fermain Bay. There is also, during the summer, a boat service from St. Peter Port harbour to Fermain Bay. The trip takes 30 minutes and the service is half hourly with a lunchtime break.

Sausmarez Manor
The main road continues south. Just before the war memorial (2.52km) on the right is **Sausmarez Manor** (not to be confused with the manor of Admiral

Sausmarez Manor

Saumarez in Câtel). Captain Philip Sausmarez died in action at the age of 37 after sailing round the world with Anson in the *Centurion*. On this voyage the Spanish *Manilla* treasure ship was captured—the richest prize ever taken. The log of this historic voyage is kept at the Manor, which is built on the site of a house erected in Norman times. In the 18C it returned to the family. Since that time the house has had Regency and Victorian additions and today it is an interesting mixture of many periods, a fine example of an hereditary seigneurie and one of very few island manor houses open to the public.

Dolls' houses

The Doll's House Collection is to be found in a tudor barn in the grounds of Sausmarez Manor, St Martin. **Open** Thur–Sun 10.00–16.00 Nov–Christmas. Closed Jan and Feb.

Anyone interested in the world of miniatures will be fascinated by this collection. The earliest of the dolls' houses date from 1830 and the present owners believe that it may have been made by an estate worker for the children. Where hard facts are not available, the owners of the collection have allowed their imagination to help them weave stories and circumstances to explain each house. There is a 'Hobbies' house which comes from Hobbies Ltd of Dereham, Norfolk, a firm which used to supply fretwork outfits, carpentry tools and patterns. This house was made in Malta about 1925 and on the walls are pictures of King George V, Queen Mary and the Prince of Wales, made from pre-war cigarette cards. The Williamsburg House is a modern American house sold in kit form, with even the wallpaper already in place when purchased. In 1970, when the *Reader's Digest* published a do-it-yourself book which contained a plan for a doll's house. A sergeant in the Royal Marines made this one for his daughter. Great ingenuity has been displayed in the furnishings, the four-poster bed is made from cardboard and biros.

There is a 'Mouse House' made c 1930 by the great toy company Lines Bros., better known as Triang. Against all natural laws the mice seem to be keeping a pet cat, which has a kitten in a boot. There is also a Dolls' House Shop which sells houses, kits, tiny shops, furniture, miniatures, DIY items and books.

By the war memorial there is a left turn for **Jerbourg Point** (2km). This peninsula is flanked by the jagged rocks of Long Pierre and Pea Stacks. Descend the slopes between granite outcrops. The Doyle monument used to stand here before it was destroyed by the Germans. After World War Two it was replaced by a column. There is an abundance of gorse and wild flowers and excellent views of Icart Point, the cliffs of Saint's Bay and Moulin Huet. Lt-Gen. Sir John Doyle

---

Fortress Guernsey

Nowadays, the Channel Islands has become a military backwater, but this is only a recent state of affairs, since for centuries the islands have lain in the forefront of British defences against invasion from the continent. This has provided a rich heritage of earthworks, castles, towers, forts and batteries. Hence, recently, the Tourist Board of Guernsey, and Heritage Committee, have co-operated in this presentation of their bailiwicks' military history over the last 2000 years. As a result an ongoing programme of interpretation, conservation and restoration of selected sites is underway along with the production of new publications and audio-visuals.

---

drained the inlet between the Vale and St. Sampson which used to divide Guernsey.

The cliff walk south of Doyle Column leads west; from it a long flight of steps descends to **Petit Port**, one of the best sandy beaches on the island, along with its neighbour **Moulin Huet**. The south coast cliff and beach scenes around Moulin Huet Bay inspired most of the pictures painted by Renoir on his visit to Guernsey in 1883 (see pp. 113–114).

To reach Moulin Huet by road, there is a left turn by the war memorial, then a second left off the main road is for Ville Amphrey. This road leads to one of the water lanes, a covered spring supplying the stream which ripples down between the granite kerbing where formerly housewives did their washing. At the bottom of the water lane is a left turn for Moulin Huet followed by a right fork.

In the centre of Moulin Huet Bay is the **Cradle Rock** and on the cliffs at the west end are the **Dog and Lion Rocks**. Notices advise people not to cross over from Moulin Huet to Petit Port at low tide because of the speed of the rising tide. Cradle Rock used to be called 'le bateau treis garces' (the boat of the three maidens) because three young local girls fell asleep there unaware that the tide was rising. As none could swim and no-one heard their cries for help, they were drowned. La Vier Port is the old name for Moulin Huet. There are attractive tea gardens in the vicinity, as well as Moulin Huet pottery, where potters can be seen at work and products purchased along with oil paintings and watercolours in the studio above the workshop. **Open** all year Mon–Sat 09.00–17.00; Sun 10.00–12.00.

Returning to the turning for Moulin Huet, the main road continues to the northwest; signposted on the right is St. Martin's church in the Rue d'Eglise.

St. Martin's Church

St. Martin's is one of the six parish churches granted by William in 1048 to the Abbot of Marmoutier in France. It is thought that the tower and chancel, which are part of the present church date from the late 12C and early 13C. The tower is dressed in pink granite. The nave has a vaulted roof and probably dates from the 15C as does the elegant south porch in decorated period style of English Gothic. The font dates from before the Reformation and then saw service as a pig trough at a local farm before being returned in 1869 to its rightful use. The church was earlier known as St. Martin's de la Bellouse and is believed to be on an early pagan site where the deity Bel was worshipped. By the churchyard gate

Statue -menhir, La Gran'mère, St. Martin's churchyard

is a figure, La Gran'mère de Chimquière, which dates from pagan times. This menhir figure appears to be wearing a cloth head-dress, the bottom of which hangs over the shoulders like a very short cape, leaving the breasts below exposed. Although this sculpture is 6C BC, just over a century ago offer-ings of fruit and flowers were still being laid before her in the hopes of fortune and fertility. Later she came to be known locally as 'Julius Caesar's Grandmother' but adults still used to put coins on her head for good luck, which the children used to rush over and collect once the depositors were out of sight.

The road to the right round the side of the triangle crosses over the main road and becomes Saint's Rd leading to **Saint's Bay**. The bay is said to have received its name from the fact that the Archbishop of Rouen landed here with the lady for whose love he had denied his vows and sought refuge in Guernsey. It is popular for morning bathing, but loses the sun in the afternoon.

Icart Point is also reached by Saint's Rd but instead of going left for Saint's Bay, bear to the right along the Icart Rd. From Saint's Bay there is a cliff path which also leads to Icart Point, the most southerly headland in Guernsey.

The cliff path continues west past the inlets, La Bette Bay and Le Jaonnet Bay. The former is inaccessible and descent to the latter difficult, but worth the effort if you like bathing from a quiet sandy beach.

The main road by St. Martin's church, continues west for Forest Church on La Rue Maze, which becomes Les Cornus Rd and then Forest Rd. Forest Church is the last turning to the left before the main entrance to the airport on the other side.

Forest Church

Another one of the six churches attached to the Abbey of Marmoutier in 1048, it used to be called La Saint Trinité de la Forêt. The church, dedicated to Ste. Marguerite, is on the site of a pagan shrine and some of the large stones in the foundation are believed to be from the Dolmen of Le Trépied des Nouettes which was once here. The present church has elements of 15C and 16C architecture in the earlier south aisle; the church was completely renovated in 1891.

German Occupation Museum

The by-road round the west and south sides of Forest Church reaches the German Occupation Museum. **Open** in summer (until 31 Oct) 10.30–17.00. In winter Sun and Mon 14.00–16.30; fee.

The German Occupation began on 30 June 1940 with the arrival of the first troops at the airport. The **Entrance Hall** of the museum contains a painting of Germans marching through St. Peter Port on this day, as well as a model of a

German officer in full uniform. There is a long showcase of weapons and equipment, including a gas mask worn by soldiers at the time.

The **Equipment Room** contains further apparatus, particularly that linked to communications, telephones, transmitters and the printing blocks used by the Occupation Forces. The **Newspaper Room** has old newspapers, evacuation posters and written orders of the German Commandant. The **Occupation Kitchen** shows some of the food improvisations available to the people and the occupiers during this grim period. The **Map and Bunker Rooms** demonstrate how the Channel Islands were the most fortified sections of Hitler's Atlantic Wall. Maps and photographs illustrate the defences which included huge battleship guns with a 37-mile range and a light railway for carrying materials from the harbour to fortifications round the north and west coasts. A tableau shows off-duty soldiers in a bunker. Next door is a tea-room.

A small granite menhir forms the corner of the wall at the junction of Forest Road and Rue de la Croisée, the nearby left turn prior to that leading to Forest Church (see above). This stone, **La Perron du Roi** (the King's Mounting Block), is approximately 1.5m high and 50cm at the base, tapering towards the top. It has three sculptured cupmarks suggesting it was connected with early pre-Christian worship. At one time it was a boundary mark of the Royal Fief and later a mounting block for the horsemen of 'La Chevauchée de la Cour de St. Michel du Valle'. Like the stones in the church foundation, it is believed to have been part of La Trépied des Nouettes.

The Rue de la Croisée winds south-west through beautiful scenery before coming to the **Petit Bot**. This small cove divides St. Martin's parish from the forest and at low tide has a large expanse of sand. The Martello tower by the granite slipway was, during the Occupation, a machine-gun post. On the east side is a chimney cave by the high-water mark which leads through the headland to a gulls' colony. On the west side is another cave with a double entrance cut into the granite cliff. **Portelet Bay** is adjacent and can be reached by a cliff path. Portelet, diminutive of French 'port', meaning bay or inlet, provides moorings for boats by its large cave, and the relative inaccessibility of the beach leaves it uncrowded. It is a good place to swim, with plenty of sand at low tide.

Returning to the cliff path, continue along the Sommeilleuse cliffs with superb views, to **La Moye Point** and **Le Gouffre** which, as the name implies, means a gulf between cliffs. The scenery hereabouts is savage and beautiful, with a turbulent sea foaming white around the rocks below. (Le Gouffre can also be reached by car from Forest Church. Follow the Rue d'Eglise south and at the crossroads bear left and then take the third right down the Rue du Gouffreé a distance of 1km.)

West along the cliff walk, the next headland is La Corbière, below and in from Le Havre de Bon Repos, 3km from Portelet. It is difficult to descend to the beach here because towards the bottom there is a danger of landslide. Venus's Pool lies at the east end of the beach and is left full of clear water like a swimming bath when the tide recedes.

The cliff path circumvents a German tower which replaces the old lookout known as La Préote and the cliffs begin to diminish in stature as the path reaches **La Creux Mahie** (3.5km). This famous cave is 57m long and 18.5m wide. The entrance is small. It used to be an island showpiece but a rock fall by the cave opening has made it dangerous and unwise to enter.

The next wild headland is Les Tielles (4km) and then Belle Elizabeth (5km).

The path goes to the cliff edge here and two needle rocks are visible below. The bay is inaccessible. Nearby is the best-preserved watchtower of this coastline, a granite building with stone chimney called Mont Herault (5.5km) and just beyond is a car park. There is access on by-roads leading south from the main Pleinmont Rd via Les Tielles Rd to Les Tielles and by Rue du Mont Herault to Belle Elizabeth. Both by-roads are approximately 400m (see above).

From the car park Lihou Island is visible across the Pleinmont headland on the right.

In view are the TV masts of the BBC Relay Station and a prominent German tower. Follow the cliff path towards another lookout tower and then enter a valley where there is a stream. For a view of the magnificent blowhole, follow the stream to where it falls and bear left along a rocky platform to a cleft; there on the left is **Le Souffleur**. The best time to see and hear it is two hours after the tide has begun to come in. When the sun is shining several small rainbows form.

Returning to the main path continue west up to a new headland, La Congrelle. Soon a German fortress dominates the headland and just off the coast is Gull Rock. There are many inlets along the coastline from here to the end of the walk at the car park by Fort Pezeries (8km).

This is the most rugged part of the whole coastline. Two kilometres offshore lies the famous **Hanois Lighthouse** which was first lit in 1862 after countless lives had been lost on the surrounding reefs. 'Hanois' is the Celtic word for agony. Beyond the car park is La Table des Pions, a ring of boulders encircling a patch of turf. Pions were young men dressed in black caps, white blouses, trousers and stockings who accompanied a ceremonial procession of dignitaries to inspect the highways and by-ways. By the time the land's end was reached the Pions were ready for refreshment which they had here.

The main road west from Forest Church turns left at the next crossroads down Rue de la Villiaze and a first right down the Rue du Manoir. This is the main road nearest the coast which runs to Pleinmont. At points to the left by-roads run nearer to the coast.

The Rue des Peltiers is on the left and bends round to join the Rue de la Prevote with a car park at the end (see above). At 10.5km left is Les Tielles (see above). Second right after this is the Rue de la Belle turning for Torteval Church (11km).

Torteval Church

Originally the church was devoted to Our Lady but the dedication was changed to St. Philip. The ancient building was demolished and replaced by the existing church in 1818. The architect was John Wilson who designed an unusual round tower and high round steeple rising from a low parapet. It houses the oldest bell on the island, cast in France in 1432.

Twelve kilometres left is Rue du Mont Herault. One kilometre further on is an important crossroads. (It is possible to turn left down the Rue des Plains and come out nearer the coastal region by Gull Rock or continue on up the Rue du Chemin le Roi which ends at the car park by La Table des Pions.) To reach Pezeries Point, the most southern point of Rocquaine Bay, turn to the right up the Rue de la Cloture, turn left at the T-junction, take the first right up the winding Rue de la Mare, and then the first left along the Rue de Pezeries.

A kilometre east of Pezeries Point via the coastal road is the fishermen's cove of **Portelet** with its boats, quaint lighthouse and cottages. In the centre of the bay is a causeway to **Fort Grey**, now a maritime museum with much information on the wrecks that have occurred in this area. 'Rocquaine' means Ledge of Rocks. The word 'Caine' has three forms, 'Caine', 'Kaine', and 'Quaine'.

Fort Grey Museum is under the aegis of the States Heritage Committee along with Guernsey Museum and Art Gallery and Castle Cornet. **Open** May–Sept every day 10.30–12.30; 13.30–17.30. An inclusive ticket can be purchased giving admission to all three.

Fort Grey, Rocquaine Bay and Lihou Island, Guernsey

Fort Grey was built in 1804 to defend Guernsey against the French. It was manned during both World Wars and served as a German anti-aircraft battery during the Occupation. The exhibits from dozens of ships that have gone down off the coast of Guernsey are fascinating and marine archaeologists, through careful excavation of wrecks, have built up an interesting picture of what life aboard ship was like at different periods during the last three centuries.

On the other side of the coastal road nearby is the Guernsey Coppercraft and Pearl Centre, useful to shoppers looking for a gift to take home (**open** daily 09.30–17.30) with traditional copperware being produced Monday–Friday.

Rocquaine Bay is the largest bay in Guernsey and sweeps round a curve of 4km to L'Erée.

Inland Guernsey

Guernsey has a number of sites—churches, manor houses, museums and cottage industries which lie just inland from the coastline. Those which have not already been mentioned lie in four of the ten parishes—Castel, St. Saviour, St. Andrew and St. Peter-in-the-Wood.

Castel

The **Church of Ste Marie du Castel** lies practically in the centre of the island, close to the crossroads La Rohais de Haut and the Rue du Presbytere. It is situated on the site of the ancient fort known as Le Château du Grand Sarazin. The Guernsey people used the word 'Sarazins' (Saracens) for Vikings, because of their cruelty. The church was built in the 12C and was a possession of the abbey of Mont St. Michel.

The north aisle is the oldest portion of the building. Early in the 19C, under the whitewash of the north wall, 13C frescoes of the *Last Supper*, and of the *Three Living* and the *Three Dead* were found. At one time a cannon was brought into the church and a breach was made in the north wall where it could be used for defence purposes. This has now been filled in. In 1878 a granite statue-menhir was discovered under the floor of the north chancel. A female figure believed to be 3000 years old, it is similar to menhirs found in ancient gravesites in France. It probably originated with the mother-goddess cult of the Neolithic and Bronze Age people. Two metres high, this statue now stands on the north side of the church entrance. On the south side is a granite trough with the sun and moon inscribed on it. The mouth holes allow water to drain off. Probably 16C, it rests on a red granite block. On nearby flat stones the Fief St. Michel held feudal court and collected dues from tenants here until 100 years ago.

Off Les Deslisles (St. George's Road) going north is, 750m on the left, **St. George's Manor**, one of the loveliest old manor houses in Guernsey. Washing in water from the 'Holy Well of St. George' in this area was a guaranteed cure for maidens suffering from eczema and an aid to them in the seeking of a suitor. At the end of this main road is a left turn into a one-way street which leads to the main crossroad of Cobo Rd.

Saumarez Park

Opposite on the left is Saumarez Park, formerly the home of Admiral Lord de Saumarez, one of the most famous Channel Islanders and a former Vice-Admiral who entered the British Navy at the age of 13.

Among his many naval successes was a battle of 1794 in which he out-manoeuvred five enemy frigates attempting to destroy his two ships. By heading

Green Lane Walks

Since 1992, the Guernsey branch of Friends of the Earth has been organising monthly walks as part of a 'Reclaim the Green Lanes' campaign, to raise public awareness of the green lanes and of the pleasure to be had walking safely away from the ever busier roads on the island. Guernsey's green lanes and water lanes are a unique legacy from a fast-disappearing past, and deserve wider appreciation. The lanes are peaceful and picturesque routes to walk and they harbour a surprising variety of wildlife habitats, providing considerable interest on the way.

The *Green Lane Walks* booklet available from the Tourist Board provides the rambler with information about opportunities to explore Guernsey's quieter lanes. There is also an organised walk on the last Sunday of every month, which starts at 14.00 and takes about an hour. Details are published in the personal column of the *Guernsey Evening Press* or the *Weekender* at the end of each month, or ☎ 01481 47679. There are also a series of walk leaflets, including cliff paths, published by the Board of Administration, which are available in the Tourist Information Centre at a minimal cost.

inshore as if to beach his ship he brought the enemy into the range of shore batteries while he slipped away safely through narrow channels. As Nelson's second-in-command he fought in the Battle of the Nile and he was the last British Admiral to fly his flag at sea in HMS *Victory*.

His Georgian Manor is now part of the National Trust of Guernsey and a home for elderly people. In the stable block at the back is sited the **Guernsey Folk Museum** (open Mar–Oct 10.00–12.30; 14.00–17.30; fee).

From the entrance, on the right is a Guernsey Kitchen of a century ago, with a lady taking a loaf of bread out of the furze oven, a table set for dinner and many examples of furniture and utensils used at this time, including bacon rack, dresser, baby's high chair, and a wooden box mousetrap. Opposite the front door is a glass case containing a changing display. On the left side is a **Victorian bedroom** with models of a farmer's wife in a half-tester bed with her new baby. Her small son and the midwife stand nearby. All are dressed in period clothes. On the day bed a baby's layette is laid out and other items include cradle, hipbath, commode and early feeding bottle. In the room off to the left is a temporary exhibition which changes its theme annually.

Leading from the courtyard is the **Cart Room**, with a collection of horse-drawn vehicles including a carroine, bosse (horse bus), vanne, spring cart, tambre, long cart with a double ox yoke which is common to Guernsey and other articles of interest including harness, panniers, straw saddle and a penny-farthing bicycle.

Upstairs in the **Plough Room** is a great plough, 12.5m long, set out for a mixed team of oxen and horse, smaller ploughs and farming equipment including seed drills and ox collars. The other end of the room has a display of a crab-pot maker's stand, fisherman's baskets and hooks.

Across the yard, opposite the entrance, is the **dairy** with wooden churns, milk cans, early equipment for measuring quantities of milk and butter moulds. Next to the stairs is a **wash house**, with copper and brass boiling pans, wooden washing machines and a selection of old irons. Upstairs, in the **tool room** is a display of different island stones used in building and as stone weights and corn grinders. In one corner are roof decorations including chimney pots, tiles and acorn finial. Along one side is a model of a quarryman using a spring-jumper to split stone. Another wall displays agricultural hand tools including wooden hayforks. Next door is the **Cider Barn** which contains a crusher driven by a horse mill and fed with apples from the loft above. The press, dated 1734, has an impressive wooden screw. On the wall, the Duke of Richmond's map (1787), surveyed by William Gardner, shows where cider apple orchards were situated. In the central courtyard is a collection of farming implements, including a hay loader and a barrel cart. Displays vary from time to time.

The main manor has a formal garden with a sunken lawn in front and the rest of the estate offers an interesting walk.

On the other side of Cobo Rd stands another famous manor, **La Haye du Puits**. It is said to have been built originally by Sir Richard La Haye du Puits of Normandy who, wishing to remain loyal to Henry II of England when Geoffrey of Anjou raised rebellion, fled to Guernsey.

In the construction he destroyed an old cromlech for which the islanders told him he would be cursed. Being superstitious, Sir Richard began to feel doomed and gave La Haye du Puits to the Church to turn into a nunnery, making it a condition that the nuns should pray that the curse be removed from him. Legend says that the guardian spirits of the cromlech were not to be appeased and the unhappy nuns became harassed and finally left. There is much superstition regarding the destruction of dolmens and it is often considered by the islanders to bring a curse upon the person responsible. Despite this many of the cromlech stones have been taken away and used in the building of homesteads down through the ages. La Haye Manor with its 18C turrets has been converted into private flats.

Some 250 metres from Saumarez Park on the Cobo Road back to St. Peter Port is the **Telephone Museum. Open** April to Oct 10.00–17.00. Free. Here you will see telephones and switchboards and other equipment used in the Bailiwick since the States Telephone Council was formed in 1896. Also close by, still going towards St. Peter Port and just by where the Friquet Road comes in from the north is Friquet Flower and Butterfly Centre. These beautiful myriad creatures are best seen on a sunny day.

St. Saviour

St. Saviour's church lies off Les Buttes where it meets Sous L'Eglise. The first mention of this church is in a charter of Duke Robert of Normandy around 1030 when he gave four Guernsey churches including St. Saviour's to the Benedictine abbey of Mont St. Michel in Brittany. This was confirmed by Duke William (later King of England) in 1048 and Pope Adrian IV (Nicholas Breakspeare, the only English Pope) in 1155.

The present church dates from the 14C and 15C and is the largest of the Guernsey country churches. It has a nave and north aisle, which are the oldest sections, with a square tower at its west end. A side chapel projects out of the nave. The vestry is contained in a small building, erected in the 18C to house a cannon and arms, at the left side of the north aisle. The height of the tower with its high weathercock is nearly 34m. Tradition has it that an argument broke out between the designers of the church as to whether the tower should be lofty or otherwise, when a stranger appeared and told them to build it as high as the church was long. He then vanished and, accepting this as a Divine command, the tower was built accordingly. During World War Two, the Germans used the tower as an observation post, constructing a chamber in the spire.

The bell-chamber is reached from inside the church by a narrow spiral stone staircase and houses two bells recast in 1680, and a third recast in 1865.

Among the church's possessions are two leather mugs dating from 1813 for taking collections and an unusual alms-box with two enormous padlocks, dating from the 17C. The church plate is of interest, for it includes a pair of silver chalices bearing the marks of the London Assay Office in the year 1664 and a pair of plates of local manufacture inscribed 'Plat a par Tenant a la pa royce de St. Sauveur 1699'. There are also large and small ewers, made in 1714 and 1729 respectively. In 1819 two clarinets were bought to accompany the singing and were replaced by a barrel organ which was still in regular use around 1850. Two men were each paid £1 a year to turn the handle and the barrels are now kept in a glass case in the church, having been replaced by a church organ. There is a menhir which serves as a gatepost at the northeast entrance to the churchyard, upon which monks have carved two crosses, one on either side. They are similar in style to the crosses appearing on the reverse of late Saxon and early medieval silver pennies.

Leaving St. Saviour's church on the left the Neuf Chemin Road runs north to

St. Saviour's Reservoir, an artificial lake shaped like a bird's claw which contains 240 million gallons of water and is controlled by a large dam. The reservoir is stocked with trout. Below the dam, at the bottom of the hill, is Mont Saint. A left fork along La Grande Rue towards the village of Perelle—400m on the right is **St. Apolline's Chapel**. Open all year round 09.00–20.00.

It is the oldest building in Europe dedicated to Apolline, the deaconess who was martyred by the Romans in 249 at Alexandria. Before being burnt alive, she had all her teeth broken and is now the patron saint of dentists and sufferers from toothache. The roof and thick wall of the chapel are made of stone, and the interior is a room 8.3m long and 4m wide with three narrow windows. A charter of Richard II, dated 1394, contains the first mention of the chapel, then known as 'la chapelle de Sainte Marie de la Perelle'. The 600-year-old building was, by the end of 1978, completely renovated and the frescoes and interior restored to their former simple beauty.

Descending the hill to Sous l'Eglise is **St. Saviour's Tunnel Museum**, one of many tunnels constructed during the Occupation, and now housing German military equipment including such items as field kitchens.

Guernsey Airport

Within 800 metres of the north-west corner of the airport are two workshops where shoppers can purchase Guernsey manufactured goods. They are the Bruce Russell Gold and Silversmiths, housed in a 16C farmhouse (Le Gron) and the Guernsey Woodcarvers, where visitors can watch cabinet-making and the sculpture of animals, birds and flowers (Les Issues).

St. Andrew's

Where Le Vauquiedor and La Brigade Road meet you see on the right Hangman's Inn and a granite slab with a cross on it. This is **Bailiff's Cross** which indicates the place where Gaultier de la Salle, a bailiff, received communion on his way to execution. His kinsman, Ranulph de Gaultier de la Salle, had accidentally killed a man whom he was arresting for murder. He fled the island and in time was pardoned by the king and returned to Guernsey. But he was imprisoned and then put to death by his kinsman Bailiff Gaultier. For this crime Gaultier was himself condemned to death and hanged at Courtil de Gibet in 1320; he may have halted at Bailiff's Cross on his way to the gibbet.

A legend about Bailiff Gaultier and his execution has it that he had tried to have a neighbour accused of theft. He hid two silver cups in his own hayrick and accused his neighbour of having stolen them. Just as sentence of death was about to be pronounced, Gaultier's servant rushed in saying: 'I have found the cups'. 'Did I not tell you not to touch that rick?' said Gaultier, making his guilt clear to all. He was himself then hanged in place of the innocent man.

Downhill, along St. Andrew's Road going west you see on the right St. Andrew's church, just after passing the incoming road L'Ecluse. The parish is the only one on the island with no coastline; the valley is noted for its beautiful flowers. The church used to be known as St. Andrew's of the Sloping Apple Orchard and is one of six assigned to the French Abbey of Marmoutier in 1048. Today's church has a square tower with a short spire at the west end of the north nave and is a mixture of 12C and 18C architecture. Like many other Guernsey parish churches St. Andrew's grew by accretion. Successive additions were made during the Middle Ages to simple stone chapels which probably replaced earlier wooden structures.

At the first crossroad after the church turn left down Vassalerie Rd (200m) to reach the German Underground Hospital.

German Underground Hospital

The hospital was built by slave workers of the Organisation Todt, some of whom perished and are buried in the concrete. The 2km of corridors which can be visited today are excavated out of solid rock—60,000 tons was removed. It took 3½ years to excavate and equip the place which was then only used for nine months. During this period thousands of tons of ammunition were stored here. The actual hospital section, which was designed to accommodate 500 patients, was only used for six weeks by German wounded brought over from France soon after D-Day. Their stay was hardly beneficial for after three weeks underground they acquired a deathly pallor. Walking the long damp passages with little to see is an unpleasant and forbidding experience, but no doubt of appeal to those interested in this period of history. **Open** April daily 14.00–16.00; May–Sept daily 10.00–12.00; 14.00–17.00; fee.

To reach the little chapel of **Les Vauxbelets** return to the crossroads, turn left and continue down St. Andrew's Rd which becomes Les Rues Frairies. At the T-junction turn left and then first right. 100m down Bouillon Rd is the entrance to the grounds of the chapel (5km). This little church, 5m by 4m, may be the smallest in the world. It was painstakingly built by Brother Déodat of the De La Salle Order of Christian Schools between 1914 and 1923 and is a near proportional copy of the Grotto and Church of Lourdes. It is decorated with ormer and other shells along with fragments of coloured pottery. Children love it. Although not consecrated, the church has been blessed by the Bishop of Portsmouth.

The Guernsey Clockmakers Workshop is close to the Little Chapel entrance where you can see barometers and clocks being made. It has a gift shop and entrance is free.

To reach the **Bird Gardens** continue along Bouillon Rd to staggered cross-roads. 200m down La Valliaze Rd on the left is this venue, designed to be of special interest to children, with a free car park and tea barn. Here you will see many aviaries rather overcrowded with a wide variety of birds including a large collection of colourful parrots, owls and vultures. Penguins are fed at 15.00 on weekdays and 16.00 on weekends. (**Open** 10.00–18.00; fee.)

St. Peter-in-the-Wood

Just west of Guernsey Airport off the main road La Route de Plaisance is a left turn by the post office down Rue des Brehauts which leads to St. Peter-in-the-Wood parish church. It stands on ground sacred before the Christian era and megalithic stones are to be found in the walls. One of these tapering stones laid horizontally in the corner of the east chancel is over 2m long, 0.5m thick and it juts out from the wall. The floor slopes upward from west to east. Note the decrease in the height of the pillars. Before 1294, when the church was destroyed by French invaders, St. Pierre du Bois was probably a two-celled church consisting of an altar house and small nave. The present larger church is mainly 14C and 15C with the sanctuary and nave being built first, a tower added on to the nave and the two side aisles or chapels being built later. Two of the south windows are different in form and size from the other nave windows; they are round-headed, contrasting with the pointed heads of the other windows. Two small chancel windows north and south show similar features. The construction here is early Norman. Because early medieval church builders preferred to patch and build where possible, it is logical to suppose that part of the south wall, the chancel walls and perhaps the lower part of the tower were left over from the earlier church.

There are several springs in the area; one is actually under the altar. The resulting rising damp has always been a problem and has lead to a lot of restoration being required through the ages. The belfry, reached by a spiral stone staircase from inside the church and wooden ladders, houses one 19C and two 17C bells. The earliest (1654) bears the inscription 'Melior vere non est Campana quam me' (verily there is no bell sweeter than me). The next one, cast in 1681, confirms this: 'Melior vere non est Campana quam es' (Verily there is no bell sweeter than he). The square tower is 35m high and commands an extensive view of the airport and of the old archery ground of the parish, Les Buttes.

To find La Longue Rocque menhir return to the post office, and go north-west along the Route de Longfrie. Carry on over three crossroads for 1.5km where, on the left side of the road, is Les Paysans Road, and just south of the house called Val des Paysans, in the middle of a field is La Longue Rocque. This is the largest of Guernsey's existing menhirs, nearly 3.5m above ground and 1m below. Menhirs such as these were symbols of fertility. Childless women used to rub themselves against them, hoping to become fruitful. Peasants also annointed the menhir with honey and beeswax, despite church edicts forbidding this superstitious custom.

Sark

The island of Sark, or 'Sercq' as it was called by the Normans, is 5.5km in length, and 2.5km in breadth. Sark is 13km east of Guernsey and hangs like a pendant on the map, with the largest northern section, Big Sark, being joined to Little Sark by a narrow land link known as La Coupée. The poet Swinburne wrote of it as 'a sweet small world of wave-encompassed wonder'.

Its exceptional beauty is a gift of nature and the islanders have endeavoured to keep it that way, forbidding the use of cars and lorries. This out-of-the-way large rock, part of the Bailiwick of Guernsey, rises straight out of the sea like a fortress, with 350 foot cliffs topped by rolling fields known as *côtils*. These are carpeted with bluebells, daisies, buttercups, scabious and white campion in the spring and early summer. During this period, flocks of migrant birds arrive and depart. It is possible to wake up one morning and see the whole island covered with thousands of migrant birds. Butterflies are abundant, and flutter from flower to flower. Granite cliffs provide a haven for myriad seabirds, with puffins breeding off Little Sark.

The main disembarkation point nowadays for passenger boats arriving at Sark is **Maseline Harbour** on the east coast. From here visitors who have come to stay are met and driven by tractor to the top of the steep harbour hill with their luggage, where they usually transfer to a horse-drawn carriage which takes them to their hotel.

Two tunnels lead to **Creux Harbour**. The first was cut by Helier de Carteret in Armada year, the second in 1866.

Day visitors without luggage who decide to walk from the jetty to the plateau have a steady climb of 70m (c 20 minutes). The jetty just below the tunnel was completed after the war and opened in 1949 by the Duke of Edinburgh. It is an excellent spot for offshore fishing once the boat crowds dissolve.

In the next bay south is the old **Le Creux** harbour which is picturesque but nowadays only used if the wind is in the wrong direction for landing at Maseline. At high tide the clear water in Le Creux is pleasant to bathe in and usually remarkably calm, particularly when compared with the tide around **Les Burons**, opposite. At the top of the plateau are the crossroads at **La Collinette**. It is from here that day visitors must decide which way to go and what to see, according to the time available.

Derrible Bay, the Hog's Back and Dixcart Bay

To reach Derrible Bay and the Hog's Back, turn left at La Collinette, follow the road which bears left at 100m and continues a further 200m to **La Forge**. At the top of the gradient is a large barn. On the right take a path that follows a hedge to the cliff top. From here a steep path on the left zigzags down to Derrible Bay (1km, 40-minute walk) which has a lovely sandy beach when the tide is out. Under its cliffs are caves eroded by the sea. Two of these lead to the bottom of **Le Creux Derrible**, and the view to the top, some 30m above, is dramatic. To look down through this creux it is necessary to return towards La Collinette and where the path breaks into the field path to La Forge turn left by a dew pond

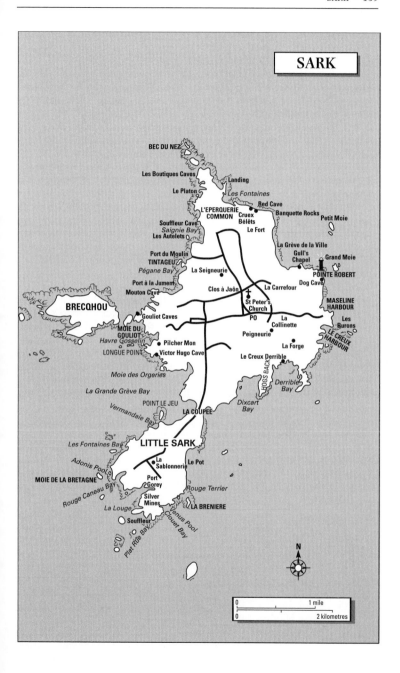

SARK

BEC DU NEZ

Les Boutiques Caves

Landing

Le Platon

Les Fontaines

Red Cave

L'EPERQUERIE COMMON

Banquette Rocks

Petit Moie

Cruex Béléts

Souffleur Cave

Saignie Bay

Le Fort

Les Autelets

La Grève de la Ville

Port du Moulin

Gull's Chapel

Grand Moie

TINTAGEU

Pégane Bay

La Seigneurie

POINTE ROBERT

Port à la Jument

Clos à Jaôn

La Carrefour

Dog Cave

Mouton Cave

St Peter's Church

MASELINE HARBOUR

BRECQHOU

Gouliot Caves

PO

La Collinette

Les Burons

MOIE DU GOULIOT

Peigneurie

LE CREUX HARBOUR

Havre Gosselin

Pilcher Mon

La Forge

LONGUE POINT

Victor Hugo Cave

Le Creux Derrible

Moie des Orgeries

HOGS BACK

Derrible Bay

La Grande Grève Bay

POINT LE JEU

Dixcart Bay

Vermandaie Bay

LA COUPEE

Les Fontaines Bay

LITTLE SARK

Adonis Pool

La Sablonnerie

Le Pot

MOIE DE LA BRETAGNE

Port Gorey

Rouge Terrier

Silver Mines

Rouge Caneau Bay

LA BRENIERE

La Louge

Souffleur

Venus Pool

Clouet Bay

Plat Rûe Bay

N

| 0 | | 1 mile |
| 0 | | 2 kilometres |

downhill through an ivy-carpeted wood. Where the path forks go left, continue to the top of the creux. It is difficult to look down to the bottom because vegetation grows out over the edge.

To reach the Hog's Back return to the fork in the path, turn left and follow the path to the ridge. Derrible Bay is on the left and Dixcart Bay on the right. On a clear day, beyond the seascape, the outline of Jersey is visible. At the end of the headland is an old cannon.

The cliff descends sharply on the west side to where a rocky ledge can be seen, offering excellent swimming and fishing. A path below an outcrop skirts the edge of an inlet to reach a rocky slope from where the ledge is accessible.

At very low tides there are caves on either side of the headland which can be investigated. However it is advisable to seek local advice before setting out to explore them.

Sark's surrounding cliffs are indented with fascinating caves, but it must be remembered that the tides run dangerously fast in this area and it is easy to get cut off. Therefore those visitors who come to Sark mainly for this purpose would be advised always to seek local information and to purchase a local guide to caves (such as that of G. and L. Latrobe) and to let someone know where they are going before setting out.

Access to Dixcart Bay is most easily obtained by turning right by the Peigneurie Cottages which are 200m down the road from La Collinette and 100m before La Forge. Continue south from the cottages down **Baker's Valley**. A footpath to the right circumvents **Petit Dixcart** and bears left down wooded **Dixcart Dale** to **Dixcart Bay** (1km, 35-minute walk). The popular and delightful beach shelves gently and is a safe bathing place for children, with plenty of sand at low tide. There is also great scope for cave exploring. On the east side, by a pinnacle rock, is one of the longest caves on the island (115m) which terminates in a circular chamber. On the north side stands a natural arch.

La Coupée and Little Sark

From La Collinette the road west (straight on) is **The Avenue** which passes the **post office** (right) and the local prison (left). Diminutive **Sark Prison**, built in 1856, is a two-man jail with a rounded roof. It is allowed to hold prisoners for a maximum of 48 hours.

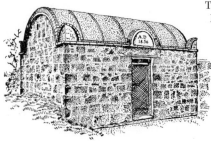

The road continues, becoming Mill Lane; to the left is a conical tower which is the old mill built by the first Seigneur in 1571. It stands on the highest point in the Channel Islands. At the end of Mill Lane (1km) turn left and follow the main road south for Little Sark.

In just over 1km is the awe-inspiring **La Coupée**, which attaches **Little Sark** to **Big Sark**. It is 80m above sea

Sark prison

> ### Sark stones
> Sark is famous for its stones which are extremely beautiful, and gems such as amethysts, emeralds, cats' eyes, crystals, agates and cornelians in varying degrees of purity have been found.

level. The causeway of concrete and iron railways was built by German prisoners under British military supervision at the end of the war.

In previous times the tenants on both sides used to say that maintenance was the responsibility of the other side. It is reported by the Serkese that children crossing over from Little Sark in strong winds on the way to school at the end of the last century did so on their hands and knees.

The roadway is now 3m wide and 100m long. On the east side there is a sheer drop to the Convanche Chasm. On the west side, the descent, although steep, can be made via steps down the eroded cliff to **La Grande Grève Bay** (2.25km, 50 minutes). There is good bathing here and, with a west wind, good surfing, as well as offshore fishing. Off **La Pointe le Jeu** at the south end of the bay are islets which are covered at high tide. Because of the noise made as the tide rises and falls over them, they are known as **The Slobberers**. In due course erosion by the sea will create a strait between the two land masses, as has happened between Herm and Jethou.

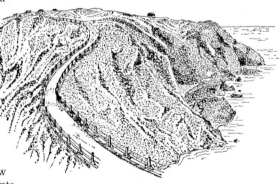

La Coupée and La Grand Grève Bay

The ribbon of road now climbs between steep banks covered with heather and thyme and soon after the summit reaches a bungalow called Clos de La Pointe on the right. Opposite, a gap in the bank leads into a field where a path crosses to the cliff top. From here a path descends to the second largest creux on the island, **Le Pot**. Descent via the Pot requires nerve but is possible. Bathing is not good but for the purposes of collecting Sark stones, this bay, the two sides of La Coupée and Derrible, are the best places.

Returning to the road and continuing to the hamlet, a left turn leads to a white gate where the lane divides. Entering the gateway, leaving the flagpole on the left there is a signpost to **Rouge Terrier**. From here, a path down the cliffs leads down to flat rocks and excellent bathing. At high tide the current runs fast between the mainland and the island of **La Brenière**, but at low tide you are able to walk across and examine this islet with its interesting arch.

Returning to the white gate, follow the path to the left; this runs between banks of gorse to a stone tower. This is an airvent of the old **Silver Mines** which were started by Peter Le Pelley, a seigneur. The venture failed miserably as the yield was small and the only export shipment sank. The mines were worked around 1835 and one shaft is said to have descended 150m below sea-level. Nearby paths lead to Port Gorey, the south tip of Sark and Venus's Pool.

The path furthest east leads eventually to Venus' Pool (4km, 70 minutes). It descends to a shaley cliff top. Continue down the headland adjoining **Clouet Bay**, descending along a sandy vein and once on firm rocks bear around to the north. Venus's Pool is tucked into the headland, on the Clouet Bay side. The pool, 6m deep and very transparent, is uncovered for two and a half hours either side of low tide. The rocks around its symmetrical edge are comfortable for sunbathing.

At low tide an interesting scramble can be made around the south coast to Port Gorey, passing **Jupiter's Pool**, **Plat Roé Bay**, **Gorey Souffleur Cave** and other pools and caves. An L-shaped gulley which makes the outer rock an island is soon reached. The top of it has a tunnel leading through the headland into **La Louge**, an inlet with precipitous walls. On the north side is a rock platform containing Gorey Pool. Further round at the point of the rocks a way up exists and it is possible to scramble right round into Port Gorey. From here a path returns to the Silver Mines.

To do this scramble it is essential to judge the tides correctly and to allow plenty of time.

Adonis's Pool, probably the most beautiful of all, is reached by following the road from La Coupée to the end and turning to the right just before the last bungalow. On coming to the fields turn left until the gorse is reached. The path here bears south-west and from the cliff tops Rouge Caneau Bay can be seen on the left, with many small pools and islands at low tide. Facing is Moie de la Bretagne, a long islet. Between the mainland and this islet, 100m below, is Adonis's Pool (3.5km, 60 minutes), just south of a large detached rock. The way round is to the right and the most difficult part is a deep gulley which has to be crossed. (To succeed make use of a boulder at the north end.) The pool is 6m deep, completely transparent and fringed with picturesque patterns of seaweed. Adonis's Pool is exposed for two hours either side of low tide and the tide rises rapidly.

The next bay north, **Les Fontaines**, can be reached from the mainland opposite Adonis's Pool by footpath. From La Coupée, walk along the main road past **La Sablonnerie Hotel** (with tea gardens and cottages); just beyond the last cottage on the right is a path which doubles back and leads to this attractive bay. Les Fontaines is very sheltered and bathing and sunbathing are excellent, particularly in the afternoon.

A long scramble from Les Fontaines Bay to Vermandaie Bay is possible at low tide but only by quick climbers, and if the longer journey to La Grand Grève is to be attempted one must start early. The arch at Pointe le Jeu must be reached before the tide turns. The scenery around this part of the coast is magnificent, particularly when a south-westerly is blowing and tempestuous seas are breaking along the reefs.

Pilcher Monument, Havre Gosselin and the west coast

From the La Collinette crossroads to the end of Mill Lane (see p. 140). At the disjointed crossroads at Vaurocque continue west, passing on the right a duck pond. The road now turns left past the Beauregard guesthouse and then right. The track comes to Pilcher Monument, a sort of granite Cleopatra's Needle. The monument was erected in memory of a London merchant, J. Pilcher, who with three companions lost his life at sea returning to Guernsey in 1868 in an open gig.

Below on the right is Havre Gosselin (2km, 25 minutes). Many fishing boats used to moor here but now it is mainly visiting yachts which use the haven. Occasionally, when wind will not permit landing elsewhere, boats from Guernsey disembark passengers here. There is good shelter from northerlies, easterlies and southerlies in this bay, but westerlies bring Atlantic rollers. Beneath the south flank of Longue Point headland is the Victor Hugo Cave. It is dangerous to visit without a guide and can only be reached by boat or by swimming. There is often a strong undertow here and at Moie des Orgeries.

Havre Gosselin Bay on the west coast was used as a harbour when easterlies closed Creux; a jetty was built in 1912. The anchorage is protected from north, south and east winds, but not from south-westerlies.

Across the Havre Gosselin Bay, looking north, an entrance to the Gouliot Caves and to the left Moie du Gouliot and the Isle of Becqhou are visible. To visit the Gouliot Caves retrace the route to the lane junction. Turn left and continue to the right. When the lane ends by a collection of bungalows, go round the one on the right and pick up a path which passes through the hedge and bears left. Go through a gate and follow the path leading to the headland opposite Brecqhou Island. At the neck before the rocky part a footpath bears away to the right along the top of the gorge which runs to the edge of a small rocky promontory. Turn left here across the sloping shoulder of rock to the worn foot track. The **Gouliot Caves** can only be visited during low ebb of a spring tide and descent is not easy. The walls and roofs of the sea-sculpted caves are beautifully studded with red, pink, yellow, green and white anemones.

To go from the harbour directly to the Gouliot Caves, cross over the Vaurocque crossroads and turn right after the duck pond through a gate. From here a path leads to the headland opposite Brecqhou. The distance to the caves is 2km; allow at least two hours for a visit and return journey to the crossroads at La Collinette. A walk to the headland only takes 25 minutes.

Brecqhou Island, the satellite of Sark, is one of the 40 private and heritable farms from which the Seigneur is entitled to receive dues.

To overlook the sandy beach of **Port à la Jument** (2km, 30 minutes), turn right at the Vaurocque crossroads instead of going straight on and at the next T-junction turn left. This road leads out towards Hotel Petit Champ and a zigzag lane which veers down to the beach. From here it is possible at low water to enter **Mouton Cave** which is 100m long and heads through the Moie to the south side. It is the most dramatic single cave on the island (a torch is required to see it properly). The beach at Port à la Jument is popular with families and it is possible to scramble at low tide round into Pégane Bay and then between the mainland and Tintageu island into Port du Moulin.

La Seigneurie, Port du Moulin and Le Platon

One of the joys of Sark is its graceful old houses, and the finest of these is La Seigneurie, the manor house, whose beautiful walled garden is open to the public from 10.00–17.00 (fee) on weekdays during the season. Dame Sibyl Hathaway (1884–1974) was a keen gardener, and the semi-tropical plants have flourished in this garden.

Sark church

To reach La Seigneurie (1.25km, 20 minutes), cross over La Collinette and continue along the avenue westwards.Turn right at the post office, passing **St Peter's church** built in 1820, with bells cast from field guns belonging to the Sark militia, the hall and the picturesque old school house on the right.

Continuing north over Clos á Jaôn crossroads, on the left are the wrought-iron gates of **La Seigneurie**. The residence of the Seigneur, Mr Michael Beaumont, is on the site of the 6C monastery of St. Magliore. Two chapels used by the monks can still be seen close to the house, surmounted by stone crosses.

The present house was begun in 1565 and enlarged in 1730 by the Le Pelley family when they purchased the island. From the central path of the walled garden there is a good view of the new signalling tower built by the Rev. W.T. Collings when he became Seigneur. When the fine trees in the grounds were threatening to block the views of the signalling tower used to contact Guernsey in emergencies, rather than cut them down the Seigneur built a new signalling tower. Behind the residence is the Gothic style Seigneurial dovecote and a collection of small cannons, including one inscribed 'Don de sa Majesté la Royne Elizabeth au Seigneur de Sercq, AD 1572' which Elizabeth I gave to Helier de Carteret for his success in establishing a thriving and loyal community on the island which had become a den of pirates and was under continual threat of invasion from the French. Elizabeth I also showed her royal pleasure by making Sark a Fief Haubert. This is the highest form of land tenure whereby the fief holder owes fealty to the Crown alone and has no intermediaries.

The present Seigneur still holds the island in perpetuity from the Queen, provided he swears an oath of allegiance and keeps a force of 40 men loyal to the English Crown, with 40 muskets at the ready. This is how the 40 tenements were founded—the Quarantaine—which have been the basis of Sark's feudal administration to the present day.

The feudal structure and the banning of cars has had the effect of suspending time in Sark, so that this smallest independent state in the Commonwealth is also one of the biggest attractions for the visitor.

Port du Moulin, 'the Port of the Mill' (2km, 24 minutes), is the nearest bay to the Seigneurie. The name arises from the days when the monks built a watermill hereabouts. At the end of the Seigneurie Wall follow a track turning left which ends in a path above L'Ecluse. This path bears left and down to Port du Moulin. On the way is a window cut in the sheer face of the rock 75m above the sheltered beach.

Vraic used for farming was at one time winched up here from the beach. Swimming is safe and pleasant at high tide. At low tide there is access to Les Autelets, three granite columns standing clear of the cliff and providing the nesting home of a variety of seabirds. At very low tide it is possible to scramble from Port du Moulin to Le Platon. The passage through the natural arch at the north end of the bay should be undertaken as soon as the descending tide allows. The next beach, Saignie Bay, has good sand and bathing for those not wishing to continue. At the far side of Saignie is Souffleur Cave which has a branch through to the next gulley. The rest of the scramble is over reefs and through crevices. The last section of the journey is the most difficult but there are places where one can clamber up onto the headland if necessary. At the end of the trek a steep path leads up from the rocks of Le Platon to the headland. This is a long scramble and one must not delay en route—again because of the tide.

L'Eperquerie Landing, Les Boutiques, Banquette Landing, Grève de la Ville and Sark Lighthouse

To reach L'Eperquerie Common continue along the road north past La Seigneurie. The common at the end of this road is covered with purple heather in the summer; in the spring bluebells and primroses abound. A track leads down to L'Eperquerie Landing (3km, 35 minutes), where Helier de Carteret and other settlers landed. On the cliff behind the landing are two old cannon and foundations of a 16C French fort.

Les Boutiques Caves follow the path leading from the Common to the most northerly point of Sark–**Bec du Nez**. Just before a tower is a deep gulley cut into the cliff with a small pathway. On the right-hand side, half-way down the gully, is the chimney entrance to the caves. The bottom of the cave slopes down to the sea and with a torch an aperture can be found into the main cave on the far side. Here two openings lead to the sea while on the right two branch caves run inland. Straight on, a long tunnel exits at the north end and the headland can be regained from here. These caves can be visted at low tide.

Midway along L'Eperquerie Common a turning to the right leads down to **Les Fontaines** (2km, 35 minutes), a rock-strewn bay with good swimming except at low tide. At the north end are two rock archways christened by Sark artist William Topliss R.A. *The Fairy Grotto* is his famous painting.

Towards the other end of the bay are **Fern Cave** and **Creux Bélêts**. From Creux Bélêts it is just possible on an ebb spring tide to scramble round and back to Red Cave (sometimes called, because of its shape, Horse Cave).

Beyond Creux Bélêts a track ascends to Le Fort. A path from Le Fort runs through a cottage yard, down a gorge with a stream on the right, west to **Banquette Landing** (2km, 35 minutes). The flat Banquette Rocks offer excellent picnic spots, afternoon sunbathing and deepwater swimming. The views are

A Sark artist

Ethel-Sophia Cheeswright 1874–1977, when she died on 30 November 1977, was 103. At her funeral service the Rev. Mallard of St. Sampson's spoke of her as '... a choice soul ... richly endowed socially and used to privileges, her artistic gifts made her famous. She chose to live in Sark for wonderful subjects for painting.' She produced a large body of work, including some oil paintings and at least one exquisite ivory miniature, but her most favoured medium was watercolour. She explored the island of Sark and the seas around, enjoying scrambling and walking over the huge cliffs and fishing for mackerel off the coast.

She spent most of World War One on the island, and all went smoothly until various representatives of the German Army turned up on Sark after the outbreak of World War Two. In February 1943 she was deported to France, and eventually was moved with other Channel Islanders from the camp in France to Wurttemberg, Germany. She was nearly 70 by this time, with very poor eyesight, yet she continued, in any way she could, to practice her art. A Red Cross nurse on occasion would take her outside the camp, where she could find a spot among the woods or hills to draw and paint. Sometimes the Red Cross were able to supply her with materials, but if not, she would save the wrappings from bread and chocolate sent in Red Cross parcels, and smoothing the creases out of them, she used them to produce sketches of the camp and the other prisoners.

She was not able to return to her beloved Sark until after the war. But as soon as she arrived she found her source of inspiration again, and was still painting in her eighties. When she was 95 she retired to live in Guernsey.

magnificent with the wild rocks of the Petite and Grande Moie just offshore. To the south are the cliff, caves and beach of La Grève de la Ville.

To reach **La Grève de La Ville** (1.5km, 30 minutes), turn right at La Collinette. Continue up the next crossroad at Le Carrefour, turn right down the Rue Pot to the T-junction. Turn right here and follow the road round to a common and then cross this diagonally to the north-east. The path to the bay is on the south side of a dale. On the beach is a natural arch called Chapelle des Mauves (Gull's Chapel) and there are many caves to explore. Dog Cave, seen at very low tide, has a total length of 75m. It has two side shoots and a barking noise is heard as the tide and wind begin to rise inside.

Sark lighthouse

This lighthouse operates automatically and viewing is by appointment only. Check with the tourism office. The views alone make this a worthwhile visit.

It is sited on Pointe Robert which is visible just before entering Maseline Harbour. To reach it by foot turn right at La Collinette and 200m further on turn right again down Rue Hotton. At the T-junction turn left and then next right. This leads east to the lighthouse itself.

Herm and Jethou

Herm

The island lies midway between Guernsey and Sark, 32km from the French coast, 32km from Jersey and 5km east of Guernsey. The island is 2.5km long and 1km wide. At high tide the coastline circumference is 7.25km. At low tide this expands as enormous areas of sand and rock are exposed. Of the island's 202 hectares, 40 are cultivated and support a Guernsey herd. The rest is made up of woods and grassland.

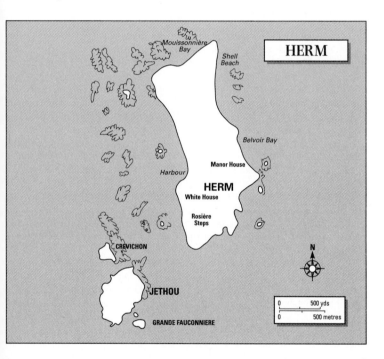

History of Herm

The history of Herm goes back to 3000 BC when Neolithic man inhabited the island. Excavations in 1840 exposed pottery, tools, weapons and ornaments which indicated an advanced Aryan culture. Other relics seem to indicate that the Romans traded here. Later the Duchy of Normandy annexed Herm along with the rest of the Channel Island archipelago. After the King of France conquered Normandy, but not the Channel Islands, the population on Herm dwindled. In 1569, Queen Elizabeth I annexed Herm to the See of Winchester but by the 17C no-one was living on the island. The export boom in quarried stone during the 19C lead to a population of 400 people living and working on Herm and the steps leading from Carlton House Terrace, London, were quarried on the island. After this export ceased, a northern England industrialist, Colonel Fielden, in 1867 leased the island from the Crown and, with the help of money he obtained from smuggling French cognac into England, built a private estate. In 1890 Prince Blucher Von Wahlstatt obtained the lease and built roads, planted trees and even tried to introduce wallabies. Between the two World Wars Sir Compton Mackenzie and then Lord Perry held the lease. During the German Occupation infantry and tank landing exercises were filmed here and shown in Axis countries under the title *The Invasion of the Isle of Wight*. In 1949 the island was leased to Major and Mrs Peter Wood. Its natural peacefulness and beauty attracts many visitors.

From St. Peter Port it takes 20 minutes by boat to reach Herm harbour. On the pier stands a 100-year-old crane, still used today. Up a pathway lined with fuchsias and hydrangeas is a little village, with stone cottages, gift shop and post office. Until recently, all postage from Herm had to carry a Herm stamp as well as a post office one to defray the cost of transport to Guernsey. When the village post office came into being in 1969 these stamps were abolished and they are now eagerly sought by philatelists. The **White House**, a colonial-style building, is now an attractive hotel with a good dining room and varied menu. In 1924–40 this was the home of the late Lord Perry. On the other side of the village is the Mermaid Tavern, a granite-built fishermen's inn with a walled garden filled with roses and geraniums. There is a snack bar and restaurant here.

Four hundred metres south of the village are **La Rosière Steps** jutting into the **Blue Lagoon**. This landing stage is used at low tide. The rest of the south half of the island from the harbour round to Belvoir Bay offers a splendid cliff-path walk from the southernmost tip of which the private island of Jethou (joined at low tide) is overlooked.

The north coastline has excellent beaches, mostly surrounding a large common, which is studded with megalithic tombs, many of which were discovered and investigated by the archaeologist Frederick Corbin Lucus during the 19C.

From the harbour a footpath north passes between an old cemetery on the east and skirts, to the west, **Monk's Hill** (Le Monceau), where a small bronze cannon stood in the 18C and was fired once a year on Guy Fawkes' night. The path now turns inland before again bearing north with Le Grand Monceau hillock to the east and Le Petit Monceau to the north-west. Along the whole length of the north perimeter of the common is **Mouissonnière Bay**.

On the beach is a megalithic tomb and on a little island stands an obelisk where the menhir La Longue Pierre once stood. Running half-way down the island from the north-east tip is the renowned **Shell Beach**. For thousands of years the sea has constantly renewed the deposits of minute, delicately coloured seashells. There are said to be over 200 varieties and 40 genera. Among the shells are some not usually found in the northern hemisphere. They would appear therefore to have survived a long journey via the Gulf Stream and the Gulf of Mexico.

Just south and adjacent is **Belvoir Bay**, also with an excellent beach and interesting shells. This bay can be reached by crossing over the island directly from the harbour. En route the 18C turreted Manor House is passed. Surrounding it are a castle keep, farm cottages and the old chapel of St. Tugual. The site of St. Tugual replaced the original church site on the small stretch of land which once joined Herm to Jethou and where St. Magloire first built a chapel in the 6C, before a storm in the 7C separated the two islands. Remains of this chapel were still on view at low tide during the last century. According to the *Histoire des Eveques de Coutances*, Herm at one time formed a parish with Sark and the Bishop of Coutances was 'patron' of the parish. In 1480, Geoffrey, Bishop of Coutances, instituted Brother William Guffart of Notre Dame du Voeu (near Cherbourg) as the curé of the parish church of St. Tugual of Herm. Today a family service is held on Sundays by the present tenant, assisted by the island children.

Puffins on the cliffs of Herm Island

Jethou

Jethou is a small island separated at high tide by a narrow channel (500m) from Herm. A hill jutting out of the sea with a circumference of 2km, it has a flat top and an area of c 8 hectares. It is privately owned and not open to the public. This island's history has been closely linked with that of Herm. A 'Druid's Stone' above the landing stage on the north marks the entrance to Fairy Wood and on the south is Keitholm Wood. Both are carpeted with wildflowers including bluebells and primroses in the spring.

The offshore islets of **Grande and Petite Fauconnière** in the south and **Crevichon** in the north are bird sanctuaries and the nesting-place of hundreds of puffins. On the flat hilltop daffodils and early potatoes are cultivated and the old quarry at Crevichon is said to have provided the steps at the Athenaeum Club in London. On the east side is a raised beach and north of Fauconnière Bay is a blow-hole or creux known as Devil's Hole. At very low tide the two islands of Jethou and Herm almost become one.

Alderney

Alderney (2068 inhab.) stands athwart the **Race**, a treacherous tide race which separates it from the mainland of France. The **Swinge** on the west side is, as the name implies, nearly as dangerous. The island is 13.5km from the coast of Normandy, 5.5km long and 2.5km across at its widest point. Having visited the only town, St. Anne, in the centre, the rest of the island is best seen by a walk round the coast, a distance of some 19km. This can be done in a day, or in a more leisurely fashion if you have the time. Many by-roads, lanes and footpaths link the centre to the coast, so that it is easy to continue a walk started the previous day.

Coach and minibus
Daily services are available offering around the island tours from the first week in July until the third week in September. Two companies offer these tours, Alderney Tours and Leisure Group and Riduna. Bookings for the former can be made at Le Boutique in Victoria Street or by ☎ 822611. Bookings for the latter can be made at The Alderney Gift Box in Victoria Street. Cost for adults at the time of going to press is £4.50 and children between 5–12 years travel half price. The trip takes approximately 1.5 hours.

Boat trips
If you would like to see the island from the sea, and some of the offshore nesting-places for sea birds, there are two boats, both licenced to carry 12 passengers that offer round the island trips of approximately 2.5 hours. They are the Voyager (bookings can be made at McAllister's Fish Shop in Victoria Street, t: 823666), and the Jung Frau (bookings through The Alderney Gift Box, Victoria Street, ☎ 823352). If you suffer from seasickness you should be warned that the sea off the island can become choppy. However, this is a really worthwhile trip especially for those interested in wildlife. Fares at the time of going to press are approximately £12 for adults, and half price for passengers under 12 years of age.

Rail trips
Since 1980 the **Alderney Railway Society** has been operating a return service between Braye Road and the Quarry on the old Mineral Railway track (every half hour at summer weekends; fee). This is the only standard gauge railway in the Channel Islands, starting operation in July 1847 when quarrying was Alderney's major industry. Rolling stock includes a steam locomotive.

St. Anne
St. Anne is the capital of Alderney, with three-quarters of the island's population. It stands in the centre of the island. During the 18C the town was formally referred to as St. Anne and called parochially by the islanders 'La Ville'. On Chevalier de Beaurain's map of 1757 the town is marked 'La Ville ou St. Anne'. Unlike those of Guernsey and Jersey, this major settlement is over 1km from the main harbour and on high ground in the centre of the island. It appears to have been selected for agricultural reasons, in that it is within easy walking distance

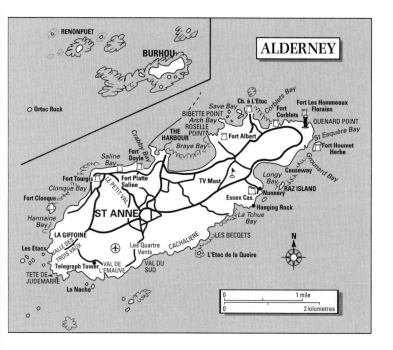

of La Blaye (derived from '*blé*' meaning a cultivated cereal crop). Here the open-field system of agriculture so prevalent in north-west Europe after the collapse of the Roman Empire in the 5C was applied. The date of its introduction on Alderney is not known.

La Blaye runs from La Giffoine in the west to La Haize in the east, adjoining and circumventing St. Anne, with the south boundary running almost to the cliff edge. It is good agricultural land and in 1941 the Germans planned to turn these 1000 vergées (the Channel Island measurement—c 182 hectares or 450 acres) into one of the main grain supply areas for Guernsey. In medieval days this land was divided into strips known as '*riages*'. Part of the west end of La Blaye has now become Alderney Airport. Beyond La Blaye were the commons separated by earthen banks where the cattle and sheep were allowed to graze, and the important fertiliser vraic (seaweed) was collected from the beaches at Clonque, Saline, Crabby and Braye bays. At Le Huret, formerly an open piece of level ground near the vicarage of St. Anne, the farmers assembled to decide when the vraic should be cut and carted.

Today the cobbled streets of St. Anne, its brightly painted shops and little houses, retain the atmosphere of an old French town. The southern section around **Marais Square** and **Le Huret** was the original settlement. This expanded when the Crown leased Alderney in the late 14C and several Guernsey families arrived to settle here. They have such names as Ollivier, Le Cocq and Simon. Meanwhile, around the same period other families bearing such names

Clock tower of the old church of St. Anne

as Herivel, Gaudion and Blott came from Normandy. Many of the street names bear witness to this immigration and the expansion of the town now took in Le Bourgage. Venelles (narrow lanes) soon provided the right of way to important wells in the vicinity as well as access to and from La Blaye. Rue des Vaches, now Little Street, became the cattle route between pastureland and the water supply.

Alderney's first courts were held in the open at Le Huret, which runs between Marais Square and the High Street. Before Marais Square was paved, there was a stream running through it in which housewives did their washing. The High Street did not become important until the 18C, although it was the main route leading to Longy, the island's ancient port.

During the 18C–19C the town of St. Anne expanded and grew in importance. In 1770 the open-air Court moved into covered quarters in the Rue de Grosnez. The Rue de Grosnez was renamed Victoria Street to commemorate the visit of Queen Victoria on 9 August 1854.

In 1763 the former **Government House** was built by Governor John Le Mesurier on the north side of St. Anne's Square, which was to become the Royal Connaught Square following a visit by the Duke of Connaught in 1905. In 1779 Peter Le Mesurier built **Les Mouriaux House**, the island's most elegant residence. On his father's death it became the Governor's home and later that of the first President of the States of Alderney. The Old Governor's House has now become Island Hall, a community centre with a library. In the square opposite is a chestnut tree planted by Queen Elizabeth II. Practically opposite Les Moriaux House, with its entrance in Petit Val, is the Alderney Pottery, which sells a range of craft products.

Alderney Society's Museum

In 1790 John Le Mesurier founded the town school and the inscription is recorded over what is now the Alderney Society's Museum which houses a collection of the island's treasures; the most important are items from the Iron Age settlement, which include Mesolithic and Neolithic implements (8000–6000BC) such as axeheads. discovered at Les Huguettes, Longy. There are also items recently found from a late Elizabethan wreck—Alderney's very own *Mary Rose*. **Open** Mon–Fri 10.00–12.30; 14.00–16.00.

The dangerous waters off the coast of Alderney has long been known as a graveyard of lost ships, and the greatest discovery in recent years has been an Elizabethan wreck that may be one of Drake's squadron which repelled the Spanish Armada in 1588.

It is recorded in State Papers that an Elizabethan vessel was cast away off Alderney in 1592 and it is probable that the newly-discovered vessel could be

The Makeshift, which would make her the only remaining ship-of-war from the reign of Elizabeth I.

Hundreds of artefacts have been raised of which half are pottery shards, but other items include muskets, knives, breastplatesand a very attractive pewter smoking pipe. Interestingly enough tobacco had only been available in England a very short time at this period. The greatest find and achievement was without doubt the raising of a cannon and its carriage in 1994. It measured 2 metres 34cm and weighed 1400lbs. The cannon has now been transported to York for conservation. This work takes about five years, after which the weapon will be returned to Alderney and put on public display.

Beside the **Old School** is the **Clock Tower**, which is all that remains of the old parish church of St. Anne, demolished when the church in Victoria St was built. The grounds of the present parish church are entered through the Albert Memorial entrance, a granite arch with wrought-iron gates, opposite Olliver St.

Parish church of St. Anne

The new parish church of St. Anne was designed by Sir Gilbert Scott and conse-crated in 1850 by the Rev. John Le Mesurier, son of the last of the hereditary Alderney Governors. It was designed in the transitional style from Norman to Early English Cruciform to hold a congregation of both the garrison and the islanders. Its proportions are extremely pleasing to the eye. Good use has been made of warm Alderney sandstone and white Caen stone against a background of well-spaced trees. The nave has 18 arches and where the transepts cross three steps lead to the chancel with its floor of black and white stone.

During the war the **Court Room** was stripped of its fine furniture. It was finally restored and opened by the then Home Secretary Major C. Lloyd George on 8 September 1955, when for the first time since 1940 the Jurats wore their formal robes. In 1957 when Queen Elizabeth II presided she was presented with a Loyal Address and this, with her reply, may be seen outside the Court Room.

Victoria Street became important with the building of breakwaters and forts and it is now the main shopping centre in St. Anne. The northern end of this street ends in a T-junction. Going left and immediately right past the Methodist church to Butes, winding paths down the hillside rejoin the Braye Road for the harbour. From the north end of the Butes are panoramic views, across **Braye Bay** and the fast tidal waters of the Swinge, to the bird sanctuary at **Burhou** and the helmet-shaped **Les Casquets**, the graveyard of numerous ships. It is here that the '*Blanch Nef*' carrying Prince William, son of Henry I, went down returning from Normandy. Today, one of these rocks still retains the name 'White Rock' in memory of the drowned prince.

The Casquets, Alderney

The coast

It is best to begin at the main harbour and proceed in a clockwise direction. The harbour was enlarged in 1847 when the construction of an enormous break-water was begun to provide safe anchorage for the British navy and merchant ships. It proved to be a white elephant costing over £1.5m and the plans for the right arm were abandoned. The annual maintenance of what was built imposes a heavy financial burden. **Braye** is Alderney's largest bay with plenty of sand surrounding a rocky centre. Two windsurfing schools operate here. Bordering the lower road was a grassy verge, Le Banquage, where vraic used to be dried. It is now the site of a new housing estate.

On the right are verdant slopes running up to Les Rochers with its TV mast. The west end of the bay has a series of buildings referred to as **The Arsenal** and a driveable road ascends from the main road at Whitegates up to **Fort Albert** (1.5km). During the war this was the most important fortification on the island, with garrison accommodation for 2000 soldiers. This fort and the **Hammond Memorial** just to the east are reminders of the dreadful life of the Todt slave labourers under the Nazi regime. Fort Albert is the kingpin of a chain of defences started in 1847 to defend the weakest points of the island. They begin in **Clonque** on the east coast and are spaced around the shoreline running north and then east to Essex. There are 13 in all and none along the precipitous south coast. During the Occupation the Germans re-fortified most of them.

The north end of Alderney between Braye and Longy Bay is low lying and makes up about one third of the island. It is here that the beaches are safest and best. The south end rises to a cliff line some 90m above sea-level. The pattern is similar to that of Guernsey. Around by the north-east wall of Fort Albert is the near-symmetrical sandy beach of Saye. This, along with the adjoining beaches of Arch Bay and Corblets Bay, between Château à L'Etoc and Fort Corblets, offer the best bathing. In 1886 Fort Corblets (2.5km) had six mounted guns which had fallen into disuse by the turn of the century. It was re-fortified by the Germans and then after the War converted into an unusual but attractive home.

Just east of the residence is the strange Rocque Bertram which is easy to climb and gives a good view of the inlet the Veaux Trembliers, Fort Les Hommeaux Florains and Cats Bay. In its heyday Fort Les Hommeaux Florains (3km) was covered with Victorian fortifications and linked by a man-built causeway, traces of which can still be seen. It was here that the famous wreck of the *Liverpool* took place in February 1902. All her cargo was salvaged when she rested with her four massive masts still under sail on the rocks. Finally, all efforts to save her hull failed and several months later she broke up. Many ships have sunk off this north coastline where the Race and the Swinge meet.

Alderney lighthouse

There was no warning light until 1912 when the Alderney lighthouse was built. Locally it is referred to as Mannez (pronounced 'Moanay'). The tower contains a lamp of 400,000 candle power with a range of 27km and a foghorn that lives up to the title 'Moanay' wherever you happen to be on the island.

Continuing round, Quénard Point marks the west end of Cats Bay. On the headland, near the lighthouse, is another fort.

A path runs from **Fort Quénard** south to Longy Bay and overlooks the Race. On a clear day the cliffs of Le Cotentin can be seen on the French mainland. At the south end of the next inlet, St. Esquère Bay, is the causeway leading to the ruins of Fort Houmet Herbe (3.5km). Its 68-pounders used to guard the rocky approaches to Gournard Bay and their mountings can still be seen. With the dangerous Brinchetais Reef so close by, the Germans did not bother to re-fortify it. Both these bays are very rocky and only the occasional sandy gully could attract the bather.

The next fort is at the end of the causeway across Longy Bay on Raz Island. It has now become a restaurant with good inland views of the Hanging Rock and Fort Essex, renamed Essex Castle (5.25km). Victorian defences, called the **Longy Lines**, extended below the hillside of the fort, but the building itself does not appear to have gun emplacements, being used mainly as a military hospital. The Germans, however, fortified it. When the original fort's foundations were being laid a prehistoric burial-ground with capstones was discovered. Bronze implements and human remains were excavated. Among the many megalithic structures destroyed during the 19C was the island's only recorded menhir, La Pierre du Vilain, which was erected by Longy pond.

Near the **Causeway** is a peat bog, indicating the presence of ancient forests. The bay itself is large and open with a long sandy beach at low tide and the best way to the west end goes across this. Here is the Nunnery, with a curtain wall over 5m high enclosing a rectangular area.

The Nunnery

The history of the Nunnery is obscure. Archaeologist Professor Kendrick writes, 'It seems possible that its ridiculous name may be a military sobriquet bestowed by the troops quartered there in the 18C'. The Nunnery is the oldest fortification in the Channel Islands and is believed to have been a 4C Roman fort. It resembles other forts of this period found in different parts of Europe and by its position probably protected a late Roman naval base. The building was substantially altered in 1793 and it is now a private residence owned by the States of Alderney.

In the area of Les Huguettes between Longy Bay and Les Rochers, during the building of a new golf course, traces of an Iron Age settlement were discovered. Several pots were restored and placed in the Alderney Museum.

Golf

The Alderney nine-hole golf course is open to visiting players. Fee, reduced ticket after 16.00. Visitors can take out short-term membership. Juniors, under 18 years, are charged at half the adult fee.

Continuing along the south coast, the path between the sea and Essex Castle begins to climb to the higher south-west section of the island. Hanging Rock, a natural column some 16m high, leans 20 degrees. Local wags have it that the rock was used as a hook by the people of Guernsey in an attempt to tow Alderney away.

Cliffs extend from Essex Hill to Hannaine Bay and a path from the post office wireless station runs between the cliffs and arable land. Some of this level and fertile land had to be surrendered for use as an airfield. Through heather and gorse, the path passes La Tchue, a difficult bay to scramble down to, and along La Haize Cliffs. Between La Haize and the headland at Les Becquets is the Vallet au Fleaume with a stream running into the sea. The islet rocks of L'Etac de la Quoire soon appear and these can be reached at low tide by taking a path running left to La Cachalière pier next to the Old Quarry.

At this point (7km) St. Anne can be reached via a track (1km). The cliff path continues past a house called 'Quatre Vents' to the Val du Sud. Several tracks called 'routes de souffrance' run across the Blaye and return to St. Anne between Cachalière and the Val du Sud. The States of Alderney have landscaped the Val du Sud through tree-planting and undergrowth clearance.

At **Val de l'Emauve** some granite rocks form a natural chair where two lovers, Jacqueline, daughter of a Seigneur, and her gallant, of humbler birth, used to meet. When this secret rendezvous was discovered, rather than be separated they leapt to their death in the sea below. Since then it has been known as 'The Lover's Chair'.

Vallée des Gaudulons and the Telegraph Tower (9.25km) are reached next, from where you can see the huge pinnacle rocks of La Fourquie and La Nache at the east end of Telegraph Bay. Descent is by path and steps. Bathing is good and the cliffs provide shelter from all but a south wind. At low tide there are good sands and at high tide care must be taken because the sea reaches the bottom of the steps and there is a possibility of being marooned on an extremity of the beach. From the headland, Tête de Judemarre, the impressive Les Etacs, or Garden Rocks, which provide nesting-places for enormous flocks of gannets, can be seen at the west end of the bay.

Fort Tourgis

Trois Vaux separates the Tête de Judemarre from Giffoine Heights as the route now continues north to one of the remotest corners of the island. From here the best view of the island of **Burhou**, about 2.5km off Fort Tourgis, is obtained. It is just over 1km long, 360m wide, and 25m above sea-level.

Birdwatchers can stay overnight on the island provided they make an application to the Harbour Officer. There is a wooden hut, which can be rented, fitted with bunks, simple furniture and cooking utensils. Visitors should take food and water. Hundreds of pairs of puffins nest here; along with storm petrels and gulls in lesser numbers. A boat from Braye to Burhou takes 20 minutes and can be privately arranged.

Just south-west of this island is the rock of Ortac where gannets breed in their hundreds. Ortac was believed by local fishermen to be the house of the spirit which ruled the wind and the water. It was customary in the last century for fishermen plying their trade in the Swinge to pause and drink to this awesome spirit.

Progress can now be made from **La Giffoine** along the clifftop through a little valley above Hannaine Bay. Since the path is overgrown it may be easier to take the rough track inland to the bitumenised road. This main road leads to a small building on the left just before the junction of a road running down to Fort Tourgis. Beside this building is a path which descends to sea-level. A rough road leads to the causeway of **Fort Clonque** (11km) which rests on an islet. Here unusual holidays can be spent in apartment rooms within the fort. **Hannaine Bay** on the south side has tongues of sand between rock masses and reasonable bathing. In Clonque Bay (derived from French '*calange*', in patois '*calanque*', meaning rocky inlet) yet another vessel, the *Emily Eveson*, went down in 1922. The crew was saved in dense fog by the bark of a dog which guided them ashore.

At the northwest end of the bay is **Fort Tourgis** (12.5km) and a burial chamber comprising two prop stones, 2m in length and 0.75m high, which support a capstone. It is the best preserved megalith in Alderney but any bones or pottery were removed generations ago. Offshore is a great rock, La Grosse. Legend has it that an enormous white bull lived there and anyone who sees this apparition in the vicinity is being warned of coming danger.

Continue northwest along a coastal track, past a German bunker, to Platte Saline. Here a road climbs the hill and another runs inland past the remains of a watermill and ascends into Le Petit Val which leads to St. Anne. The track past Saline Bay is invigorating when a west wind blows and the sea pounds against the shingle. Fort Platte, by the middle of the bay, now blends into the industrial background of the gravel works and Fort Doyle (13.5km) at the northwest end which has recently been renovated for youth activities.

Crabby Bay separates Fort Doyle from **Braye Harbour** by 500m. Here the sand is grey, probably from the stone dust which was dumped from York Hill Quarry when it was being worked. An interesting way to return to St. Anne from **Crabby Bay** is via the wooded route of **La Vallée** which leads past many of the island's charming houses and gardens.

Index